THE GREATEST CHAMPION THAT NEVER WAS

THE GREATEST CHAMPION THAT NEVER WAS

The Life of W. L. "Young" Stribling

Jaclyn Weldon White

Foreword by

Bert Randolph Sugar

Boxing historian and member of the International Boxing Hall of Fame

MERCER UNIVERSITY PRESS

MACON, GEORGIA

MUP/H828

First Edition

Books published by Mercer University Press are printed on acid-free
paper that meets the requirements of American National Standard for
Information Sciences—Permanence of Paper for Printed Library
Materials.

Mercer University Press is a member of Green Press Initiative
(greenpressinitiative.org), a nonprofit organization working to help
publishers and printers increase their use of recycled paper and
decrease their use of fiber derived from endangered forests. This book
is printed on recycled paper.
Library of Congress Cataloging-in-Publication Data
White, Jaclyn Weldon.
  The greatest champion that never was : the life of W.L. "Young" Stribling /
Jaclyn Weldon White. -- 1st ed.
    p. cm.
  Includes index.
  ISBN 978-0-88146-252-4 (hardcover : alk. paper)
  1. Stribling, Young, 1907-1933. 2. Boxers (Sports)--United States--Biography. I.
Title.
  GV1132.S7W45 2011
  796.83092--dc23
  [B]
                                2011024691

This book is lovingly dedicated to Dr. James C. Bryant. More than a decade ago, Dr. Bryant became fascinated with the story of Young Stribling. He spent many years conducting meticulous research in preparation for the book he planned to write. Unfortunately, he passed away before he could do so.

Using the enormous amount of information he collected, I have tried to create a book of which he would be proud.

Acknowledgments

The staff of archivists in the Genealogical and Historical Room of the Washington Street Library, Middle Georgia Regional Library System, has helped me in more ways than I can count. They've never hesitated to go the extra mile, even when my requests put them to great trouble. Muriel Jackson, Willard Rocker, Anne Rogers, and Dr. Christopher Stokes are not only consummate professionals, they are now dear friends.

Foreword

In one of those little tricks history continually plays on us to see if we were really paying attention—in a manner similar to the factoid that has become enshrined in our memories and history books that Charles Lindbergh was the first to cross the Atlantic when, in reality, he was the 19th, albeit the first to fly solo—we tend to omit the name W. L. "Young" Stribling in any list of great boxers merely because he never became a champion.

And yet, in any list of "great" boxers, be it in record books or induction into the International Boxing Hall of Fame, Stribling's name is there even if it has little meaning other than a few graybeards who have not yet been run over by errant trolleycars.

All of which is patently unfair to the memory of this great fighter.

Now comes Jaclyn Weldon White who, in this well-researched and richly detailed book, rights the wrongs done to the memory of Young Stribling.

Ms. White's biography is like an artichoke—the more she peels away, the more we discover. Her story is one of a fighter who started out as a skinny, elbowy bantamweight and fought his way up the fistic ladder to the cusp of both the light heavyweight and heavyweight titles. Of a dedicated fighter who found the time to be a devoted family man even as his career progressed. Of a fighter so skilled that none other than former heavyweight champion James J. Corbett, the father of "Scientific" boxing, called "the best heavyweight fighter for his pounds that ever lived." And of a fighter whose dark good looks, closely resembling those of Jack Dempsey, made him one of boxing's—if not all of sports'—beau idols.

Had there been an investiture, Young Stribling would have been crowned light heavyweight champion by acclamation.

However, as Ms. White tells us, fate has a fickle habit of bestowing its fame on someone it later takes by the scruff of the neck and hurls overboard. That, too, is part of the story of W. L. "Young" Stribling, a tale well-told in one of the most readable books to come down boxing's pike in many a year.

—Bert Randolph Sugar
June 7, 2011

The Greatest Champion That Never Was

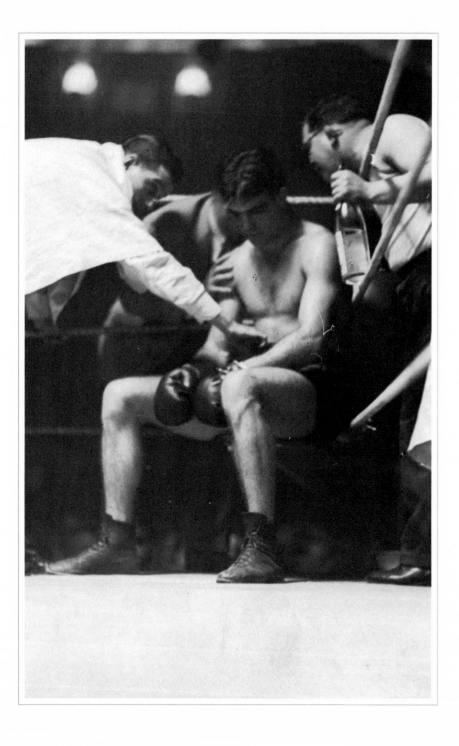

1

The title fight was held in Columbus, Georgia, an unusual location far from the big northern cities that were the centers of the boxing world. Fans and sportswriters from all over the country poured into the small town in late September of 1923. The hotels were filled, and visitors crowded the shops and restaurants.

Mike McTigue was the light heavyweight champion of the world, but the real drawing card was his opponent.

William Lawrence "Young" Stribling, known as W.L. to his family, was an eighteen-year-old schoolboy from nearby Macon. Stribling, who had his first professional fight only two years before, had captured the interest of sports fans all over the country. With an astonishing record of 77 wins and only 3 losses, his meteoric rise through the boxing ranks was impossible to ignore.

The stocky, dark-haired McTigue had been born in County Clare, Ireland, but grew up on the tough streets of New York. This would be his first defense of the title he had won only six months earlier by defeating Battling Siki. Siki, a man who evidently enjoyed tempting fate, had taken on the Irishman in Dublin on St. Patrick's Day. No one was surprised when he lost.

Stribling had traveled from Macon with his parents. His father was his manager, and his mother often acted as his trainer. The family settled into their training quarters in Columbus a week before the fight. Although they preferred concentrating on training, they couldn't escape the press or the fans. Stribling was so popular that his training camp was always filled with sightseers, and he was recognized everywhere he went.

McTigue and his entourage checked into the Ralston Hotel on September 27. While they stood at the reception desk, they noticed a tall, handsome boy in an orange and green letter sweater standing with an older woman near the door. Several people crowded around them, clamoring for the boy's autograph.

"Who's that?" McTigue asked the desk clerk.

"That's Young Stribling and his mother."

The champion gave a derisive laugh. "He doesn't look like he's ever been in a fight," he said, speaking loud enough that W.L. could hear him.

As the Striblings walked past a minute later, W.L. said in a low voice to McTigue, "You don't look like you ever missed one."

Columbus grew busier by the day. Each train into Terminal Station brought another load of fans. Dignitaries from surrounding cities mingled on the crowded streets with boxing enthusiasts from all over the country. Sportswriters and columnists, Damon Runyon and Ed Curley among them, traveled south to cover what was being described as the greatest boxing match to ever take place in that region.

Crowds began gathering at the stadium by 2:00 on Friday, October 4, even though the fight wouldn't take place for another five hours. The day had begun cloudy and humid, but the sun broke through in the afternoon, sending the temperature well into the 80s. The growing crowd hardly seemed to notice the heat. An Army band from nearby Fort Benning played rousing music, and spirits were high.

At 7:00, the fighters made their way into the ring. When the two men stood side by side, the comparison was remarkable. McTigue was nearly ten years older than Stribling. His face bore the marks of his many fights—his nose was crooked and his eyes narrowed by scar tissue. He scowled at the crowd that clearly favored his opponent.

In contrast, Stribling stood straight and fit. His movie-star handsome face, golden in the light from the setting sun, was unmarked. Tanned and muscular, he was the picture of health and confidence. He smiled and waved at the crowd, and the thousands jammed into the stadium responded with wild cheering.

How did this boy who had begun his senior year of high school only a month before end up in a boxing ring with a veteran fighter surrounded by thousands of cheering supporters while his fellow students were concerned with nothing more serious than a history test or a Saturday night date?

There's no magic formula for producing a legendary athlete. What set of circumstances determines who will maintain the status quo and who will push the limits of birth and time? History can't provide us with a definitive explanation for William Lawrence Stribling Jr.'s extraordinary talent and achievements, but part of the reason certainly lies with his parents.

Bainbridge, Georgia, was an insignificant market town tucked away in the southwest corner of the state in the late nineteenth century. A handful of commercial buildings lined the unpaved streets and, in one of these modest structures, Augustus Raymond Stribling operated a dry goods store and tavern.

Gus, as he was known to everyone, had the reputation as an honest businessman and, more important in some quarters, a bartender who poured with a liberal hand. He married Louisa Singletary from nearby Thomas County on December 21, 1884, and, on August 16, 1886, their first child, William Lawrence Stribling, was born. They called him Willie. And by 1897, he had five siblings—Irene, Early, Hoy, and twins Sallie and Roscoe.

As soon as Gus decided he was old enough, Willie began helping in his father's store. Stocking shelves and assisting customers was boring work for a high-spirited boy. In his spare time, he found excitement reading his father's *Police Gazette* magazines.

More tabloid than magazine, the *Gazette* carried lurid stories and illustrations of sensational murders, sports, and tales of the Wild West. Willie's favorite articles were the boxing stories that fired his imagination with the pugilistic heroes of the time. His favorite was John L. Sullivan, who reigned as heavyweight champion from 1882 to 1892.

Willie longed with all his heart to be a prizefighter. He spent hours doing strenuous exercises and did everything the magazines recommended to improve his physique. He grew strong and muscular, but his height never reached more than 5'6" and he had to accept the fact that his short stature would prevent his dream from coming true. But that goal was soon replaced by another. Willie wanted to see the world.

Louisa Stribling died between 1897 and 1901, leaving Gus alone to raise six children. Life wasn't easy for the family, but Willie still had big dreams. More than anything, he wanted to see what was waiting for him outside of Bainbridge, and he had read in the magazines that a fabulous world's fair, the Pan American Exposition, was being held that year in Buffalo, New York.

So four months before his fifteenth birthday, he packed some clothes, slipped away, and hopped a freight train to the port city of Brunswick on the Georgia coast. There he arranged to work for his passage on a northbound steamship and, a few days later, stepped off the boat in New York City.

It was a world he had never even imagined existed. He had never seen so many people, and there hadn't been any tall buildings in South Georgia. But he loved the bustle and excitement that swirled around him.

He worked his way to the upstate city of Buffalo by doing odd jobs and exercising his considerable charm. The journey took him through miles of rural countryside that looked a little like home, but there was nothing familiar about his destination.

The Pan American Exposition sprawled across 350 acres of rolling countryside north of the city. Admission was fifty cents—a lot of money for a fourteen-year-old boy—but that half dollar took him through the gate into another world.

Lush landscaped grounds surrounded a paved plaza lined with exotically colored buildings. At the north end of the plaza the Electric Tower reached 410 feet into the air. Blue and white and ultra-modern, it celebrated the hydroelectric possibilities of nearby Niagara Falls and was the focal point of the fair.

The noise was nearly deafening to someone accustomed to the quiet of a country town. The rush of flowing water never ceased. Music poured forth from exhibit halls, and an ever-changing variety of bands played marches and popular music in the ornate bandstands scattered throughout the grounds. A foghorn sounded at intervals, and vendors selling popcorn and peanuts shouted the glories of their wares.

Amazing sights were everywhere he turned, but the place that most interested Willie Stribling was the Midway where 296 concessions vied for the fairgoers' nickels. Games of chance crowded in beside panoramas depicting the frozen North Pole and darkest Africa. A Philippine settlement stood beside the Streets of Mexico. A Cairo street, complete with an elaborate mosque, wound through the Beautiful Orient.

The Scenic Railway, a precursor to today's roller coaster, carried thrill-seeking passengers up steep hills, along sharp curves, and down stomach-raising dips. Sandwiched between the Old Plantation and the Glass Factory, the Trip to the Moon simulated spaceship travel, complete with howling wind and thunder and lightning. It was such an extraordinary experience that many fairgoers were convinced they had actually made the trip into space.

The Midway was more crowded and even noisier than the exhibit area. Music blared from a dozen different locations. Bells clanged, barkers delivered their spiels in singsong voices, and laughter filled the air. Willie loved it.

Jobs were easy to come by at the Exposition, and Willie soon found work as a utility boy in the Japanese Village. It was mostly scrubbing floors, but it paid a decent wage and would do until something better came along.

His real challenge was finding a place to live. Buffalo was stretched to its limits that summer. Hotel rooms were almost impossible to find, and boardinghouses were filled to capacity. Local residents began renting out rooms, and a tent village was erected at the edge of the fair. There's no record of where Willie stayed, but it's certain his accommodations were modest and crowded.

Scrubbing floors paid the rent, but it wasn't the kind of job he wanted to do for long. Entranced by the Midway, he longed to be in the thick of the action and soon persuaded the manager of Darkness and Dawn to hire him as a groaner.

The Darkness and Dawn illusion was billed as a trip to the afterlife. Patrons were shown the delights of heaven and, after a harrowing ride over the Chasm of Fire, introduced to the horrors of hell where souls screamed and groaned to the accompaniment of rattling chains. Hell was, of course, the most popular part of the trip and was where Willie, hidden in a coffin, groaned in misery and rattled chains.

It was delightfully scary for the patrons, but hiding in the dark didn't suit Willie's personality. Outgoing and energetic, he longed for a more public position. Within weeks, he had moved on to a job as a barker at the same illusion, his engaging smile and soft Georgia drawl promising passersby the thrill of a lifetime.

When he wasn't working, Willie literally had the entire world at his disposal. While the exhibits were fascinating, he preferred spending his time with the performers and was particularly taken with the acrobats. After a while they began teaching him simple tricks. Willie practiced and mastered each one, then went back for more. His small muscular body was perfectly designed for flips, turns, and feats of balance and by the end of the summer he had become a fairly accomplished acrobat himself.

September 5 was designated "President's Day" at the fair. President William McKinley was coming to the Exposition to deliver a major address, and excitement ran high. His arrival that Thursday morning was as impressive as anyone might have hoped. President and Mrs. McKinley crossed the Triumphal Causeway and entered the grounds in an open, horse-drawn carriage. They were accompanied by mounted troops, an honor guard, and a military band. On the Esplanade, surrounded by a raucous, cheering crowd, the president delivered a major speech on trade among the countries of the Americas.

But the visit wasn't over yet. The next day he and his entourage traveled by train to see Niagara Falls, where proud city leaders explained the endless possibilities of hydroelectric power, then returned to the Exposition for a public reception in the Temple of Music that afternoon.

McKinley had been shaking hands in the reception line for about ten minutes when Leon Czolgosz, an unemployed Detroit factory worker, approached him. Czolgosz carried a revolver in his right hand, concealed by a handkerchief. When McKinley reached to shake his hand, Czolgosz fired twice. Both bullets struck the president, and he collapsed as onlookers rushed to help him and to subdue the shooter.

The Darkness and Dawn exhibit was less than 500 yards from the Temple of Music, but no one on the noisy Midway heard the shots. However, word of the attack reached them in minutes.

The injured president was rushed to an ambulance and taken to the on-site hospital. It required an armed guard with fixed bayonets to get

Czolgosz out of the building through the angry crowd and into a local jail.

At first, it was believed the president's injuries weren't life threatening and after surgery he was transported to the nearby home of John Milburn to recover. For a few days he seemed to improve, but then an internal infection set in and he began to fail. He died in the early morning hours of September 14, and forty-three-year-old Vice President Theodore Roosevelt then became the youngest man ever to hold the office of president.

Czolgosz, a self-proclaimed anarchist, later declared, "I killed President McKinley because I done my duty. I didn't believe one man should have so much service and another man should have none."

He was brought to trial on September 23, convicted, and sent to Auburn State Prison to await execution. There, after expressing remorse, he was put to death by electrocution on October 29, 1901.

McKinley's death nearly overshadowed everything that the Exposition had accomplished. Instead of establishing itself as a progressive, dynamic city, Buffalo was now the city of assassination. The Exposition continued, but the huge crowds never returned. As attendance dwindled, many of the fair workers were laid off.

The Pan-American Exposition officially closed on November 2, but Willie Stribling was on his way home to Bainbridge well before that. A southern boy with no experience of the extreme northern winters, he wanted to be out of Buffalo before the first snow fell.

2

The quiet, dusty streets and agrarian rhythms of Bainbridge were tame after the excitement of the Buffalo Exposition. Willie went back to work in his father's store. The work hadn't changed, but now he could break the boredom by entertaining himself and his friends with stories of his summer up North. He loved to show off his newly acquired acrobatic skills. Sometimes he would walk the whole length of a bowling alley on his hands and knock over all the pins at the end to win a CocaCola.

During the summer of 1903 sixteen-year-old Willie Stribling took a train to visit relatives in the tiny settlement of Ochlocknee in neighboring Thomas County. It was there he met Lillie Mae Braswell, a vivacious, dark-haired sixteen-year-old girl with flashing blue eyes and an irrepressible spirit.

She was the tenth child of well-to-do farmer A. A. Braswell. Her mother had died four years before, leaving her father to raise his large family alone. Braswell was a strict patriarch who wasn't impressed by the young man from Bainbridge. But Lillie didn't let her father's disapproval stop her. She had never met anyone like Willie. He was a natural leader, brimming with self-confidence, and she knew from the stories he told that he had seen and done more than any other boy of her acquaintance.

The elder Braswell believed that Willie was too young for marriage and had too few prospects. Mr. Braswell had more important and prosperous suitors in mind for his daughter. But Lillie was determined, and Braswell eventually gave in to her and reluctantly allowed Stribling to court his daughter, hoping she would soon come to her senses.

But the two young people were in love. Whenever Gus gave him time off, Willie took the 30-mile train ride to Ochlocknee. His courtship of Lillie Braswell might have continued that way for months or even years, but another World's Fair was being planned for 1904. The Louisiana Purchase Exposition was scheduled to open in St. Louis, Missouri, in the spring, and Willie Stribling was determined to make the trip.

This time he didn't make a secret of his plans. Gus didn't like the idea at all—he needed the boy in the store—but Willie couldn't be dissuaded. On Valentine's Day, which fell on Sunday that year, he told his father he had decided to leave that very day for St. Louis. The two argued, but Gus couldn't talk him out of the idea.

Finally Gus tried diversion. "Don't you have a date with that little girl in Ochlocknee tonight?"

Willie admitted that he did, but said he planned to break the date.

Gus was quiet for a moment, then he did something completely out of character. He handed his son his purse. Inside was $80.

"Here. Go on to Ochlocknee and keep your date," he said.

Surely Gus didn't expect Willie to spend such an exorbitant amount of money on one date in Ochlocknee. Perhaps it was his way of giving his blessing to the trip without having to declare it out loud.

Willie did go to Ochlocknee that afternoon, but it wasn't for a date. His plan was to say good-bye to Lillie and then leave for St. Louis. He had dressed carefully, wanting to look his best for the coming trip. His short hair was neatly parted in the middle and combed flat against the sides of his head, and he wore a suit and a white shirt with a stiff starched collar.

He arrived just after church and went straight to the Braswell home where Lillie was waiting for him. Willie hadn't seen her in over two months, and she was prettier than he had remembered. Her lustrous dark hair was piled high on her head, and she wore a high-necked dress with a fitted bodice that showed off her trim figure.

He couldn't imagine leaving her. In fact, as soon as they were alone, he proposed and she accepted. That question was settled, but there were a lot of details to consider. They knew that her father would never allow the marriage to take place. And even though he wanted to make Lillie his wife, Willie still had adventure on his mind. So a few hours later they slipped away from her house, hurried to the railroad station, and boarded a train for Bainbridge.

Willie rented a horse-drawn buggy at the station and drove them straight to the Bainbridge Baptist Church. During the short trip, they had a discussion about likes and dislikes.

"Honey," Lillie asked, "do you love milk?"

"No," he answered. "I don't love milk."

"Neither do I," she said with some satisfaction.

And that exchange set the tone for their marriage. They generally liked the same things and were young enough that they could change to suit each other.

At the church they found the minister, John Roberts Jester, who agreed to marry them. An hour later, just before the evening service ended, they stood before the congregation and took their vows.

Then the newlyweds boarded another train. This one was northbound and would eventually take them to St. Louis. Lillie was nervous leaving her home for the first time, but she loved and trusted Willie and was ready to follow his dream with him.

A. A. Braswell was furious when he learned of the elopement. He declared he would have nothing more to do with his wayward daughter and the worthless young man who had stolen her away.

The St. Louis Fair was the largest event of its kind ever seen. More than 100,000 people a day came through the gates. Willie, a veteran of the Pan American Exposition, took it in stride, but Lillie was wonderstruck. The huge Plaza of St. Louis was lined with exhibits, beautifully landscaped grounds, and a series of lagoons. Gondolas and motorized launches ferried people from shore to shore, and land travel was provided by a fleet of rickshaws pulled by Chinese runners.

There were forty-five full-service restaurants within the grounds, along with vendors selling hot dogs, ice cream cones, and other treats. Music poured from bandstands—everything from marches to the new craze of ragtime.

They located lodging, and Willie found work easily. His experience at the Buffalo fair stood him in good stead with the Midway providers. The young couple still had Gus Stribling's purse with most of the $80 intact, and they were careful to guard their small nest egg.

Soon after they arrived, Willie sought out the European and American gymnasts who performed daily. He spent a great deal of time with them when he wasn't working. Another newly married woman might have resented his taking time away from her to spend with the acrobats, but Lillie was just as fascinated as her husband was by their feats, particularly when she learned that women regularly took part in the gymnastic demonstrations.

While Willie had already perfected a number of acrobatic feats, they now realized that Lillie could participate as well. She had always been a strong, athletic girl, and this was her chance to show it. The young couple practiced alone in their room in the evenings and dreamed of performing together. But by June, Lillie's tumbling days came to a temporary halt when she learned she was pregnant with their first child.

They stayed in St. Louis for the rest of the summer, but by the fall they were more than ready to go home. It was time to start their family.

3

Willie's brother Hoy and his family lived on Planter Street in Bainbridge, and the young Striblings moved in with them. While her siblings were excited that she was home and expecting a baby, Lillie's father still refused to see her.

Willie was a family man now, even if he was still a teenager, and he needed a grown-up job. He found work selling insurance, but not for long. He sold his first policy to a man who died soon afterward and decided right then that it wasn't the job for him. He turned his attention to photography instead.

The day after Christmas of 1904, Lillie gave birth to a strong, healthy boy. Willie took one look at his son and was convinced that his own dreams could be fulfilled through him. He rushed out and had birth announcements printed. They read "Born to Mr. and Mrs. W. L. Stribling, Sr., a future heavyweight champion of the world, the day after Christmas, to be called William Lawrence Stribling, Jr."

Willie and Lillie never disagreed about how they would raise their son. Physical fitness was high on their list of priorities, and they began training the baby with that goal from a very early age. While he was still an infant, Lillie rolled him around on the bed, as she put it, "like a piece of dough." By the time he was four and a half months old, the baby, whom they called W.L., was capable of holding up his own weight with one hand.

Gus Stribling's bad luck with marriage continued. In March 1905 his wife Mamie died at the age of 23. Nine months later he married for a fourth and final time. His bride was young Mattie Little, sister of his second wife.

Willie was becoming quite a successful photographer. Carrying his heavy equipment with him, he traveled all over the Southeast, taking family photographs and group pictures at picnics, churches, and schools.

He hand-colored the prints, a very popular process at the time, and was on his way to making a good living.

When he was home, he worked with Lillie to teach their young son the basics of acrobatics. And he never lost his certainty that W.L. would become a world champion boxer. Before he was a year old, the baby was given his first pair of boxing gloves.

They had been careful of his diet from the very beginning and, as soon as he graduated to table food, they decided to raise him as a vegetarian. They weren't dictatorial about it—he was occasionally given lean meat—but the bulk of his diet was whole grains, fruits, and vegetables. Willie firmly believed he was laying the foundation that would produce a perfect specimen of good health.

Their second son, Herbert Graham Stribling, was born on March 23, 1907. After only a few months, Herbert was included in the training sessions with his older brother.

Like other traveling men, Willie was always looking for diversion on the road, and he often found it in the theaters. Vaudeville was nearing its golden age, and most theaters presented two performances a day, both featuring nine or ten acts. As he sat in theater after theater watching dancers, acrobats, and comedians frolic on the stage, a plan began taking shape in Willie's mind.

Photography was definitely better than selling insurance, but it was not the career he had dreamed of as a child. Why, Willie wondered, shouldn't he and his family become vaudeville performers? After all, he and Lillie had practiced acrobatics numerous times and had taught the children a few tricks as well. They could do the same things on stage and travel the country.

Never shy, Willie approached the manager of the El Teatro Theater in Montgomery about giving his new act a try. The manager was reluctant, but when Willie offered to perform for free, he agreed. And if the act was good he promised he would do what he could to get them a spot on the circuit.

That was all Willie needed to hear. He started planning the act and sent for his family then and there. Most wives receiving such a summons would believe their husbands had lost their minds, but Lillie trusted

Willie and was ready to support him in anything he wanted to do. A few days later she and the boys arrived by train.

Willie took the act's name from his youngest son's middle name, and the Novelty Grahams debuted in February 1908 at the El Teatro Theater. When the curtains opened, eleven-month-old Herbert was revealed sitting on a pedestal in the center of the stage. He seemed quite content there, showing no sign of uneasiness, and he never moved.

Then he was joined onstage by the rest of his family. The baby sat absolutely still while his mother, father, and older brother cavorted around him, doing handstands, headstands, somersaults, and back flips. After a few minutes, Herbert was included in the activity. His placid expression never changed, even when Willie tossed him into the air or balanced him in his hand on one foot.

The audience loved them, and the theater owner knew a hit when he saw one. He immediately agreed to pay the little troupe for the rest of the week and wired his headquarters for bookings.

The Striblings were on their way. None of the family could sing or dance, but Willie had a keen sense of humor and they gradually refined their act. It slowly evolved from an acrobatic display to a comedy act with the acrobatics as a backdrop.

Willie and the boys wore bright green gym suits while Lillie's outfit was bloomers and a sleeveless top. She looked fit and statuesque beside her short, stocky husband. As they flipped and twisted across the stage, tossing the boys high in the air, Willie kept up a snappy patter, which Lillie punctuated with numerous jabs at his expense. Then Willie pummeled a punching bag while his wife made less than flattering comments about his appearance and skill.

Audiences roared with laughter, and before long, the Four Novelty Grahams were the grand finale on the bill, leaving the audience cheering for more.

Lillie assumed the role of manager for their act, scheduling the bookings and accepting the checks. While they never headlined on the biggest circuits, the Striblings did well in vaudeville. Their salary was upward of $150 a week, and they were popular enough to have bookings scheduled throughout the season. One critic called them "Katzen-jammers in stage clothes."

Show business was glamorous from the outside, but for insiders it was a hard life. The Striblings were in different towns every few days, often traveling at odd hours of the night. Each week they had to adjust to a new theater, and a different hotel or boardinghouse.

But they managed to create their own routine. Lillie began schooling the boys at a very early age, and she and Willie, still kids themselves, often joined in the children's games. They read the Bible together before every performance and, when schedules permitted, attended church together on Sunday mornings.

Willie's photography expertise came in handy making publicity posters and postcards for the troupe. One card showed Herbert perched atop a pedestal with his legs crossed and W.L. leaning against it. Both boys, dressed in Sunday suits and broad-brimmed hats, smiled broadly for the camera. Another postcard advertised the family as "One of the Greatest Novelty Acts in the Business."

One of those postcards made its way to Ochlocknee in 1910. Dated June 20 and postmarked Philadelphia, it was mailed to Lillie's sister Sallie. The message was simple: "Hello we will be Home soon."

The Striblings' rare visits home were exciting for them and the folks in South Georgia. They usually stayed with Cuy and Belle Harrell, Lillie's sister and brother-in-law. The farmhouse was a small one, and they had to leave their large traveling trunks on the front porch. During the short visits they tried to see everyone in the family, entertaining them with stories of faraway places and famous people. Sometimes they performed their act at the local school.

On their 1910 trip home, Lillie saw her father for the first time since her marriage six years earlier. Hard feelings were put behind them as the two reconciled and Braswell met his grandsons for the first time. It was a joyous reunion and a timely one because he died less than two years later.

Gus Stribling had given up his dry goods store by 1910 and now owned and operated a bicycle accessory and repair shop at 211 Water Street. Newspaper advertisements billed him as the Old Reliable Master Mechanic.

As always, the time at home was too short. As fall approached, the Striblings boarded a train with their trunks and were off for a new vaudeville season. They appeared on bills with some of the great performers of their time, including the promoter Flo Ziegfield, W. C. Fields, and Houdini, but Willie was more impressed with the famous athletes they encountered. He was especially thrilled when they shared the stage with James J. "Gentleman Jim" Corbett, the former heavyweight boxing champion.

They appeared in the Northwest and, by late winter of 1912, were in San Francisco where Willie took the boys to see a boxing match between middleweights Frank Klaus and Jack Dillon. It was a rough, brutal fight, and afterwards Willie declared that his son would never be that kind of brawling boxer. He would be a fighter with class.

For several years their act had included comic boxing matches between Willie and Lillie that usually ended with Lillie knocking out her husband. In 1912 that changed. It was an easy step from that to having five-year-old Herbert and seven-year-old W.L. put on gloves and square off against each other. The boys fought in a small makeshift ring while Willie "refereed" three one-minute rounds.

Audiences loved the new act and laughed uproariously when the younger boy knocked out his older brother. Even more laughter was elicited when Herbert occasionally delivered a roundhouse punch to the referee.

In later years, Herbert enjoyed telling people that, when he and his big brother argued, he would just bide his time until their mock stage fight. Then he would let W.L. have it with everything in him. Since the act called for Herbert to win, W.L. couldn't fight back.

Later that year, the Striblings took their act across the Pacific. Lillie was hesitant about leaving the country, but Willie persisted and she eventually gave in. However, she did say "I told you so" when outbreaks of bubonic plague caused them to flee China.

In 1912 they appeared in 42 states. When Willie wanted to go abroad again, Lillie wasn't eager to do so, but he prevailed once more and they took their act to Cuba. They enjoyed their time in the island country until riots broke out in Havana and the Striblings fled to a sailing ship in Havana Harbor.

They toured the United States during 1913 and a year later began a South American tour with another appearance in Havana. This time an earthquake hit nearby Santiago de Cuba, but they weren't hurt. They moved on to Venezuela, but had to leave Caracas in a hurry in the wake of a revolution there. Fortunately their trips to Colombia, Chile, Argentina, Brazil, and Mexico were much less eventful.

In late 1914 the Striblings were back touring the United States. Once again, they changed their act. The boxing match between the brothers was replaced by something new. Willie now issued challenges to all comers in every town. Any boy in W.L.'s weight class was welcome to fight him. If a contender could last three rounds with the strapping ten-year-old, he would win a $10 prize.

There was almost always a local tough guy ready to accept the challenge, but the prize was awarded only once. The rest of the fights ended long before the three rounds were over. W.L. grew more and more confident, easily dodging wild swings and dancing around the ring. He wasn't marked in a single fight.

W.L. was injured only once during the vaudeville years. During a 1915 performance in Jackson, Tennessee, his foot slipped while he was attempting to stand upright on his mother's head, and his hand was hurt in the resulting fall. Lillie iced it, but the pain continued. The next morning his parents took him to a nearby clinic where the doctor examined him.

"It looks bad. How did you do this?"

W.L. hadn't cried since the injury happened, but he was worried. "It's not broke, is it?"

The doctor pressed his hand. "Does that hurt?"

"Y . . . yes. It hurts. Is it broke?"

"Maybe."

W.L. fainted. When he was revived, Willie asked what caused him to faint. "Did it hurt that much?"

W.L. shook his head. "No. But you always told me I wouldn't be able to box if I broke any bones. So that just meant the end of everything for me."

Willie gave him a quick hug and suggested a compromise. "You look out for your body, and I'll look out for your mind."

17

After X-rays, they determined that his hand wasn't actually broken. He just had a bad sprain that would heal in a few days.

Things were going well for the Striblings, and they were planning a European tour when world events made them reconsider. Germany's threats of aggression couldn't be ignored any longer. In April 1917, the United States declared war on Germany.

The Striblings had been traveling now for over nine years, but with Europe out of reach for the time being and war imminent, they decided it was time to find a nice place and put down roots.

4

The Striblings had always expected to return to Bainbridge after their travels, but when the time came to leave the road they chose the city of Macon instead. The opportunities for earning a good living seemed better there than in rural South Georgia. In 1917, Macon was a bustling town with a population of 50,000. Eleven railroads serviced the new Terminal Station, and the posh new Dempsey Hotel welcomed visitors. Horse races were held in Central City Park, moving pictures were shown in the Capitol and Rialto theaters, and vaudeville performances were held at the Grand Theater. Macon was also an educational center with both Mercer University and Wesleyan College located there.

The United States' entry into the war had brought even more people into town. Camp Wheeler, a military training center that would house 60,000 men, was being built on Holly Bluff across the Ocmulgee River in East Macon. The city had to extend water, electrical, and rail service to the site, and the pace of work on the camp in 1917 was frantic.

The Striblings moved into a boardinghouse at 817 New Street in June, and Willie found a job driving a bus for soldiers and civilian workers between Camp Wheeler and Macon. Lillie was soon hired as a clerk at the McEvoy Book and Stationery Company on Cherry Street. Herbert and W.L. spent the summer getting acquainted with their new home and meeting some of the neighborhood kids.

W.L. quickly found a group of sandlot baseball-playing boys who called themselves the Cherry Street Sluggers. They were a ragtag bunch who had no uniforms and only a few pieces of equipment, but they welcomed W.L. to the team. At twelve, he was an outgoing, friendly boy, but more importantly for the Sluggers, he was bigger and more athletically inclined than anyone else on the team.

One dusty summer day, the Sluggers rode their bikes out to the Vineville playground where they were to play a game against that team. Things went smoothly for a while, but the home team eventually grew tired of trailing the Cherry Street boys. A scuffle broke out, and Slugger Sidney Dasher got into a dustup with Vineville's Ed Clayton. The two were rolling around on the ground, both trying to land a few punches, when the playground supervisor Mrs. George Beggs stepped in and stopped the fight.

But tempers were still up and insults were flung from one group to the other. That's when W.L. stepped forward.

"I guess I'll take on anyone who thinks he can beat me," he challenged.

Since Stribling was taller and stronger than any of the Vineville boys, none of them were interested in fighting him. The only one who came close to matching him in size was a boy who was visiting from Atlanta. He didn't have any real loyalty to the Vineville team, but didn't want to be seen as a coward, so he reluctantly stepped up to face W.L.

"I haven't got anything against you," he said, "and I don't care so much about fighting, but if you want to fight, I'll take you on."

That was enough for Mrs. Beggs. There wasn't going to be any brawling on her playground. She ordered W.L. and his team to leave.

"We can't have this sort of thing going on here."

"Yes, ma'am," W.L. said.

Without another word, he and the rest of the Cherry Street team climbed on their bikes and left the playground. Mrs. Beggs figured she had seen the last of the big kid from downtown, but she was wrong.

The next afternoon, he rode his bicycle back to the playground just to see her. He apologized for his part in the ruckus. And instead of leaving once the apology was made, he stayed awhile to visit with her. Mrs. Beggs was charmed by the polite youngster, and the two talked and laughed together until evening. After that W.L. was a frequent visitor to the Vineville playground, taking part in whatever seasonal game was under way.

By September, Camp Wheeler was ready, and soldiers from the surrounding states began arriving in large numbers. The enlisted men were quartered in eleven-man tents, and hundreds of frame buildings had been erected to serve as mess halls, administrative buildings, infirmaries, and officers' quarters. But the officers often preferred staying in downtown Macon, and people joked that there were so many of them quartered at the Hotel Dempsey it should be renamed Fort Dempsey.

The Stribling brothers enrolled in Alexander I Elementary School, and on the first day of school Lillie dressed them in suits with large white Buster Brown collars. Then the two went off to meet their new classmates.

They felt somewhat awkward in their new roles as schoolboys. Even though they had traveled the world, and seen and done things their classmates had never even dreamed about, their odd upbringing had kept them from attending school with other students.

That first day their more casually attired schoolmates ridiculed the Stribling boys for their fancy outfits. By the end of the first day, someone had scribbled "Sweet William" on W.L.'s white collar and "Baby Herbert" on his brother's. That was the last time the boys wore their finery to school.

But the Striblings had long ago learned to get along with a variety of people and were soon at ease in their new circumstances. Their classmates liked them, and they did well in their studies and excelled in any sport on the playground.

The war raged on in Europe, but it seemed very far away from Macon. The Striblings were living a more stable life than they had at any time in their marriage. Willie joined the Macon YMCA so that the boys could take part in sports, particularly boxing, there.

The year 1918's debut in Macon was a dramatic one. The weather had been unseasonably warm, and on Friday, January 11, torrential rain and high winds tore through the South. Telegraph and telephone lines were down all over town, and the Ocmulgee River overflowed its banks, flooding some areas with up to six feet of water.

Just after dark, a tornado touched down in East Macon. In Camp Wheeler, sixteen tents attached to the base hospital were blown down, exposing convalescing soldiers to the storm. Three men were killed, and many were injured.

The storm was bad enough, but the Arctic cold front that followed the next day was worse. Friday night the temperature plummeted fifty degrees, from 63 to 13. Most of the city was still in the dark due to the storm. Now residents had the cold to contend with as well. The Striblings were safe and stayed warm, but many of their neighbors weren't as fortunate.

The national coal shortage and frigid temperatures sent the demand for the fuel skyrocketing. With the temperature nearing zero on Sunday night, the mayor opened City Hall as a shelter for citizens without heat. But nowhere fared worse than Camp Wheeler, where the floors of the remaining tents were covered with ice and soldiers had little more than small fires to keep them warm.

In the spring soldiers who had trained at Camp Wheeler left Georgia for France where they became part of the Rainbow Division. Within months, the Allies were turning the tide of the war in Europe. In July the Germans were in retreat and by August the outcome seemed decided.

Summer was playtime for W.L. and Herbert. They boxed and played basketball at the YMCA. They took part in countless pickup games of baseball in the city playgrounds and, on really hot days, rode their bikes to the Forty Foot, an abandoned rock quarry that now served as a swimming hole.

When the first warplanes made their appearance over France they captured the imagination of the whole world. Although airplane travel was still rare in the United States, each day more planes were built and flown. Everyone knew that air travel was the wave of the future, and Macon wanted to be a part of it. So that summer a portion of the Central City Park racetrack was converted into a landing strip for daily cross-country flights. On August 1 the first flight landed there, and the news made the front page of the paper.

The boys returned to school in the fall. W.L., who would turn 14 in December, was a couple of years older than his classmates. He should have been entering high school, but because of the unconventional schooling he had received on the road, he was still attending elementary school.

The war was ending in September, and encouraging news was printed in the papers every day. But the cost had been terrible—15 million soldiers and civilians had died. And there was more death to come.

In August, the Spanish flu broke out in Boston and quickly spread to neighboring states. While the death tolls were high, the epidemic stayed north and west of Macon. It wasn't until the first of October that it arrived in Georgia. Four days after the first case was reported at Camp Hancock in Augusta, 3,000 soldiers were infected and 52 had already died. The flu spread through the state with alarming speed.

The University of Georgia suspended classes indefinitely, and the City of Atlanta banned all public gatherings, including schools, libraries, churches, and theaters, for two months. These precautions helped slow the disease, but didn't stop it.

The first cases appeared in Macon in mid-October. The city was hit hard, but the Striblings escaped the disease. By the beginning of November, the quarantines ended and the fear of the epidemic gradually faded, but the disease had claimed over 20 million people worldwide.

The war in Europe was almost over. When word came at two in the morning on November 11 that an armistice was to be signed later that day, the citizens of Macon filled the streets, shouting in celebration. Sirens sounded, whistles blew, and people cheered. When Germany and the Allies signed the truce at the eleventh hour on the eleventh day of the eleventh month, there was peace in the world and pandemonium in Macon.

5

With activity at Camp Wheeler winding down, Willie took a job with an automobile dealership. The boys were passing all their courses, and Lillie was happy with the life they had found in Macon. She had made new friends there, but had rediscovered old ones as well.

Lillie and Hettie Barfield had grown up on neighboring farms in Ochlocknee, and it was only natural that they should continue their friendship when they both found themselves in Macon. So the Striblings often had Sunday dinner with Ernest and Hettie Barfield.

The Barfields' son James, who was six in 1918, idolized W.L. The older boy was handsome and athletic, but more important to James, W.L. actually paid attention to him. When the families were together, he never failed to spend some time with the little boy, joking around or showing him some easy boxing moves.

In early May the Southeastern Aeronautical Congress was held at the recently constructed landing field at Central City Park. For two days airplanes soared and swooped in the sky above Macon. There were daily balloon ascensions and flying demonstrations, and exhibits of Allied aircraft and captured enemy planes. Ten thousand people attended the show on the first day, and it's likely the Stribling boys were among the spectators.

One big news item that summer in the Stribling household was that, on July 4, Jack Dempsey beat Jess Willard and won the heavyweight boxing championship of the world. Ruggedly handsome and fond of the limelight, the twenty-four-year-old Dempsey became an overnight sensation and was suddenly every young boy's hero. The boxer was the talk of the schoolyard when the boys returned to school in the fall.

Willie left the new car dealership and took a position at the Used Car Clearing House in downtown Macon in 1920. The same year the family moved into a rental house at 869 Mulberry Street, and W.L. started Lanier High School in September.

Lanier High occupied a big, three-story building at the corner of Orange and Pine streets. It didn't have a cafeteria in those days, and many of the students brought their lunches. Since W.L. lived only a few blocks away he usually went home for the noon meal.

Most boys would have been uncomfortable being two years older than the others in their grade, but W.L. had learned confidence early in life. He might not have been as scholastically advanced as the other fifteen-year-olds, but what he lacked in educational ability he made up in athletic prowess. Taller than most of the boys and heavily muscled, he couldn't help occasionally showing off how strong he was.

"Hit me in the stomach as hard as you can," he had challenged the other boys.

When they obliged and the punches caused him no discomfort, he would just laugh.

Every boy in school was required to join the Reserve Officers Training Corps (ROTC). W.L. became part of the program that year under the direction of Major Stanley G. Saulnier and drilled with his company in Forsyth Street Park across from the school.

Nearly sixteen, W.L. was noticing girls for the first time. He dated several, but none of the relationships were serious. Evenings out usually included picking up the girl at her house, riding the streetcar downtown, and seeing a moving picture. Douglas Fairbanks and John Barrymore were the idols of the silent screen that year.

But W.L. enjoyed sports as much, if not more, than dating. He played baseball and basketball with his friends every chance he got, and Willie never stopped pushing him to practice boxing. W.L. actually preferred basketball—he liked the speed of the game and the camaraderie with the other players—but his father insisted that he concentrate a good portion of his time on boxing, and W.L. did as he asked. After school he trained at the YMCA, working on the bags or sparring with anyone available.

Willie was so serious about W.L.'s future in the ring that he hired several boxing tutors for him. The last one was Edward Beaufort Everett, a Mercer Law School student who had learned boxing in the navy during the war.

W.L. liked the older boy and was fascinated by his stories about his time as a sailor, but Everett sometimes got a bit too aggressive in their sessions and W.L. had to scramble to defend himself against his free-swinging tutor. Willie finally decided that Everett was too rough for the 120-pound W.L. and took over training his son himself.

Along with school and sports, the Stribling boys were responsible for certain chores around the house. One of these was washing the dishes. It was a mundane task, but they livened it up for themselves and they loved an audience. They had learned showmanship as toddlers.

When their cousin Polly Braswell visited Macon one summer, she was amazed at the show that took place in the kitchen. W.L. washed the plates, then flung them across the room where Herbert deftly picked them out of the air, dried them, and put them away.

W.L. was popular, a good student and a promising basketball player, and he would have been happy enough to just go to school and knock around with his friends. But Willie was tired of waiting. As 1920 drew to a close, he decided that W.L. had learned all that his boxing mentors could teach him, and it was time to move forward with the career he had always envisioned for his son.

There was no professional boxing in Macon at the time, but the sport was thriving in Atlanta. In December Willie heard that Atlanta promoter Max Abelson was looking for someone to fight a preliminary bantamweight bout with a boy he called Kid Domb. Domb was primarily a street fighter and was billed as the king of Atlanta's newsboys. Willie wrote to Abelson offering W.L. as an opponent. In return, he received an invitation for W.L. to take part in the match and a round-trip train ticket to Atlanta.

So, instead of going to school on January 17, 1921, W.L. accompanied his father to Terminal Station where they boarded a train for the two-hour trip to Atlanta.

There were three bouts scheduled at the Atlanta Auditorium that evening and Stribling's was the first. Just before they entered the auditorium, one of the rough-looking men hanging around the door called to W.L.

"Hey, kid. A lot of people are going to be watching you. You got stage fright?"

W.L. looked at him with surprise. He was a bit nervous about his first real fight, of course, wanting to do well. But the idea of being frightened of an audience was a foreign concept for a boy who first appeared on stage at the age of three.

The crowd paid little attention to the unknown boy from Macon when he climbed into the ring, danced around a bit, and then took a seat on the stool in his corner. Willie, in a brown suit with his hair slicked down and parted in the middle, stood behind him, talking continuously. He was interrupted only once when the ring announcer "Fat" Elrod came over to make sure he had the boy's name right. Was it Stribling or Stripling?

Then the introductions began. Since no one in Atlanta had ever heard of W.L., he only received a smattering of applause from the audience. Kid Domb's reception was much warmer.

Willie kept speaking softly in W.L.'s ear, keeping his mind on the fight and off the audience. When the bell rang to start the first round, Willie jerked the stool out from under him and gave him a little push toward the center of the ring.

"I'll never forget how it felt to be cut loose from Pa after fifteen years," W.L. said years later. "It was like dropping off a precipice into darkness."

But he was only disoriented for a moment. Then his instincts and training took over. Graceful, clean-cut, and remarkably quick, he soon earned the respect of the crowd. By the middle of the first round, the audience was on its feet and remained there until the match ended, cheering for the unknown Macon fighter. W.L. easily defeated Domb, winning all four rounds.

He didn't get any prize money for his first win, but neither he nor his father minded. It had been a great debut, and when Abelson approached Willie after the fight and suggested another match in February, he eagerly agreed.

They took the train back to Macon that night and W.L. was in school the next day. He was happy about the outcome of his first fight—it was good to win—and he was relieved that he hadn't been marked in the fight so he didn't have to explain any cuts or bruises to his schoolmates.

The next day, Atlanta sportswriter Guy Butler was the first to call W.L. "Young" Stribling to distinguish him from his father who bore the same name. In the *Atlanta Constitution* his fighting was praised and W.L. was described as being as cool and confident as a veteran of a hundred matches.

The *Telegraph* carried an article about the match two days later, and W.L.'s picture first appeared in the Macon newspaper. In boxing shorts, his bare arms crossed and muscular, the boy stared straight into the camera without smiling. The photo was accompanied by a three-inch column that briefly described his fight with Kid Domb and predicted great things to come for the young boxer.

6

W.L. was no stranger to fame. A vaudeville veteran, he had seen his name in print numerous times, so the story and photo in the local newspaper didn't mean much to him. But he did receive some good-natured kidding about it from his friends.

His father was excited. He knew they were on their way. He intensified W.L.'s training over the next few weeks. Herbert had been trained right along with his brother, and now Willie decided that both boys were going to be professional boxers.

On Wednesday, February 9, the boys left school early and the whole family drove to Atlanta. The weather had been unseasonably warm for February, spawning the type of storms typical for springtime. Macon had experienced off-and-on rain for several days. Now as they drove northward, it grew heavier. When they reached Atlanta, the rain was coming down in sheets. They were all soaked by the time they got inside the auditorium.

But their discomfort was soon forgotten. W.L.'s match with Kid Nappie was a preliminary bout, but the two treated the crowd to four rounds of hard-hitting boxing. In the first round, Nappie delivered a hard right cross to W.L.'s jaw. It was the first time the boy been hit hard in a match and it stunned him for a moment, but he recovered almost immediately. Then he smiled. From then on he was in no danger from the other fighter and won the judges' decision.

The drive home through heavy rain was a long one. The downpour never relented, and by the next morning, Macon's Ocmulgee River had overflowed its banks. The water continued to rise as the day went on. The levee along Central City Park held, so the Striblings were safe in the downtown area, but large sections of East Macon were flooded and many people lost their homes that day.

W.L.'s second match received even more local newspaper coverage than his first. And it also sparked interest in boxing in his hometown. Sportswriters started calling for the establishment of a boxing club in Macon to show off the city's talent.

Meanwhile W.L.'s career was picking up speed. He defeated Tim O'Dowd in Atlanta on February 15, knocking him out in the first round. And W.L. and Willie were on the road again a week later for a match in Milledgeville, 30 miles northeast of Macon. Boxing fans in his hometown had been wanting to see W.L. fight since first reading about him, and a number of them made the automobile trip to the neighboring town that afternoon.

W.L. was scheduled to box Kid Sullivan, another Atlanta youngster, but there was a surprise for the audience before that match. Fourteen-year-old Herbert Stribling made his boxing debut that night against Little Bulldog. While it was only a three-round paperweight fight, the younger Stribling boy put his heart into it and won the decision. Then it was W.L.'s turn. The bell rang opening the first round, and W.L. and Sullivan met in the center of the ring. W.L. led with a hard right to Sullivan's jaw. This was followed by a left to the body and another right to the head. Sullivan slumped to the canvas without ever throwing a punch and the match was over. Stribling's hometown followers had gotten to see him fight—but only for one minute.

Willie didn't allow W.L. much time for a social life since he expected him to spend most of his free time in the gym. But there was no way his father could keep W.L. from noticing girls. In the spring of 1921 one of the girls he noticed was dark-eyed, black-haired Clara Kinney.

Clara was a child of privilege. The only daughter of William Oscar (W.O.) and Clara Guerry Kinney, she had grown up with four older brothers and was known to her family as Sister. The Kinneys lived in a big house on Cherokee Avenue designed by noted architect Neal Reid. It was an impressive place with a sizable staff of servants, including a cook, butler, and housekeeper. While her father ran a profitable cotton brokerage, her mother concentrated on various civic issues, including the beautification of the city. And now that women had won the right to vote, Mrs. Kinney was considering a run for City Council.

Clara was enjoying her high school years. Involved in several clubs and activities she never seemed to have a spare moment. Although they had both attended Lanier High that year, Clara hadn't really noticed W.L. until the spring. One afternoon she was walking with a friend when they passed a tall, muscular boy. He was handsome enough to be a movie star with his wavy dark hair and blue eyes, and Clara was intrigued.

"Who is that?" she asked her friend.

"He's a prizefighter."

"What's that?"

"He hits people," her friend said.

"He does not," Clara said, believing she was being teased.

But her friend explained about boxing and W.L.'s fights until Clara believed her. She wasn't especially taken with the idea of fighting, but once she met W.L., she was so impressed that she didn't care.

"I wouldn't have cared if he had been a grave digger," she said later.

The postwar years were a progressive time. In late March it was announced that a paved road from Atlanta through Macon to St. Simons Island off the coast of Georgia would be finished by the fall. The Striblings were interested since they frequently traveled to Atlanta for boxing matches. And the Kinney family was pleased with the southern leg of the route because they vacationed every summer in a big two-story house on East Beach on the island.

Although he still worked at the used car lot, Willie's real interest was training his sons and scheduling matches for them. The boys were both in demand and were now known by the nicknames bestowed on them by the press. W.L. was called "Young" Stribling, and Herbert was being referred to as "Baby" Stribling.

Their parents had nicknames, too. Even though they were only in their mid-thirties, in the newspapers Willie had become "Pa" Stribling, and Lillie was now "Ma." The nicknames stuck. Soon everyone, family and friends included, called them Pa and Ma Stribling.

W.L. continued his winning ways through the spring, and Pa started looking for tougher opponents. He found one in Dick Leonard, a

Savannah native who held the Georgia featherweight title. They traveled to Savannah for the match on March 30, and Pa pumped up W.L., telling him, "The tougher they are, the better." W.L. was in great form that night and ready to take the championship away from Leonard.

Entering the ring in Savannah was a new experience for him. Leonard was a hometown boy, and the crowd was hostile toward the newcomer from Macon. W.L. smiled at their reaction, but he found it disturbing.

The boxers were evenly matched, and the fight was a good one. In fact, a portion of the audience switched allegiances during the match. When the referee awarded the win to Leonard, the crowd was boisterous in their disapproval. Even the *Savannah Morning News* declared that the match had been a draw. But the decision stood, and W.L. had his first loss.

The following week W.L. was back in the ring in Atlanta. He went ten rounds with Battling Mishound and won every one but the first. However, he was tired and it showed. He had fought six matches in two and a half months, and it was time for a rest.

For the next month W.L. almost lived the life of a normal high school boy. He went to classes, hung out with friends, and went out with several girls. When his parents allowed, he drove the family car around town, delighting in the experience. But he never completely stopped training and was in the gym for at least a little while almost every day.

Boxing had been banned in Macon for fear of corruption, but W. L. Stribling had demonstrated that boxers could be clean-cut, upstanding young men, and local fans were anxious to see him in action. The local demand for the sport was growing. So the Neel American Legion Post stepped up to meet the need and became the official boxing sponsor in Macon.

In mid-April the City Council gave the Legion permission to use the newly completed City Auditorium for boxing matches, but permission came with a few strings attached. If anything illegal or immoral happened during the matches, the sport would again be abolished in Macon.

Pa Stribling was selected to arrange and promote the matches for their opening session, and he tackled the task with great enthusiasm. The

Legion promised "nothing but clean fights" and vowed to keep anyone or anything questionable out of the matches. They also declared they wouldn't tolerate fixed bouts or "stalling" by the boxers themselves.

The kickoff for the Legion's six-month fighting season was scheduled for May 5, 1921, with a match between Lou Gomez of New Orleans and W. L. Stribling. It was just what Macon's fight fans had been waiting for, and anticipation was high.

W.L. trained at the gym every night in preparation for the fight. As time grew short, more and more spectators crowded into the YMCA to watch him skip rope, shadow box, and routinely take on half a dozen sparring partners every night, going at least one round with each.

Placards were posted in town and throughout Middle Georgia. When tickets were put on sale at all the Macon drugstores, they went fast.

General admission was a dollar and a half, but Lanier High School students and American Legion members were offered special one-dollar tickets. Ringside seats were priced at two dollars and were so popular that most were snapped up as soon as they became available.

Over a thousand people jammed the City Auditorium that warm May night. In addition to fight fans, Lanier students—both boys and girls—turned out in big numbers to see their classmate in his Macon debut. Clara Kinney, however, was not among them. Although she was smitten with W.L., she had no desire to watch men hit each other until one of them fell down.

The three preliminaries that Pa had arranged were exciting and kept the audience entertained until the feature match. W.L. entered the arena in a matter-of-fact manner. As he approached the ring he stopped beside his mother, who was sitting at ringside. After the two exchanged a few words, he kissed her and then climbed between the ropes. Pa took his usual place in his son's corner.

The gong sounded, and W.L. and Lou Gomez squared off. The two swapped a few blows and appeared evenly matched in the opening round. But then W.L.'s superior ability began to show, and the crowd began to cheer. Gomez was floored in the third round and took a count of nine before getting to his feet.

When the fight resumed, W.L. attacked with a barrage of blows and Gomez went down again. This time he was out cold. W.L. had won his first hometown match.

In Friday morning's *Telegraph*, sportswriters raved about Stribling's performance and the clean, efficient way the American Legion had run the fight program. They predicted that the sport of boxing had a bright future in Macon.

Three weeks later, Macon hosted another boxing program, and W.L. was again in the feature match. This time he met Dick Leonard, the Georgia Featherweight Champion who had beaten him in the controversial fight in Savannah the month before. Once again, Macon turned out in force.

It was the local fans' first chance to see the younger Stribling boy. Herbert boxed one of the preliminary bouts and won an easy victory over Harry Allen.

W.L. couldn't help but remember the Savannah match and his loss, but that night it was Leonard who faced a hostile crowd and Stribling didn't disappoint his fans. Leonard outweighed him by four pounds, but W.L. had the advantage in height and speed. His footwork was dazzling, and his punches, especially his fast left hand, won him point after point.

At the end of ten rounds, W.L. was an easy winner and held his first title—Georgia Featherweight Champion. The title wasn't recognized outside of the state, but W.L. and his father felt as if they had won a major victory.

Leonard demanded a rematch as soon as it could be scheduled, and within days Pa Stribling announced that W.L. would face him again on June 7 in Atlanta, neutral territory.

W.L. and Clara Kinney started dating casually that spring. When Clara asked her parents if W.L. might come to call, her father first investigated the young man. He asked around town and heard only positive things. W.L. was a well-mannered, responsible boy who had the reputation of being a gentleman.

Clara's parents were charmed by him from their first meeting. The only holdout was her grandmother, Fanny Guerry, who had moved in with the Kinneys after she was widowed the year before.

Mrs. Guerry seemed determined to dislike W.L. from the beginning. In fact, she made up her mind not to ever meet him.

"I don't know what a prizefighter is," she said more than once. The implication was that, whatever it was, she wanted nothing to do with it. When she heard W.L.'s car in the driveway, she would hurry upstairs to her room and remain there until he left the house.

Clara had a strict ten o'clock curfew, but that gave her and W.L. plenty of time to see movies or attend the baseball games they both loved. As the weather warmed, they would go out to Lakeside Park in East Macon for boating and picnicking. Dances were held there in the evenings, and the orchestra played "Song of India," "Look for the Silver Lining," "Ain't We Got Fun," and other popular songs of the day.

W.L. was as fond of Clara as she was of him, and the situation would have been perfect if only her grandmother would give him a chance. The rest of the family had repeatedly asked Mrs. Guerry to simply meet the young man, but she refused. Finally W.L. conspired with Clara to bring about an encounter.

One evening, he parked his car some distance up the street and made a stealthy approach to the house. Clara quietly let him in the front door, and he came face to face with Mrs. Guerry in the parlor. As soon as she saw him enter the room, she hurried to the stairs, but he got there first, standing right in front of her so that she couldn't pass.

He smiled the smile that rarely failed to charm. "Mrs. Guerry, I've wanted to meet you for a long time, but I've always missed you."

This woman made it clear she wasn't about to be charmed. "Please let me pass," she said with no hint of warmth.

W.L. wasn't about to give up. "Oh, do you want to go upstairs?"

"Yes."

Without another word, he swept her up into his arms and carried her up the staircase. She locked her arms around his neck to keep from falling, but by the time they reached the second floor, she was giggling like a girl.

"You can put me down now," she told him.

He did so, then said gallantly, "I'm so glad to meet you, Mrs. Guerry. I hope you're going to like me because I love Clara very much."

35

From then on, Fanny Guerry was W.L.'s strong supporter and wouldn't allow anyone to speak against him.

7

W .L. fought three more matches in June 1921, including the rematch with Dick Leonard. He won all of them, two by knockouts. On July 4, his fight with Kid Bartlett of Charleston was the feature bout of the Legion's program in Macon.

The weather that day was hot and humid—typical for Macon—and Central City Park was the center of activity for the holiday. Picnickers spread blankets in the shade of the huge live oak trees, and a series of automobile races were held on the track early that afternoon. W.L. and Herbert slipped away from their parents to watch the speeding cars. Someday, they decided, they would drive race cars, too.

The boxing matches followed the races. A ring had been erected inside the ball park, and 3,000 people gathered there. Another 2,000 climbed onto the boxcars parked on the tracks behind the park to watch the action for free.

Herbert Stribling fought Little Tom Jones to a draw in a four-round preliminary bout, and then came W.L. and the main event.

Kid Bartlett had come to Macon with an impressive record, which included a recent defeat of Savannah's Dick Leonard. In fact, Pa had told *Telegraph* sportswriter C. E. Baker that Bartlett was "a bad actor" who was likely to give W.L. a real fight. He even suggested that Bartlett might win.

But evidently no one told W.L. that he might be facing a defeat. Although the fight went nine rounds before Bartlett's manager threw in the towel, sportswriters agreed that Stribling dominated every one. The only criticism of the young Macon fighter was that he fought too carefully. Instead of just rushing his opponent with all the strength and power he had, he held back, choosing his best punches and scientifically placing them where they would be most effective and score the most points.

W.L. had one more fight in July. He and his family drove to Atlanta in a new Ford automobile where he took on Cy Young at the Business Men's Athletic Club.

The crowd, which numbered about 1,000, was divided in their support of the two boxers, but just before the match, W.L. did something that endeared him to the audience. As he approached the ring, he stopped where Ma sat at ringside. He leaned down, embraced, and kissed her.

"I'll get him, Mama," he said.

Then he returned to the aisle and stepped into the ring in time to be announced. The applause was deafening. With that one gesture—one he performed before nearly every bout—he had won the hearts of the Atlanta crowd.

W.L. seemed unconcerned about the ultimate outcome of the match. He delivered devastating blows and easily avoided much of what Young tried to throw at him. So relaxed was he that, when he dodged to avoid his opponent's punches, he would grin as if he found the whole experience great fun.

He won by a knockout in the eighth round. Then he and referee Hume McDonald lifted the defeated fighter out of the ring so that he could be carried into the locker room.

W.L. Stribling was only sixteen years old in July 1921 and had fought fourteen matches since his professional debut seven months before. His fame was growing, but it was time for a rest. And P. A. McArthur of the Macon YMCA had just the place in mind for that. On July 14, W.L., his classmate Charlie Holmes, and McArthur left Macon for the mountains of North Carolina.

The Blue Ridge Assembly was a YMCA student training facility. For two weeks, the three young men attended leadership classes in the big, white-columned buildings. But whenever time allowed they were outdoors, hiking the mountainous trails, splashing in the clear streams, and enjoying the natural beauty of the Appalachian Mountains.

But then it was back to Macon and back to work. A week after he returned home W.L. fought Joe "Kid" Peck in Central City Park, taking a ten-round decision from the power fighter.

Pa was succeeding as a promoter and had also begun building his own small stable of local fighters, including Hooty Flahive and Herbert. But W.L. was the undisputed star of the group. It was an unusual day when Pa didn't receive a letter or telegram from someone trying to arrange a match between W.L. and some hopeful young contender.

It was only natural that Pa began looking around to expand his sphere of influence, and the capital city of Atlanta was the next logical step. In August 1921 he made his first move in that direction by arranging some bouts for W.L. through the sponsorship of the Atlanta Post of the American Legion.

At the time, Walk Miller was the undisputed master promoter of boxing in Atlanta. His fighters, from bantamweight to heavyweight, appeared on nearly every boxing card presented there, and he didn't appreciate any encroachment on his turf.

But he knew how popular Young Stribling was becoming in Atlanta, and he wasn't about to turn down a good drawing card. So in spite of Pa's inroads, Walker arranged for W.L. to fight Freddie Boorde, the acknowledged Featherweight Champion of the South, in Atlanta on August 15. Older, taller, and heavier than Stribling, Boorde had been fighting professionally for nearly three years. It was even rumored that he was scheduled to fight in New York's Madison Square Garden in the fall.

With the featherweight championship on the line, Miller heavily advertised the Boorde–Stribling bout. He even had a decorative belt made—a beautiful woven creation of red, white, and blue, bearing the championship inscription. It would be awarded to the winner of the fight, and since he was certain that Boorde would take the match, he was confident the belt would stay in Atlanta.

Advance ticket sales were brisk, and Macon was well represented at the contest. When Young Stribling, as he was billed, stepped through the ropes in the Atlanta Auditorium Armory that Monday night, there were plenty of hometown fans among the 6,000 people in the auditorium to cheer him on.

The title match was the fourth bout of the evening, beginning around 9:30. Boorde was the strongest, smartest fighter W.L. had ever faced, but when the final bell rang, the judges gave the unanimous decision to Stribling. He was now the official Featherweight Champion of the South and had a dazzling new belt to prove it.

The audience cheered and whistled and many of them rushed to the ring to congratulate the new champ, but W.L. evaded them. He left the ring and hurried to embrace his mother. He kissed her, then handed her the championship belt. The crowd roared its approval of this loving gesture.

Boorde's manager demanded a rematch, and he and Pa began immediate negotiations. But W.L. had other things on his mind. Champion or not, he was still a sixteen-year-old boy, and school would be starting back soon. He planned to try out for the Lanier High basketball team and was eager to see Clara Kinney, who would soon be returning from St. Simons.

But the Striblings didn't go straight home. They hadn't been to South Georgia in some time, so soon after the Boorde fight they drove to the little town of Cairo, near Ochlocknee, and stayed a few days with Ma's relatives. W.L.'s fame hadn't gone unnoticed in that part of the state. W.L. and Herbert worked out several times at the Cairo Athletic Club, and their sparring matches drew quite a crowd. People were eager to see the new Featherweight Champion of the South.

Labor Day might have been the unofficial end of summer in much of the country, but Macon never saw relief from the heat until October or later. On Labor Day 1921, the high temperature was 97°. There was baseball that day in Central City Park, and in late afternoon there was boxing.

Pa Stribling had put together an entertaining card featuring thirty-six rounds of boxing. four thousand people filled the stands to watch three preliminary matches and a semifinal bout, but most of them were there to see the feature fight between Young Stribling and Fearless Ferns.

Rumor had it that Pa's Atlanta rival, Walk Miller, had sent Ferns to Macon for the Labor Day match in hopes that he beat Young Stribling. Such a defeat would decrease the Macon fighter's popularity in Atlanta and just might derail the elder Stribling's plans for expanding his empire in that direction.

It was all speculation, of course, and might have been dreamed up by an overzealous sportswriter or even suggested by Pa himself, but the stories sparked more interest in what was already an eagerly anticipated fight.

Ferns, whose real name was Powell Corley, had boxed professionally for less than a year, but he had only lost one of his nine bouts. He was taller than W.L., had a longer reach, and was expected to give the local boy a tough time.

The fighters were evenly matched and in the end the judges declared the fight a draw, but the crowd wasn't disappointed. They had witnessed a masterful display of the sport.

After the last boxing match in the park, the baseball games resumed, but attendance dwindled. People were already making their way home through the twilight. Summer was over, and school started the next day.

W.L. was happy to be back in the school-day routine. He was a sophomore that year and Clara Kinney was a junior, and the two were becoming a steady couple. W.L. enjoyed socializing with the other students and put in enough time with the books to do well in his studies, but Pa made sure he still had regular workouts in the gym.

Charlie Morgan was director of athletics at Lanier High and coached the boys' basketball team. He wasn't much older than the boys he coached. In fact he attended Mercer University and played on the college's baseball team during the time he worked at Lanier.

W.L. was eager to try out for the Lanier Poets basketball squad. He excelled at the game, which he had first learned at the YMCA, and Coach Morgan soon recognized the young man's abilities. W.L. easily made the team, and his work on the court earned him a regular spot at forward.

W.L. was busy that fall and winter. In addition to his studies and boxing training, he regularly drilled with the ROTC, where he had achieved the rank of corporal of Company B. Now he added basketball practice to his already crowded schedule.

Clara was busy as well. She worked on the yearbook staff and, in December, joined a few other girls to form the Junior Dramatic Club, which gave several performances at the Wesleyan College Conservatory auditorium.

W.L. fought eight more times that year, including a rematch with Fearless Ferns in which he stepped up to the next weight class and won the Southern Lightweight Champion title. The win earned him another fancy belt contributed by Walk Miller. He wrapped up 1921 with a career record of twenty-five professional fights, winning twenty-one, drawing three, and losing only one.

8

W.L.'s photograph graced the cover of the *Pugilistic News*, an Atlanta-based boxing magazine, in January 1922. In the accompanying article he was praised for his skill and given another nickname—the "Heart of Georgia." Great things were predicted for him.

In fact, great things were already happening to the Striblings. They were finally able to purchase a house of their own—a wooden bungalow at 821 Second Street—and Pa was becoming so successful in promoting fights that he had left the used car business behind and set up an office in the Macon Athletic Club. When space above a restaurant on Cherry Street became available, he leased it and turned it into a gym for his stable of fighters.

Ma was no longer working at the stationery store, but her home and family kept her very busy. And when business required Pa to travel, she stepped in as trainer in his absence. She was just as demanding as her husband and even occasionally climbed into the ring to spar with W.L. or Herbert.

W.L. did his best to keep current with his studies, but he often missed classes in order to appear in fights. On January 23 he was again matched with Freddie Boorde, this time in Birmingham, and his featherweight and lightweight titles were on the line. Boorde was so confident of the outcome that he told reporters W.L. would leave Birmingham when the fight was over, but those shiny belts would stay right there with him. However, the match ended in a draw, and Stribling's titles were secure.

Boxing took a lot of his time, but W.L.'s overriding interest that winter was basketball. He proudly wore his orange and green Lanier letter sweater and enjoyed nothing more than romping around the court in a fast contest. He approached the sport with the same focus and determination he brought to the boxing ring and was a skilled, exciting player.

Sometimes doing both was difficult. The Poets were undefeated with a 7 and 0 record. On Friday, February 3 they were scheduled to play Gordon Institute, but W.L. was fighting Battling Budd the day before. He was determined to do both.

Every afternoon he worked out with the basketball team. Then at 6:00 p.m. he reported to the Macon Athletic Club to train for the upcoming fight. The only concession Pa made in light of the boy's work on the basketball court was to discontinue his roadwork for the week.

It was an exhausting time, but W.L. came through it well. He won the fight with Budd on Thursday night and was on the court with the Poets the next evening when they posted a lopsided 38-18 victory over Gordon. He even emerged as one of the stars of the game. W.L. was fast on his feet and could elude the most determined guard. He and Buncie Skinner were responsible for much of the team's scoring. To watch him, no one would have ever guessed that Stribling had fought a 10-round boxing match the night before.

In early February, Pa received a last-minute invitation for W.L. to fight in Galveston, Texas. Excited by the opportunity for his son to expand his reputation outside of Georgia, he was eager to schedule the match, but for once W.L. resisted. He would not only miss several days of school, but would be absent when the Poets played Albany, one of their toughest rivals. No matter how much Pa tried to persuade him, W.L. wouldn't be moved. His father was disappointed but finally declined the offer, and W.L. was with them when the Lanier team won the game on February 10.

Knowing his son wanted to devote most of his time to the Poets, Pa only scheduled one more fight for W.L. during basketball season. He defeated Charles "Sailor" Blanque in Birmingham where the crowd was so impressed with his performance that they swarmed the ring after the fight. It took W.L. twenty-six minutes to free himself from their enthusiastic congratulations.

Soon after the Blanque fight the Macon newspaper ran an advertisement for the Macon Athletic Club, featuring a picture of W.L. in a fighting stance. The ad announced that the club now offered boxing and wrestling lessons, taught by Pa Stribling and Harry Stevens.

The Lanier Poets finished their season undefeated, then turned their sights on a state title. On February 23, 24, and 25, the school hosted the first Georgia Interscholastic Athletic Association tournament. The games took place in the city auditorium, and on the last day of the tournament Lanier played Tech High School of Atlanta in the state championship game.

W.L. played his usual skillful game, but fouled out in the last minutes. The boy who so loved the game ended up on the bench, tears in his eyes, but his team won without him by a score of 39-38.

Pa was more interested in boxing than basketball. It was time, he believed, for W.L. to move from the lightweight classification into light welterweight. To that end, he scheduled his next match with Larry Avera.

Avera, a professional since 1919, was managed by Walk Miller. A compact, muscular blond, he outweighed W.L. by several pounds. The March 7 fight in Atlanta could have gone either way. Avera began aggressively, coming at W.L. with a barrage of punches. He bloodied Stribling's lip in the first round—the first time the boy had been marked in a match. But as the fight went on, Avera appeared to tire while W.L. rallied, and the lead changed hands several times.

At the beginning of the tenth round, the crowd was treated to some unexpected excitement. Immediately after the fighters shook hands to start the final round, Avera gave W.L. a light blow to the head. Pa saw it as a cheap shot and was through the ropes and into the ring before the referee could stop him.

He rushed Avera, berating him. Believing he was being unjustly accused, Avera grew equally angry. But before the incident escalated into a physical confrontation, W.L. stepped between them and herded his father out of the ring. Then the fight resumed, and when it ended the judges ruled the match a draw.

Legendary golfer Bobby Jones was just coming into prominence in 1922, as much a youthful wonder in the golf world as W. L. Stribling was in prizefighting. Jones had qualified for his first U.S. Open in 1920 at the age of eighteen. By March 1922, he had twice won the Southern Amateur Tournament, but hadn't yet entered the professional ranks.

That's when Macon's Idle Hour Country Club persuaded him to pair with club pro Jack Oke against two internationally known golfers—U.S. Open champion Jim Barnes and British Open champion Jock Hutchinson.

The match, which was played on Saturday, March 11, was quite a feather in Macon's golfing cap. It was Jones's first time in the city, and his appearance generated a lot of excitement. However, the Striblings didn't take much notice of the event. Golfing was one sport they hadn't yet tried.

Pa had scheduled three more March matches for W.L. and was pushing him to train harder and harder to be sure he would be in good fighting form. Socializing and studies had to be crowded into the little time that was left over.

But W.L. wasn't ready to limit himself. With basketball finished, he tried out for the baseball team and made it. But he could only do so much with the time he had, and he was missing a number of days at school. Although nothing was said at the time, his absences were being noticed.

He won his next two fights, but his match with Battling Budd was another story. The two had met twice before. One fight ended in a draw, and Stribling won the other. The two might never have fought again, but when Walk Miller wrote to Pa Stribling, declaring that Budd was the Southern Welterweight champion, it was all Pa had to hear. He fired back a letter of his own, declaring that W.L. was ready to go fifteen rounds with Budd anywhere and anyplace Miller desired.

The time Miller chose was Tuesday night, March 28, and the place he selected was the Forsyth Street Arena in Atlanta. Although a number of Macon fans made the trip, the majority of the big crowd was pulling for the hometown favorite, Budd.

Budd moved aggressively on his opponent the moment the opening bell rang and never looked back. Stribling's usual practice of staying on the defensive and striking from that position didn't work that night. For the first time in his career, W.L. was soundly beaten. The judges awarded him only one of the ten rounds and no one was surprised when the referee raised Budd's hand in victory.

W.L. stood to one side in the unaccustomed position of loser, a small, sad smile on his face. Then he braced himself, walked over to Budd, and congratulated him. Even in defeat, he didn't forget his manners.

Pa told reporters after the match that he believed the fight was actually a draw in spite of the judges' decision, but Atlanta and Macon sportswriters alike had no doubt that Budd had been the winner. More than that, they all agreed that losing was the best thing that could have happened to the seventeen-year-old.

A loss was bound to happen, they said in print and in private, and it was good that it finally came. Up until now, W.L. had felt nearly invincible. The controversial match with Leonard in Savannah hadn't really seemed like a loss. But now, with his first real loss out of the way, he wouldn't have to worry about avoiding it and could concentrate on becoming a better, more skilled boxer.

The Striblings drove home that night, arriving in Macon well after midnight. Although he got little sleep, W.L. was in class the next morning and reported for baseball practice in the afternoon.

Pa's ultimate goal that year was to have his son fight Southern Welterweight Champion Jake Abel. But in order to be considered for that contest, W.L. would have to convincingly defeat the two other most likely contenders—Larry Avera and Battling Budd, both members of Walk Miller's stable.

W.L. fought Budd twice in May, and each match ended in a draw. The fans were unhappy with the decisions, but W.L. had other things on his mind. While he might have one foot in the adult boxing world, the other was firmly planted in high school.

In early May the annual Lanier basketball awards were given out. W.L. and the other members of the title-winning team were all present and received a gold basketball charm from the school. The Macon National Bank also had gifts for them— each boy received a medal and a victory dollar.

W.L. treasured that little basketball charm. He carried it with him for many years afterward. It was more important to him than the championship belts, titles, and the stories that now appeared regularly in the newspapers.

The baseball season was now in full swing, and the Lanier team had two games scheduled for May 5 and 6 with Richmond Academy. W.L. and the rest of the team practiced hard, but the baseball team didn't have the same degree of talent that the basketball team did. W.L. played left field and was an adequate, although not spectacular, hitter.

The Poets decisively lost the series with Richmond Academy, and W.L., who wasn't a starter, only played sporadically. He didn't get a single hit, and on the one occasion that a ball sailed into his part of the outfield, he wasn't able to catch it. For once, W.L. encountered a sport in which he did not excel.

9

S tribling was back in the ring on May 24, defeating Joe Marks in the Macon City Auditorium. A week later he took a 10-round decision from Larry Avera in Americus, but he still hadn't achieved the victory that Pa believed he needed. So once again a match was scheduled with Battling Budd.

The fight would take place in North Carolina where the law required that it be a "no-decision" match, meaning that there would be no winner or loser unless there was a knockout. On June 12 the two fighters met for the sixth and final time in Charlotte. Both tried to achieve that winning knockout but weren't able to do so, and the match was officially classified as having had "no-decision."

But that didn't keep the sportswriters on hand from discussing the fight and reaching a consensus among themselves as to who won. The next day, the *Atlanta Constitution* announced that Budd had won. This was called a "newspaper decision" and was common practice in the 1920s.

W.L. had some free time after the Budd fight to enjoy the summer. He and his friends saw movies—they laughed at the antics of Buster Keaton and were amazed by Valentino's heroics—and spent long, lazy afternoons swimming and boating at Lakeside Park.

It was at Lakeside that W.L. got into the sort of casual altercation familiar to most teenaged boys. One Friday evening, H. M. Brice, a young fireman, accused Stribling of pinching him. W.L. denied it, and a scuffle ensued in which each young man threw one punch. That was the end of it—at least W.L. thought it was.

But he was about to learn one of the drawbacks of fame. Instead of passing off the tussle, Brice swore out a warrant, charging W.L. with assault and battery. Stribling was shocked when he learned about the warrant the next day, but his parents insisted he had to take care of it immediately. He went down to the sheriff's office and turned himself in, scared and embarrassed. Nothing more came of the incident, but W.L. learned a valuable lesson.

Even though W.L. never defeated Battling Budd, Pa finally got him a match with Jake Abel. The setting couldn't have been more favorable to the Striblings. The contest would be the feature fight in Macon on the Fourth of July.

Pa immediately started W.L. back on a strenuous training schedule, but his son wasn't ready to give up all of his other interests that summer. He still went out with friends, took his sweetheart Clara on dates, and even had time to pursue other sports.

On June 26 he took part in the North Highlands playground tennis tournament, battling Joe Norris for the tournament championship. The match was a long one, going to deuce a record-setting thirty-five times in the scorching heat before Norris finally won.

Jake Abel, the Southern Welterweight Champion, was a clean-cut, wholesome young man, the opposite of the rough, rude boxer stereotype, and had been fighting professionally for nearly ten years. A World War veteran, he had been the American Expeditionary Forces Welterweight Champion.

He was 29 years old in July 1922, and W.L. was only 17. The difference in ages was worrisome to Stribling's fans, some of whom were afraid that the match with the experienced champion was coming too soon. Based on Abel's record of 53 wins and 17 losses, they feared W.L. would be outclassed this time. Sportswriters suggested he would do better with another year's experience before this kind of test.

But Pa wasn't worried. He assured reporters that his boy would be ready and would beat the Atlanta champ. Typically, W.L. had nothing to say about the upcoming bout and just went about the business of training under his father's watchful eye.

Every morning he did his usual five miles of roadwork. After a rest and lunch, he played a few sets of tennis or a game of handball. Then, when the temperature dropped a bit in the evening, he spent a couple of hours at the Athletic Club sparring with local fighters.

As always Ma was close at hand. Her job was to oversee his diet, sticking mostly to fresh fruits and vegetables. W.L. didn't complain about the strict nutritional regimen, but he did long for ice cream. It was his favorite treat, and after every match, he was allowed a quart of it.

The training went well that summer. As the fight neared, W.L.'s punches grew in intensity, and one by one, the local boys refused to spar with him anymore. By the Saturday before the fight, Pa had to import a young boxer from Fort Benning in Columbus to go the final practice rounds with W.L.

The town was excited about the upcoming fight. Ticket sales had been brisk. The gloves to be used in the match had been on display at R.S. Thorpe's store for a couple of weeks and had attracted a number of curious folks, most of whom had never before seen boxing up close.

Nearly 5,000 people were expected in Central City Park for the July 4 festivities, but cloudy skies and occasional rain showers early in the day cut that number in half. But the rain stopped around noon, and they were able to get the scheduled baseball game in. Then the diamond was transformed into a sporting arena with the ring located just behind home plate. The boxing matches started at 5:00.

Herbert Stribling won the opening fight with Pi-Line Price. A big group of his schoolmates were present to see the win and raucously cheered him on.

Three more preliminaries followed, and at ten to six W.L. and Abel entered the ring. The fighters were greeted by wild applause and shouting from the obviously partisan crowd. W.L. proudly displayed the Lanier High School colors—an orange and green silk belt with his black trunks.

There were no judges for the match. The decision rested in the hands of referee Ed Alexander, a police lieutenant from Savannah. Alexander was a former prizefighter, promoter, and boxing manager, and both sides had declared they believed him to be fair and impartial.

Stribling's superiority was evident from the beginning. Although the close fighting seemed even, W.L. landed several body blows in the first round that caused Abel pain, and he continued on the offensive throughout the fight.

At the end of ten rounds, Alexander didn't hesitate. As soon as the final bell rang, he lifted W.L.'s hand in the air. The crowd showed its approval of the decision, but they saved a good deal of applause and admiration for Jake Abel, who had never given up and fought a clean, determined fight.

W.L. Stribling was only seventeen years old the day he took the Southern Welterweight title from Jake Abel. In eighteen months, he had progressed in class from bantamweight to welterweight. He had fought 43 matches, winning 32 of them. Nine were draws or no-decisions. He had only lost two and was never knocked down. It was an impressive record for any boxer, but one that was almost impossible to believe for a schoolboy.

Pa incorporated W.L.'s win into his promotional business. His letterhead stationery featured three pictures of his son, a brief listing of former opponents down one side and the heading: "Welterweight Champion of the South, under personal management of 'Pa' Stribling."

The rest of the summer was a blur of training and fighting. W.L. had four more matches and won them all. Then on Labor Day, September 4, he was back in Central City Park facing Kentuckian James "Red" Herring.

The championship was on the line, and this time, the young Macon fighter wasn't favored to win. Herring had fought all over the country, racking up a record of 125 fights. Of that number, he had only lost four. He was a formidable opponent.

It was hot that afternoon—the temperature had soared to the high 90s and the air was so humid it was difficult to take a deep breath. But the heat didn't seem to affect W.L. at all. When he stepped into the ring the Lanier High School band played the school's alma mater, "Glory to Lanier," and he waved at the crowd, smiling and relaxed.

It was a hard-hitting, aggressive fight. W.L.'s first left jab brought forth a small stream of blood from Herring's nose, but the Kentuckian quickly retaliated. The give-and-take continued through ten rounds when the referee declared the match a draw. He hadn't won, but the title still belonged to Stribling.

The next morning it was back to school. A junior that year, W.L. was promoted to Platoon Sergeant of Company C in the ROTC program, and he was looking forward to playing basketball that winter. He would have liked to play football as well. He tried his best to persuade them, but his parents refused to allow him to take part in such a "dangerous" sport.

Clara was thrilled to be back at school. She was the center of a whirlwind of social activities and honors—senior class president, a football, basketball, and ROTC sponsor, and a member of the drama club and yearbook staff. Raised to believe that her destiny was being a wife and mother, she wasn't particularly concerned about schoolwork. For her, high school was a party interrupted every now and then by classes.

While W.L. enjoyed school, too, Pa never let him forget that it came second to his career in the ring. He fought and won twice more in September. And, on the 25th, the Striblings hosted a reception at the newly renovated Young Stribling Athletic Club at 613 Cherry Street. The reception was a chance for the public to see the club's new furnishings and equipment. Athletic exhibitions were put on, and refreshments were served while Pa signed up new members. Each membership came with the promise of boxing and wrestling instruction and a regular schedule of gym work.

The Striblings not only had a new health club, they would soon have a brand-new house as well. Property on the east side of the river was being developed into an exclusive neighborhood. In September, Pa purchased a lot in North Highlands at 109 Nottingham Drive, and work was soon under way on a modern brick bungalow.

A second bout with Red Herring was scheduled for October 4. Before it took place, the Kentucky boxer wrote a letter to the sports committee at the Macon American Legion, declaring himself more than ready to meet and beat Young Stribling. He had, he reported, scored two knockouts since they fought to a draw on Labor Day.

"I have solved the Stribling style," he wrote, "and this time I am going to put over the K.O."

W.L. smiled when he was shown the letter a few days later. "Red believes he can knock me out, but he's due for another surprise. I'll be in there for a knockout this time."

The first game of the 1922 World Series between the New York Giants and the New York Yankees was played on October 4, but the big event in Macon was the Stribling–Herring fight. While neither man scored a knockout in their second meeting, W.L.'s performance was impressive enough to sway the referee and he was declared the winner. Years later, Stribling would say Herring was the toughest man he ever fought.

Pa was growing impatient for matches that would bring his son the national attention he craved. He was pleased that W.L. continued getting offers to fight in the Southeast, but he wanted more. The Southern Welterweight Championship wasn't enough.

In October, he got his wish. Young Stribling not only left the state for a bout, he left the country. The same week that Ty Cobb, known in his home state as the world's greatest baseball player, returned home to Augusta after another spectacular season, Pa and W.L. were on their way to Cuba.

10

Prohibition might have been the law in the United States, but not in Cuba. Only 90 miles from Key West, Havana had become a tourist Mecca for well-to-do Americans. Liquor flowed freely in the upscale restaurants and nightclubs, and the casinos, racetracks, and boxing rings offered glamorous entertainment all day and late into the night.

The Stribling men arrived in Havana on October 9, and Pa sent Ma a telegram as soon as they landed, letting her know they had gotten there safely. W.L. wasn't scheduled to fight until the 14th, so they had a few days for training before the match. They even had time to visit some old haunts from their vaudeville days.

Eight thousand spectators were present in Havana when Stribling fought Young Wallace. Sportswriters had predicted a close fight, but it didn't work out that way. W.L. was never behind on points and won by a knockout in the tenth round.

By the following Wednesday Pa and W.L. were back in Macon, but W.L. didn't return to class. Instead, he and his father left the next afternoon for the Tennessee mountains where he had a fight scheduled for Friday night. This match, however, would be different from any he fought so far.

Some months before, Pa had gotten a letter from Casey Hanegan, secretary for the National Sanatorium for Disabled War Veterans in Johnson City, Tennessee. He asked if there was any chance that W.L. would appear in a match for the patients at his hospital. He apologized that there were no funds to pay for his appearance since the hospital was a government facility.

Pa immediately accepted the invitation, saying they would be pleased to appear "for the benefit of the disabled heroes who are certainly entitled to anything for which they ask and if we can contribute to their happiness, it will be our pleasure to do so."

It was the perfect time of year to visit East Tennessee. The weather was growing cooler, and the changing leaves painted the mountains with color. The Striblings were welcomed as if they were visiting royalty.

W.L.'s opponent for the charity match was a fresh-faced high school student named Tiger Toro. He had a reputation as a good amateur, but his fight with Stribling would be his first professional one.

Eight hundred disabled veterans made up the enthusiastic crowd. They were eager for an exciting fight, but from the first bell it was clear that the two fighters were badly mismatched. Toro was completely out of his league. Stribling could hit him at will, and all Toro could do was try to defend himself.

W.L. recognized the situation for what it was. But rather than beat the younger boy mercilessly and go for what would have been an easy knockout, he adroitly turned the remaining rounds into something of an exhibition, demonstrating his own skill, but not injuring his opponent in the process.

The next day Casey Hanegan sent letters to several leading Georgia newspapers, commending the "Macon Flash," as some were beginning to call him, for graciously entertaining the war veterans at the sanitorium.

"Last night Young Stribling made our dreams come true and acquired 800 fast friends," he wrote. He described Pa as "one of the finest of all the boosters for the disabled veterans."

W.L. returned to school the next week. While he tried to catch up on his studies, his father continued scheduling fights for him.

On November 9, W.L. met Jack Denham, an Atlanta police officer, in the Macon City Auditorium. It was Stribling's first time in the middleweight class and everything went his way that Thursday night. He won every round. When it was over, Denham raised W.L.'s hand in victory before the judges even voiced their opinion.

W.L.'s boxing career was on fire, but his academic situation wasn't as healthy. His frequent absences from school were being documented, and on November 9—the same day as the Denham fight—the Bibb County Board of Education considered the matter.

A. L. Miller, the board chairman, was the first to raise the subject. He was concerned, he said, because W.L.'s father took the boy out of school "at will" to go to other cities or even other countries where he fought for money. He stressed that he wasn't criticizing W.L.'s conduct or reputation in any way, but questioned whether Pa had the right to completely disregard the school's attendance rules.

If Miller expected the rest of the board to share his concern, he was disappointed. One by one, the other members expressed their admiration for the boy.

"I have found that those who excel in athletics usually excel in their studies," Mayor Luther Williams said. "I believe that's true in this young man's case."

Superintendent C. H. Bruce supported that. "His teachers say that he is studious and is keeping up with his work."

Another member contributed the fact that no matter how late the night before W.L. returned from an out-of-town match, he would be in class the next morning "the freshest student there."

Miller finally dropped the matter. "I give up," he said. "I can see that this board is made up of fight fans. You're all against me."

The Cuban sporting public had been so impressed with Young Stribling after his first Havana appearance that promoters there lost no time in inviting him back. Less than a week after the Board of Education meeting, W.L. was out of school again. On Tuesday, November 12, he and Pa left Macon for Cuba, and the following Saturday night W.L. fought Tony Marullo in Havana's Mariana Stadium.

It was the boy's first fifteen-round fight, and Pa was a little anxious as to how he would handle the longer match, but he needn't have worried. Marullo was so badly bested that the referee called the fight in the twelfth round and awarded the victory to W.L. Four days later Stribling was back in class at Lanier, but he had missed another week of school.

Jack Dempsey, reigning World Heavyweight Champion, hadn't put his title on the line in over two years, spending his time instead appearing in vaudeville. People around the country who had never attended a prizefight were thrilled to sit in a theater and watch the handsome champion on stage. He was so popular that, in late November 1922, a New York theater promoter offered him $1,000,000 to box in three exhibition matches. It was an astronomical amount of money, and reading about it in the *Telegraph* just strengthened Pa's resolve to push his son to greater and greater achievement.

Pa's goal might have been lining up more bouts for his son—W.L. fought and won two matches in the first week of December—but W.L.'s attention was focused again on basketball. That year both the Lanier High and Mercer University teams would practice and hold their home games in the City Auditorium. Coaches Charlie Morgan and Josh Cody and several assistants worked for weeks painting backboards and court lines. When the Poets arrived for their first practice, it was like walking into a brand-new gym.

Only two members of the last year's championship team were absent. Rufus Smith and Atwood Wilder had graduated the previous summer, but Vernon Skinner, Malcolm Green, Oscar Long, and W.L. were all there and ready to play. The rest of the team was chosen from a dozen more players who had shown up for tryouts.

The Poets opened their season Friday night, December 14, against Barnesville A&M. The game wasn't even close, ending in a 66-14 victory for Lanier. Skinner was the high scorer, but W.L. posted a respectable 12 points.

After the game, players and students celebrated. Clara and W.L. joined their friends at the local confectionary shop where there was excited talk about a second championship season. The team was sure they were on their way to another state victory.

Christmas was approaching. Store windows were decorated, and newspapers carried advertisements for special gifts. Victrola record players were among the most extravagant items being offered that year. There were several models available, and all of them were priced over $100.

But the season had its charitable side, too. Many businesses, civic organizations, and churches teamed up to make sure the orphans in Macon's numerous institutions had special food and gifts for Christmas.

The Georgia Industrial Home, Appleton Church Home, Masonic Orphans Home, and several others were recipients of the city's goodwill.

It was a rare day that month when W.L.'s name or picture didn't appear in the sports sections of the Macon newspapers. There were stories about the Poets' practices and games, and articles announcing Stribling's upcoming boxing matches.

Photographs of him were printed with regularity. He was shown in street clothes, boxing shorts, and in his Lanier basketball uniform. There was even one picture of him at six months old standing aloft on his father's outstretched hand.

W.L. won his last two fights of 1922. It was a happy time for him. He enjoyed school. He was an up-and-coming prizefighter, a basketball star, and he was dating one of the most popular girls in town. But trouble he had thought had been put to rest was about to be resurrected.

11

W.L. was back in the ring on New Year's Day. The match at the Macon City Auditorium was his first in the light heavyweight class. His opponent Jack Middleton came into the fight with a string of twenty-five wins behind him, but Pa was confident his boy was up to the challenge.

And he was right. Two minutes into the first round, W.L. drove Middleton back against the ropes. Then a left to the jaw, followed by a hard right uppercut sent the man flying through the ropes. He landed several feet below the ring, bruised, disoriented, and unable to return to the fight, Stribling winning by a technical knockout. It was an impressive showing by the Macon boy, but a little disappointing for fight fans who had expected a ten-round, not a two-minute event.

The next day, W.L. was back in school, and at 2:45 p.m, he reported to the auditorium for basketball practice. The Poets' schedule was crowded that month. On Friday, January 5, they defeated Washington High School. The following Thursday night, they traveled to Moultrie for a win and, the next evening, beat Georgia Military Academy at home. W.L. was the high scorer in that game, and in praising him, one sportswriter declared that "everything in the game worked around Stribling."

The Poets were rolling along undefeated and seemed poised to take the state championship for the second year in a row. But there were forces at work hoping to change the makeup of the winning team.

Charles Tolbert coached basketball at Atlanta's Tech High. It was his team that had been defeated in the 1922 GIAA tournament when the Lanier Poets took the championship. Tolbert had been paying close attention to what was happening in Macon, and he decided that W.L. Stribling shouldn't be a part of the Lanier squad if they returned to the tournament in that year.

In early January he announced that he would protest Stribling's eligibility when the GIAA met later that month. He based his objection to W.L.'s participation in high school sports on the fact that he was a professional fighter. It meant, he insisted, that Lanier had a professional athlete as a member of what was supposed to be an amateur team.

Macon fans were outraged. They contended that a high school student who regularly attended his classes, kept up with studies, and was in good standing with his school shouldn't be barred from taking part in any school activities, including athletics. They believed that Tolbert's protest was not so much concern over the rules as a reaction to Tech High's 1922 defeat by Lanier.

The debate continued with school officials, sportswriters, and politicians all offering opinions, but only the GIAA could settle the question. And they wouldn't meet for several weeks.

For months Macon sports fans had been urging the American Legion to put some better-known fighters on their boxing cards. They had seen plenty of men from the surrounding area. Now they wanted someone with a national reputation to fight in their town.

Pa Stribling had always had a keen ear for the audience. He got busy and wired Leo P. Flynn, a well-known New York boxing promoter. The result was a January 18 match in Macon between W.L. and George Shade.

Shade was well known in both New York and San Francisco as an able fighter. In fact, after fifteen knockouts on the West Coast, he acquired the nickname "the Pacific Coast Knockout King." He agreed to travel to Georgia to show the southerners what boxing was all about.

Arranging such a fight wasn't cheap. Unlike the local boxers who would drive into town for a bout and then drive home for the price of a couple of meals, Shade was expensive. It would cost nearly $1,000 to bring him to Macon. Admission prices would have to be raised to cover the expenses, and Pa hoped that the local fans were willing to pay more. If not, the Legion stood to lose a lot of money.

W.L. had been engaged in light training all year, but now he had to get serious about the upcoming fight. By the third week of January, Pa demanded that he give up basketball for a while and concentrate on boxing. Once again, W.L. was back in the gym every afternoon. While he was absent from basketball practice, Charles "Sherlock" Holmes filled in for him.

Both fighters were in top form the night of the fight. Shade outweighed Stribling by eleven pounds, but W.L. had two inches over him in height. Over 2,500 fans were on hand in the Auditorium that Thursday night, among them several famous out-of-towners. Baseball great Ty Cobb had driven down from Augusta for the match. Georgia Tech coach W. A. Alexander and his Auburn counterpart Mike Donahue were there, along with a number of Atlanta sportswriters and editors.

They all hoped for a good fight, and no one was disappointed. The match went the full ten rounds, but Stribling dominated throughout. His greatest advantage was speed. He danced and dodged around the ring, moving in and out, delivering almost surgical-like strikes. When it was over, the referee held up Stribling's hand and the big crowd roared in approval.

Many people saw the Shade match as Stribling's first real test in the middleweight division, and the overwhelming opinion was that he had acquitted himself very well. Even George Shade agreed, saying that the younger man was the fastest he had ever seen and that he had won fairly.

W.L. was back at school the next morning and in his usual position at right forward Saturday night when the Poets took on and overwhelmed the team from Columbus High and Industrial School. Once again, he was the high scorer with 16 points, but a cloud hovered over the victory.

Stribling and everyone else in Macon knew that the Georgia Interscholastic Athletic Association was scheduled to meet in Atlanta on the 29th and his eligibility for high school sports would be on the agenda.

W.L.'s name came up in another setting that month—a very unlikely one. The Bibb County Grand Jury had been in session since November. As their term was coming to a close, they chose to examine boxing in Bibb County. Ever since the Legion began sponsoring the matches, there had been occasional complaints. A segment of the population considered boxing to be a crime rather than a sport. Some critics even went so far as to try and get charges of assault and battery filed against the combatants.

The Grand Jury decided to look into it and, as part of their investigation, they had attended the Stribling–Shade fight. Soon afterward they released their findings and declared, in part, that "contests of superior strength and skill, when conducted upon a high plane like the one between Young Stribling and George Shade on January 18, are a wholesome and worthy sport."

They further recommended that there should be no profanity at these contests and that, if more women were encouraged to attend, there would be no need for the separate seating for ladies now seen at most matches.

The next day Pa and W.L. traveled to New Orleans for a match with Tony Marullo on January 26. They stopped in Atlanta where W.L. worked out at the Progressive Club. This wasn't to get him in shape for the fight as much as to allow Atlanta fans to get a good look at him. Pa knew they would soon be back in that city.

The New Orleans debut was a successful one. Stribling so outclassed Marullo in the fifteen-round match at Frankie Edwards' Coliseum Club that the fight was stopped in the ninth round and W.L. declared the winner.

In the audience that night were boxer George Kuhn and his manager John Cox. They had been badgering Pa for months to allow Stribling to fight Kuhn. When the match wasn't scheduled as quickly as they wanted, the two accused the Striblings of cowardice. Pa was growing tired of the interchange, and while they were in New Orleans he signed a contract with Cox, agreeing to a February match between the two fighters in Macon.

The GIAA met in Atlanta on Monday, January 29. In a five-hour session that stretched nearly to midnight, they adopted a new constitution that required, among other things, that competing athletes had to be less than 21 years old. It wasn't until late in the evening that the question of Stribling's eligibility was raised.

There was much discussion, but the group wasn't able to reach an agreement. Finally, they referred the matter to their arbiter, Georgia Tech coach W. A. Alexander, the same man who had recently attended the Stribling–Shade fight. They requested that he render his decision by February 18. In the meantime, W.L. was allowed to continue playing with Lanier.

W.L. had two more fights scheduled before Alexander's decision was released. He and his brother both had matches in Atlanta on January 30. Herbert beat Charlie White in the four-round opener that evening. After another preliminary match it was time for the feature bout.

As W.L. was climbing into the ring, Herbert called to him.

"Wait a minute, W.L."

"What is it?"

"Do you remember those sleeve supporters you brought me from Cuba? Well, a man wants to trade me a knife for them. Do you think it would be a good deal?"

Before W.L. could answer, Pa shooed Herbert away, but the encounter emphasized the fact that the younger Striblings were still schoolboys with schoolboy concerns.

The fight between Stribling and Harry Krohn was one-sided from the beginning. Krohn won only one round, and by the end of ten, his eyes were nearly swollen shut. No one was surprised when Stribling was declared the winner.

In February, W.L. was once again able to concentrate on basketball. On February 2, the Poets took on Albany High in the City Auditorium. Most sportswriters had been predicting that W.L. would be declared ineligible by Alexander and had announced that this could very well be one of Stribling's last games with the team.

With that possibility looming, the night was transformed into something of a farewell party, with the school band presenting a half-time concert in his honor. And W.L. rose to the occasion. He played like it was his last chance to shine. His floor work was remarkable—three times he dribbled the ball the entire half court, evading all the Albany players and scoring.

But the good-bye was premature. W.L. did play at home again. Even though the match with George Kuhn was only two days away and Pa would have preferred having his son training in the gym, W.L. insisted on appearing with the Poets in their February 6 game against Marshallville. The team outdid themselves that night, and the final score was 60-17 with the Poets on top.

Pa had recently found an effective and profitable method of promoting his son. That week W.L.'s picture appeared in an advertisement for Goldsmith's Athletic Goods. W.L. was shown in boxing shorts in a fighting stance, and the time and date of the Kuhn fight were listed at the bottom. The advertising copy stated that the gloves on his hands were Goldsmith boxing gloves. The Striblings were now in the endorsement business.

Kuhn's charges that Stribling was afraid to fight him had gotten a lot of space in the papers, and there was a larger crowd than usual at the auditorium on the evening of February 8. A special section had been set aside for the ladies and it was full, as was the rest of the house. After round one, which appeared to be even, W.L. took the remaining nine. So decisive was his victory that, when the referee lifted Stribling's arm to declare him the winner, Kuhn helped him. He then embraced W.L. in congratulation. The subject of Stribling's cowardice was settled.

W.L. continued traveling and playing with the Poets as the month went on. When they took on Savannah High, W.L. clipped a rabbit's foot to his shorts and maybe that did the trick. The Poets won that one by two points. And on the 16th, Lanier hosted Chattanooga's City High School. They won 44-32, and the Poets concluded their second undefeated season.

That was W.L.'s last game in Macon with his beloved team. Two days later, Coach Alexander ruled that Stribling was ineligible to participate in any GIAA athletic contest due to his professional status as a prizefighter. Macon fans were disappointed, but resigned.

So Lanier competed in the GIAA tournament starting February 21 without the services of their star forward. The Poets made it all the way to the final game of the tournament, but Atlanta's Boys High won the championship. W.L. was there in the stands with them until the final second, cheering right along with his classmates.

With basketball season over, Pa expected W.L. to concentrate his full attention on boxing, but the Poets weren't ready to quit just yet. On February 25, Coach Charlie Morgan announced that he would be taking the team to the National Interscholastic Basketball Tournament in Chicago in April. The whole team was excited and none more so than W.L. Stribling. Since this event had nothing to do with the GIAA, he would be free to play once more with Lanier.

Pa had received several offers of fights for the first week of April, but W.L. wouldn't even consider them. He told his father he would have to refuse. He was going to the national basketball tournament with his teammates.

Held at the University of Chicago, the tournament attracted 40 teams from 24 states and the games were broadcast over radio. In the first round, the Poets played Mesa, Arizona. Although they got off to a quick start and a big lead, Mesa came back strong and eventually won 38-28. Lanier had been eliminated in their first game.

But even with the loss, the boys were having a fine time. Rather than return home, they chose to remain in Chicago through the rest of the tournament and were in the stands for the final game when Wyandotte High of Kansas City won the championship by beating Rockford, Illinois.

12

Clara Kinney's senior year was progressing exactly as she had expected. Popular and outgoing, she never lacked for something to do. When the yearbooks came out in the spring, there she was—Best All-Around in the Senior Girls' Who's Who. She expected the good times to last right up until the minute she graduated in June. When she got word that Miss Maggie Darrow, principal of the school, wanted to see her she assumed it would be another good thing.

Clara sat in front of the principal's desk and smiled expectantly.

"Do you plan to graduate?" Miss Darrow asked her.

Of course, she planned to graduate, Clara said. She had already bought her senior ring and been fitted for the white dress she would wear for the ceremony.

That's when Miss Darrow delivered some shocking news. Clara's grades were so poor that there was a very good chance she wouldn't graduate with her class.

For once in her life, Clara Kinney actually had to study. She cancelled most of her social engagements and devoted herself to her textbooks. She wasn't happy about it, but she knew she had no real choice. She had to graduate.

Ordinarily Clara's self-imposed exile would have seriously impacted W.L.'s social life as well, but he was so busy with boxing that spring that it didn't create much of a problem. In fact, he might have had a hard time working her into his schedule.

The Striblings moved into their new house overlooking the Ocmulgee River before the hot weather arrived. They were doing well financially. Along with the profits that came from the Stribling Athletic Club and Pa's work as a promoter, W.L. was bringing in a great deal of money from his matches and endorsements. It seemed natural that Pa managed all of the income and made the investments for the family.

Professional boxing was becoming popular throughout the country, but nowhere else had it reached the heights it had in New York City. And no promoter of the sport was bigger than Tex Rickard.

He had led a colorful life, working as a cowboy, a Texas town marshal and prospecting for gold. He had made a fortune running gambling houses in Alaska and San Francisco before becoming a fight promoter in New York. And it said something about W.L.'s growing reputation that, when Rickard visited Savannah in April 1923, he spoke to reporters about the young Macon fighter.

"When the Striblings come to New York," he declared, "I'll give the boy a chance. He may be the real article. His record would indicate it."

But New York was a dream for the future. Pa was taking W.L. along a step at a time. He won three relatively easy matches in April, but there was nothing easy about taking on Frankie Carbone in Atlanta on May 4.

The match was the first one fought in Spillers' new arena at Ponce de Leon Park, and a good crowd showed up that evening. Frankie Carbone, a short, stocky New Yorker, battled fiercely from the beginning. Although Stribling tried to keep up, staying in gamely to the end, by the tenth round he was slow and groggy and Carbone was the clear winner. It was only W.L.'s third loss in seventy-three fights.

After the match, Stribling experienced some pain in his left arm, but he paid little attention to it. He had had minor injuries before, and all of them had healed quickly. He expected nothing less this time.

With no fights scheduled for the next couple of weeks W.L. was able to enjoy the last weeks of school, reconnecting with friends and seeing Clara when her studies allowed.

His next fight was with Al Nelson on May 17 in Atlanta and was billed as a title match for the Southern Middleweight Championship. It was an unofficial title. A number of matches had been advertised as such, including W.L.'s recent losing bout with Frankie Carbone, but this time the NuGrape Company had donated a diamond-studded belt with a solid gold buckle, giving the claim some weight. The belt would go to the winner to keep as long as he held the title.

It was the only boxing match anyone could remember where the victor scored not one, but two knockouts. One sportswriter commented it was the "queerest fight ever seen."

Stribling appeared stronger than Nelson from the start, winning the first two rounds. In the third Nelson nearly collapsed in W.L.'s arms in a clinch. Stribling pushed him away and Nelson went down. The referee stood over him, counted him out, and raised W.L.'s arm as the winner.

But the crowd didn't like the decision. They believed that Nelson had been pushed down, not knocked down, and therefore had been fouled. W.L. just shrugged and volunteered to fight again after Nelson rested as long as he needed. The crowd thought that was a good thing, but the judges weren't sure.

After discussing the matter at length, they declared that since all of them ruled that Nelson had been knocked out, the match was officially over. If the fighting continued, it would have to be considered a second, separate match. More consultation ensued, but all sides finally agreed.

After a fifteen-minute rest, Nelson and Stribling reentered the ring to begin the second bout of the night. This one turned out to be worse for Nelson than the first. W.L. floored him in the second, and he didn't get back up. The fancy belt went home with Stribling, the winner of two title fights in one night.

Clara's studying paid off. When the Lanier High School Senior Class graduated in June, she was among them. The boys wore suits, and the girls were lovely in long white dresses with colored sashes. Clara received her diploma, proud that she had managed to accomplish what she had set out to do. Now the whole summer stretched out before her to be enjoyed.

While his friends enjoyed their vacations, W.L. concentrated on staying in shape. His career was heating up, and the quality and fame of his opponents were growing with every match. Pa now had his eye on a shot at Mike McTigue, the light heavyweight champ, but he knew that W.L. would first have to prove himself by leaving his familiar southeastern surroundings and taking on some national contenders.

On June 14, Macon celebrated the Centennial of its founding. Clara's father, W. O. Kinney, was named King Cotton and presided over the event. There were pageants and performances spotlighting the town's history. The finale was a huge parade with marching bands and elaborately decorated floats.

A small part of the citywide celebration was a night of boxing at the Auditorium. In the main event, W.L. took a ten-round decision from Pennsylvania boxer Jack McCarron.

Later in the month he fought Vic McLaughlin to a draw in Savannah, then faced Happy Howard in Shreveport, Louisiana. He won a fifteen-round decision over Howard, but the victory wasn't without cost.

W.L. led off with a right in the twelfth round, and Howard responded with a hard left that caught W.L.'s right elbow and fractured the elbow. Stribling never complained about the pain and the fight continued. But he kept his right hand and arm pressed against his side and fought the remaining three rounds with one hand.

The next day doctors set his arm and encased it in a cast. Examining him further, they discovered that his left arm was also broken. From the partial healing they found there and his history of pain since the event, they concluded that the injury had taken place when he fought Frankie Carbone in early May. W.L. had been boxing for over a month with a broken arm and had fought several rounds of the Howard fight with *two* broken arms!

The doctors forbid him to fight for at least two months. A rematch with Frankie Carbone that had been scheduled for July 4 in Macon had to be cancelled.

However, another match took place that day hundreds of miles away that attracted the attention of the whole country. Heavyweight Champion Jack Dempsey, who had been criticized for not giving anyone a chance at his title for two years, fought Tommy Gibbons in Shelby, Montana, that afternoon. Gibbons was the first man to ever go a full fifteen rounds with Dempsey, but in the end the decision went to the champion.

W.L. was sidelined for all of July and August, but Pa never slowed down. He was still working on a match with Mike McTigue, and on July 6 he began an extended trip throughout the Northeast. He visited New York City, Albany, Buffalo, Cleveland, Cincinnati, and Allentown,

Pennsylvania, and was the guest of several prominent promoters. They had all heard about the sensational young fighter from Georgia, and Pa was able to arrange a number of fall and winter fights for W.L.

The cast on Stribling's arm was removed in late July. After X-rays the doctors reported that the breaks were knitting well and he could resume training in September.

Negotiations continued between the McTigue and Stribling camps. They finally agreed that the two boxers would meet on October 4 at the Driving Park Stadium in Columbus, Georgia. The fight would be a ten-round affair, and the world light heavyweight title would be on the line. Harry Ertle, who had officiated at the Dempsey–Carpentier match in 1921, was named referee.

Another part of the contract stated that McTigue would be paid $10,000 the day before the fight to guarantee his appearance. W.L.'s guarantee wasn't anywhere near that large, but he would receive a share of the proceeds and the Striblings thought it was a fair arrangement. It wasn't money they wanted. It was the title.

13

W.L. began his senior year the day after Labor Day, 1923, but he was back in the gym that afternoon. He had put on some weight over the summer and now tipped the scales at 165. As the McTigue fight neared, Pa intensified his training. He now ran five miles a day at Central City Park and worked out every afternoon and evening in the Stribling Athletic Club.

Pa didn't restrict W.L.'s training to gym workouts. While he appreciated the benefits of sparring, he believed that actual fights were the best preparation for a big match. So on September 10, Stribling fought and defeated Sailor Martin in Miami, and nine days later he knocked out Jimmy Conway in Rome, Georgia.

Macon and Columbus were only 75 miles apart, and many local fight fans were expected to make the trip to see Stribling take on Mike McTigue. Tickets for the match sold well in Macon where the Central of Georgia Railroad planned to run a Stribling Special train to and from Columbus for fight fans. Leaving at 11:00 a.m. on the day of the match, it would arrive in Columbus by 2:00 p.m. After the fight the train would return its passengers to Macon before midnight.

A large crowd turned out on Thursday, September 27, for Stribling's last Macon workout, watching as he played a quick game of handball, did some limbering-up exercises and finished with six fast rounds of sparring with several different partners. The last round was with Joe Burman, one of Pa's new fighters. W.L. put everything he had into it and sent Joe stumbling backward into the ropes several times.

The next morning the Striblings and several boxers who would serve as W.L.'s sparring partners drove to Columbus where a training camp had been set up for them. They were joined by Ben Smith, a well-known California trainer whom Pa had hired to work with his son the last week before the fight. Mike McTigue and company arrived in Columbus the same day.

Both the McTigue and Stribling training camps were open to the public, and every day hundreds of spectators gathered to watch the fighters work out. It was warm in Columbus that first week of October, with temperatures reaching the upper 80s every day. Coming from Macon, where it was, if anything, even hotter, Stribling wasn't bothered by the typical southern weather. But McTigue, who hailed from the cool country of Ireland and lived in New York where the temperatures had already dropped with the seasonal change, suffered in the heat and accompanying humidity.

Several days before the fight McTigue's manager Joe Jacobs went to J. Paul Jones, the American Legion organizer, with a surprising proposal. He wanted to change the terms of the match. Instead of a title bout, he asked that it be changed to a "no-decision" fight.

Such a change would have, in essence, turned the Stribling–McTigue fight into an exhibition match unless one of the contestants was knocked out. No one knew why Jacobs had made the request, but there were rumors that it had to do with a future fight with Georges Carpentier.

Earlier in the week, Carpentier had defeated Joe Beckett in London, and, it was said, his manager had wired Jacobs an offer of $50,000 for a title fight. However, if McTigue lost to Stribling, the offer would certainly be rescinded.

Jones didn't care about Jacobs' reasons and not surprisingly refused his request. The contract called for a title match, and that is what they were going to have in Columbus.

Columbus was ready for the fight. In the 20,000-seat Driving Park Stadium, an 18-foot ring and ringside seating for 1,000 people had been erected. General admission tickets wouldn't become available until the day of the match, but advance reserved ticket sales had already topped $10,000. People began pouring into the city several days before the match, and hotels and restaurants were already full.

The press was well represented. Most of the newspapermen, including reporters from a number of Georgia papers, were predicting a good fight but an ultimate victory for McTigue.

A huge crowd was expected at the stadium. The promoters had hired the William T. Gloer Detective Agency to put operatives on the ground at the stadium to protect the spectators from pickpockets. Everything was in place. The fight was scheduled for 7:00 p.m. on Thursday, October 4. Then came news that no one had expected.

Late on October 3, McTigue's manager called for a meeting with the Striblings and the Legion representatives. When everyone arrived at the Ralston Hotel just before midnight, Jacobs announced that McTigue had injured his left hand and wouldn't be able to fight the next day. He returned the $10,000 advance—which he had received only hours before—to Major Jones.

If Jacobs expected the others to calmly accept his decision, he was disappointed. The reaction was quick and angry. Neither the Striblings nor the Legion officials believed McTigue was really injured and saw this as another attempt to avoid a title match.

Within an hour the Legion had called out four doctors who examined and X-rayed McTigue's hand. They reported that although they found an old imperfectly healed fracture of his left thumb, there was no evidence of a recent injury or any condition serious enough to cancel the fight.

Even at that time of night word spread like kudzu through the city. Residents who had expected the fight to put their town on the map were outraged. Fans and sportswriters who had traveled to Columbus from all over the country at some expense felt cheated.

Furious fight fans spilled out of parlors and hotels into the Columbus streets. Tempers flared and indignation built. Within hours an angry mob formed in front of the hotel, demanding that Mike McTigue come out and face them. Some carried hastily printed yellow placards with his picture on them. They shouted "coward" and "cold feet" until McTigue could stand it no longer and stepped out onto a balcony overlooking the street.

At his appearance the grumbling erupted into a roar. "Cold feet" was shouted again and again. Finally McTigue exploded. He shook his fist at the mob and screamed, "I'll fight him! I'll fight him with one hand and beat him!"

Later that morning, Jacobs announced the fight would take place as planned. When reporters asked about his fighter's injured thumb, he told them that a local anesthetic would be administered to deaden the pain. He predicted that McTigue would beat Stribling in three rounds.

So the match was to go on, but the damage had been done. The attendance was nowhere near the expected record crowd. Many fans had left the city soon after the cancellation was announced. And others, like those planning to take the Stribling Special from Macon that morning, weren't able to go because Central of Georgia cancelled the special train when word of McTigue's withdrawal reached them.

But the Macon fans were still going to have access to the up-to-the-minute details of the fight. The local newspapers combined efforts with the Associated Press to provide a telegraph wire from ringside to the front office of the *Telegraph*. As the information was wired, blow-by-blow descriptions of the action would be called by a newspaper employee on a megaphone to people gathered on Cherry Street. It wasn't ringside, but it was the next best thing to being in Columbus.

McTigue wasn't the only one with health concerns. W.L. had been ill for several days with bronchitis, but neither he nor Pa had revealed anything about it, fearing the public might interpret it as an excuse for a poor showing. On the afternoon of the fight, W.L.'s temperature registered over 100°, but he never considered not going through with the match.

Spectators began arriving at the stadium by two that afternoon. Many had come directly from McTigue's hotel and emotions still ran high. But the Columbus police were there in force, backed up by a number of military police from Fort Benning to assure order and safety.

The day had been overcast, but by 3:00 the sun made its first appearance. The temperature began to rise and soon rose into the 80s. The Fort Benning 29th Regiment Band played enthusiastically as people found their seats and prepared for the action.

There were several preliminary bouts before the main event, and the sun had set when McTigue and Stribling made their way into the ring at 7:00. Both looked fit and ready. Stribling was taller than the champion and outweighed him by three pounds. The raucous crowd clearly favored Stribling.

After all the buildup, the fight itself was almost a disappointment. One sportswriter later said Stribling won after eight rounds of fighting all by himself. McTigue spent most of the match in a defensive posture. W.L. tried to force the action—moving in on his opponent as soon as the bell rang—but the champion would grab his arms and hold on. The referee spent a good deal of his time breaking up clinches.

McTigue only showed signs of fighting in two rounds. The remaining rounds were, according to the newspapermen at ringside, all Stribling's. When the final bell sounded and the fighters returned to their corners, the crowd was confident Stribling had won. They exploded, chanting his name.

But instead of summoning W.L. to the center of the ring, referee Harry Ertle stood alone for a moment, then simultaneously pointed to each fighter, gesturing that the match was a draw. W.L. stared at him, as astonished as the spectators at the call.

The crowd yelled for Stribling, and furious fight fans rushed forward to voice their anger at the verdict. Ertle, surrounded by police, quickly left the ring and McTigue followed, similarly protected. But the crowd surged forward, breaking through the ring of police, and one of the MPs hustled the referee back into the relative protection of the ring. Then the local and military officers set about clearing the arena.

McTigue and his manager did make it out of the stadium and into a car, but angry fight fans surrounded them the whole time. They shouted their displeasure at the fighter, and some tried to push forward to get to him.

Major Jones climbed into the ring and demanded that the referee declare a winner. Ertle ordered a confused Stribling to stay in his corner, then motioned for the newspapermen at ringside to join him. Twelve of them made it through the ropes and went into a close huddle with the referee and Jones.

Ertle asked who they believed had won the match, and they all answered at once, shouting to be heard over the uproar. They were unanimous in believing Stribling had been the winner, taking eight of the ten rounds, and they demanded that the referee do the right thing.

Ertle held up his hands, "Please, gentlemen, give me time to think."

After a moment, he called W.L. to the center of the ring. As the boy stood there with his head bowed in embarrassment over the ruckus, the referee raised his hand and declared him the winner. A roar of approval rose from what was left of the audience, and Ertle hurried from the ring.

W.L. was exhausted. Confused and somewhat deflated by the strange episode at the end of the fight, he climbed through the ropes and left the stadium with his parents while the cheers continued.

W.L. Stribling was the light heavyweight champion of the world, but he held the title for only three hours. Once he was back in the safety of his hotel room, Ertle reversed his decision. He said he had declared Stribling the winner only because he had believed his life was in danger. The match was a draw and that was final.

There was tremendous public outcry, and sportswriters from all over the country condemned the decision, declaring that Stribling had won. But none of that mattered. The match was officially a draw and McTigue retained his title.

McTigue and Jacobs were out of Columbus by the next morning, but the Striblings stayed a few more days. The people in that city somehow felt responsible for what had happened and wanted to do something for the young man they believed had won the fight. So on the evening following the fight, the American Legion hosted a banquet for him and his family.

A few days later, the Macon Chamber of Commerce held their own banquet to honor Stribling. Some two hundred people filled the dining room of the Hotel Dempsey. Clara Kinney and her parents were seated at the head table with the Stribling family.

14

The aftershocks of the McTigue–Stribling fight were felt in boxing circles all over the country. The Columbus American Legion, which had lost money on the match, was still trying to decide how to refund the ticket money to fans whose train to Columbus was cancelled. Sportswriters began referring to Stribling as the "uncrowned champion," and Joe Vila, sports editor of the *New York Sun and Globe*, demanded that the New York Athletic Commission institute an investigation.

While the controversy still raged, New York promoter Tex Rickard stepped in. Responding to the interest in the Macon fighter, Rickard announced that he was beginning negotiations to bring Stribling to Madison Square Garden that winter. McTigue was noticeably absent from the schedule.

W.L. got over the uproar quicker than everyone else and was back in class on Monday morning. It was good to be with friends, but some of the fun of the previous years was gone. Since the GIAA had disqualified him from interscholastic athletics, he was no longer a member of the basketball team and wouldn't be going out for the baseball team either. Most of all he missed seeing Clara Kinney during the day.

She was now a day student at Macon's Wesleyan College. While she and W.L. were still a couple and saw each other frequently, they no longer spent time together every day.

The situation wasn't improved by Pa and Ma's attitude toward the girl. It wasn't that they didn't like *her*, they simply didn't want W.L. involved with any girl at that time. They believed he needed to concentrate on his boxing career, and they disapproved of anything that distracted him from that.

Although Pa enjoyed talking with the press about enrolling W.L. in college the next year—Georgia Tech was the school he most often mentioned—his real efforts were directed toward arranging more matches for his boy. They had received more than two hundred offers for W.L. to fight since the McTigue match. Pa was sorting through those and had also been busy setting up deals for W.L. to endorse various businesses and products.

W.L. fought and won twice in October. And on Halloween, he and his father went to New York City to meet with several boxing promoters. The typical high school boy might have been overwhelmed by such a trip, but W.L. wasn't typical. During their vaudeville days, the Striblings had often played New York, so the big buildings and crowded streets weren't a surprise for him.

But this time their circumstances were different. Rather than arriving in town largely unnoticed as members of a moderately successful comedy troupe, Pa and W.L. were met by reporters and actively courted by some of the most powerful people in the city.

They had a long meeting with Tex Rickard, who was eager to set W.L. up with a match in Madison Square Garden. But there was a problem to be resolved. The New York Boxing Commission rules didn't allow anyone under the age of 21 to take part in a match longer than six rounds and all six-round matches were semifinal, not feature fights. With Pa unwilling to consider the possibility of W.L. participating in a preliminary match, even if it was in Madison Square Garden, it looked as if Rickard wasn't going to be able to arrange a fight for him.

However, there was so much interest in the young Georgian that Rickard and others decided to pursue the possibility that the Commission might waive their rule for Stribling. The rules had been established, they pointed out, to protect young boys and prevent them from being mismatched with grown men. But this boy didn't appear to need any protection.

Only one jarring incident occurred during their northern visit. The two went to Madison Square Garden to see a fight. Before the match, the referee invited W.L. into the ring so he could introduce him to the crowd.

With a grand gesture of his arm, he announced, "I present to you the marvel of Georgia—"

Shouts of "Ku Klux! Ku Klux!" from some in the audience drowned out the rest of what he was saying. The anger wasn't directed so much at

W.L. as at the situation in Columbus where, some northern newspapers had suggested, Ertle and McTigue had narrowly escaped lynching.

It wasn't the warm welcome he was accustomed to, but W.L. didn't respond in anger. He simply stood there and smiled and within moments the majority of the audience was applauding him. Later some even apologized for the crowd's behavior.

The Striblings went to Philadelphia and attended another boxing match the next night. This time their reception was warm. Once again, W.L. was introduced, and the Philadelphia audience gave him a great ovation. Afterward Pa suggested to reporters that W.L. might attend the University of Pennsylvania the following year.

The Striblings were back in New York two days later so that W.L. could appear before the Boxing Commission. The boy acquitted himself well, but in the end the Board still refused to relax the rules for him. If W.L. boxed in New York before his twenty-first birthday, he would be restricted to six-round preliminary matches.

Hearing the decision, Pa was disappointed. In the past he had flatly refused to consider having W.L. appear in anything but a feature fight, but now stopped short of ruling out a six-round appearance at Madison Square Garden. W.L. wouldn't be fighting in New York for a few years, he said, unless he was offered extremely lucrative terms.

The Striblings were happy to be back in Macon. It was a good time of year for Middle Georgia. The summer's stifling heat had finally disappeared, replaced by cool, dry air and bright blue skies. Hot weather clothing was packed away, and people pulled out sweaters and heavier fabrics. The laziness of summer was gone, and the whole city crackled with energy.

W.L. and Pa returned to Macon, but were soon on the road again. In late November the whole Stribling family traveled to Boston where W.L. was scheduled to fight Joe Eagan on the 26th. Their train was met at Back Bay Station by a crush of reporters, all eager to see the young Georgia fighter the Boston papers called "Billy" Stribling. More reporters were waiting at the hotel.

For the next several days, the press followed the Striblings around Boston. Every move W.L. made was reported, and almost as much attention was paid to his parents, who were described as looking like the boy's older siblings.

As usual Pa was the spokesman for the family. A master at playing to local interests, he told reporters that W.L. would be attending college the next year and was considering Yale. And W.L.'s attendance at the Harvard–Yale football game seemed to lend a certain credence to that possibility.

He was at the Saturday afternoon game in Boston because two Montezuma, Georgia, boys, students at Harvard, had invited him. This, too, was chronicled in the press. The "Georgia Flash" had become Boston's latest media darling.

One person, however, was less than thrilled with the attention being lavished on the Georgia fighter. Joe Eagan, who hailed from nearby Worchester, was to be W.L.'s opponent on November 26. Even though he was a local boy, he was nearly lost in the media storm surrounding Stribling.

Eagan was stung by the way the press was virtually ignoring him. When someone finally asked his opinion of the upcoming fight, he angrily promised to pummel Stribling so badly that his mother wouldn't even recognize him.

But that prediction turned out to be just an empty boast. When the two fighters met at the Boston Arena Monday night, everything went Stribling's way. He won over the audience and the judges taking seven of the ten rounds.

Back in class at Lanier the next week W.L. tried to catch up on his studies, but his schoolwork was beginning to reflect his absences. He missed even more class time in December when he traveled to Tennessee and Florida, winning three fights in a row.

There was a break in his schedule around Christmas that year, and he and Clara Kinney were together as much as they could be. They attended holiday parties, went to dances, and saw movies.

The respite didn't last long. On W.L.'s nineteenth birthday, he, Pa, and Herbert set out for New Jersey where W.L. would fight Dave Rosenberg on New Year's Day.

Pa had arranged for W.L. to train at Freddie Welsh's Health Farm in Summit, New Jersey, before the Rosenberg fight. The place had gained national prominence when Jack Dempsey had made it his training headquarters in 1921.

Dempsey was still a frequent visitor to the farm, and he made an appearance there while the Striblings were in residence. W.L. even got in a couple of workouts with him. The champ liked the young fighter, whom he called Bill. Not only was W.L. a polite, pleasant young man, but he and Dempsey shared a love of practical jokes. After only a couple of days together, the two were regularly playing pranks on each other— and anyone else they could find.

The farm was well equipped and a great place to work out. However, the Georgians hadn't planned on the snow that blanketed the grounds the whole time they were there. W.L. and Herbert soon found themselves slogging through the frozen stuff during their daily roadwork.

But the snow wasn't all bad. It was a novelty for the Stribling boys. Soon after their arrival they demanded and got a sled, and the two spent hours gliding down the hills and tumbling into snow banks, acting like the teenaged boys they were. Pa let it go on for a while, but then called them back to the gym.

On December 29 W.L. and his father were dinner guests at the Newark Athletic Club. Pa, never at a loss for words, entertained his fellow diners with stories of their early years as traveling acrobats and their future plans. He was still suggesting that W.L. might attend Yale, but this time he added that his son planned to go on and become a surgeon. It must have been a surprise to W.L., but the sportswriters who were present jumped on the information and added it to the growing legacy that was the Young Stribling story.

The match with Rosenberg took place on New Year's Day at the First Regiment Armory in Newark. It was a sold-out event with all 7,000 seats filled. Pa and Herbert positioned themselves in W.L.'s corner while Ma, who had arrived from Georgia the day before, took her usual place at ringside.

Spectators and reporters alike were fascinated by this seemingly sweet southern woman who stoically watched as her son traded blows with other fighters. Reporters clustered around, peppering her with questions. Then someone suggested that most women wouldn't want to see their son fight.

"I can't understand why women think boxing is dangerous," Ma told him. "They can't injure each other seriously. A knockout is temporary. What's a little blood? Football seems much more dangerous to me."

When W.L. entered the arena minutes later, he stopped to kiss his mother, then climbed into the ring. The recent newspaper coverage had made him something of a folk hero, and spectators were excited to see him in the flesh. In black satin trunks with an orange and green trim that Ma had sewn on only minutes before, Stribling was just as handsome as they had heard.

At almost six feet tall, he was a perfect specimen of a nineteen-year-old boy with a friendly, open face to match. But when the first bell sounded, the boyish face suddenly changed to that of a determined, almost savage man. He was totally focused on the task at hand and that task was fighting the other man into submission.

Although W.L. had become a fan and press favorite, he was still an underdog coming into the fight. But the northeastern fighting establishment got a wake-up call that day. Aggressive and single-minded, Stribling dominated the match from the beginning. Rosenberg never backed down, but the young Georgian was too much for him. At the end of the twelve rounds, the audience cheered him and he slipped from the ring to embrace his mother.

"You were all right, darling, all the time," she told him.

New Jersey law prohibited the declaration of a winner by the referee or judges, but the "newspaper" decision went solidly for Stribling. W.L. was pleased with the win, but his greatest satisfaction came from the fact that the northern sportswriters were beginning to see him as a genuine talent and a real threat.

The family made it back to Macon on January 3 in time for W.L. to catch the Lanier Poets basketball game at the City Auditorium. While he enjoyed watching the action on the court and cheered as loudly as any fan in the stands, it wasn't in his nature to sit on the sidelines. When he was approached that night about playing with the newly formed Macon

YMCA Blues basketball team, he immediately agreed and debuted with them the next night.

One of the often-touted advantages to living in Macon was the temperate weather the city enjoyed most of the time. That first week of January 1924 had been typical for the area with temperatures rising into the lower 60s most days.

But there was a quick change in the weather that Friday. The day began seasonably with a low in the middle 30s, but from that point the mercury fell instead of rising. By noon thermometers read 29°.

When the Macon Blues took on the Miami YMCA at the Sport Arena Friday night, the outside temperature was 22°. And conditions weren't much better inside the unheated arena where it was below freezing. The Blues won, but no one really cared. It was a miserable game for players and spectators alike.

Pa and W.L. had tickets on the 11:35 p.m. train leaving Macon the following Monday night—this time W.L. had a fight scheduled in West Palm Beach—but Ma insisted that he go to school that morning. He hadn't been back to Lanier High since the Christmas holidays and knew he was behind in his work, but W.L. never expected what happened when he arrived at school that morning.

Before the first bell rang he was summoned to the principal's office where Professor Walter P. Jones told him they were dropping him from the school's rolls.

"We can't teach you anymore," he told the shocked student. "You and your parents will have to go see Superintendent Bruce if you want to be reinstated."

W.L. went straight home and told his parents. He wanted them to go with him to the superintendent's office, but Pa had other ideas. Instead of meeting with the superintendent of schools, he called a local sportswriter.

Pa was furious. If his son wasn't allowed to return to the school he loved, Pa told the reporter, the family would immediately put their house up for sale and move to New Jersey or Philadelphia. The only thing that could prevent their leaving was intervention by the Board of Education.

"They're meeting later this week," the reporter said. "Are you going to be there?"

"Can't do it," Pa told him. "The boy's fighting in Florida that same day."

But even without them being there, Pa said he hoped the Board would do the right thing.

Since he didn't have to be in school, W.L. accompanied his father to the gym where he spent the rest of the day. Several reporters found him there and tried to get his reaction to being dropped from the school rolls, but the boy had nothing to say to them. Pa, however, was more than happy to share his opinion of the situation.

"My son has to have an education. If it isn't to be had in Macon, we'll find it elsewhere."

Told that Principal Jones had said that they had removed W.L. from their rolls due to excessive absenteeism, Pa was indignant. "Nobody ever complained to us that he wasn't attending school enough."

When the Striblings boarded the train for Miami that night, they left a storm of controversy behind them. The Board of Education's regular meeting was in three days, and while the Striblings wouldn't be there, many others in the community planned to be present.

15

Reporters joined the local citizenry that jammed the Board of Education meeting on Thursday afternoon. Representatives from the American Legion and the YMCA were there, hoping to be heard. But no comments were taken from the audience.

There was, however, considerable discussion among the members about the Stribling situation, and opinions differed—some pushed for the Board to uphold the principal's decision while others wanted W.L. reinstated.

Chairman A. L. Miller pointed out that the law fixed the ages for public school at six to eighteen years old. So, he concluded, at nineteen W.L. had in essence voluntarily removed himself from school by missing so many days.

Superintendent C. H. Bruce took responsibility for the principal's actions, stating it was at his direction that Professor Jones had removed Stribling from Lanier's rolls. He revealed that he had been watching the boy's attendance all year.

"By the middle of October he had attended classes only 11½ out of 35 school days," he said. "I told Professor Jones to give him another chance, that possibly he would do better."

But his record didn't improve. Stribling was present only five days in November and eight in December, and he had also failed to complete much of his schoolwork.

"That's when I decided to take action," Bruce said, "and instructed Mr. Jones to drop him from the rolls."

He had also instructed the principal to have W.L. and his parents report to him.

"It's common practice to drop a student from the rolls for absenteeism," Bruce explained. "When that happens, it's usual to have the student and parent meet with me to discuss the matter. If the child promises to do better, they're allowed to return to school."

But the Striblings hadn't come to Bruce's office for reinstatement. They had not contacted him in any way.

"If W. L. Stribling had come to my office on last Monday agreeing to cancel his fighting engagements and agreeing to get down to business with his schoolwork, he probably would have been taken back. But instead he went to Miami, Florida, to be gone another week."

That revelation closed the discussion. The Board quickly endorsed Professor Jones' removal of Stribling from Lanier's rolls and moved on to other matters.

The same night the Board of Education met, W.L., now officially out of school, fought Mike Nestor in Miami. With heavyweight champ Jack Dempsey looking on from ringside, Stribling knocked out the New York fighter in the sixth round. Afterward, Dempsey told reporters that Stribling would one day be a world champion.

Instead of returning home, the Striblings stayed over the weekend in South Florida, and W.L. fought Norman Genet in West Palm Beach on Monday night. The match began well and seemed to be going W.L.'s way, but during the sixth round he was disqualified for hitting after the command to break. He had already been warned twice by the referee for the same thing, so when it happened a third time he was disqualified and Genet was given the win.

W.L. accepted the decision philosophically, but Pa lost control. He jumped into the ring and began shouting at referee Phil Prichard. Prichard shouted back. Pa finally grew so exasperated that he punched the referee. It could have turned into a free-for-all, but W.L. and several other people rushed in and separated the two men.

After the official and unofficial fights that night, the Striblings left West Palm Beach and joined Ma in South Georgia. They had always enjoyed visiting relatives in the area, but now they were landowners.

They had recently purchased a farm in Ochlocknee and hired Ma's brother Monroe Braswell to live there and manage the place for them. A deacon in the Ochlocknee Baptist Church, Monroe was probably her favorite brother. Although he was only a few years older than she was,

Ma called him "Uncle Gus" and his wife "Aunt Annie." While her husband looked after the livestock and the land, Aunt Annie took care of the housekeeping duties.

The farmhouse was a bungalow with a large front porch, a screened-in side porch, and several bedrooms so there was plenty of room for them when the Striblings visited. It wasn't showy, but it was well kept and comfortably furnished. There were also a barn and a garage on the property and sufficient acreage for hunting. Ma and Pa loved spending time there because it felt like going home. The boys liked it because it gave them the opportunity to run the fields, fish, hunt, and ride horses. And everyone loved Annie's cooking.

Offers kept pouring in, but there were too many to accept. Everyone wanted W.L. Stribling to appear in their town, and Pa had him booked for fights well into the spring. He even received an invitation to appear in *The Passing Show*, a New York musical comedy that was touring the South. The show's producers were willing to guarantee W.L. $1,000 a week for his appearance, but he was too busy to take them up on the offer.

Herbert was also scheduled for regular matches, and the family members were now so busy that they were having difficulty finding the time to operate their athletic club. They leased it for a year to the Central of Georgia Railway organization to be operated as the Right Way Health Club, but Pa would still maintain an office in the Cherry Street building and W.L. would have full use of the facilities for training.

Pa might have threatened to move his family out of Macon because of the problems with Lanier High, but they didn't start making plans to leave immediately. And Pa made a point of reassuring friends there that they would always love the town. If he and his family did choose to leave Macon, he promised them, the news would first be released in the local newspaper.

No matter where the Striblings lived that winter, it was generally agreed that they would soon be traveling to New York again. W.L.'s debut in Madison Square Garden seemed imminent. Although Pa was excited about seeing his son in such a glamorous venue, he kept W.L. in less famous rings while they waited.

On January 19, W.L. defeated Harry Fay in Indianapolis where he and his parents were welcomed as celebrities by the mayor and his wife. Nine days later, he went to Atlanta to fight Billy Shade.

The city of Atlanta was lobbying hard for the Striblings to relocate there. The Chamber of Commerce had calculated that Young Stribling was worth $150,000 in promotional benefits to Macon. They were sure he would be even more valuable to Atlanta.

In late January Atlanta's mayor Walter Sims had written an open letter to the Striblings that had appeared in the Macon newspaper:

> "There are many in Atlanta who have watched your achievements in the boxing ring with a great deal of interest. Your career to this time has been rather a steady and manly climb toward the top and then a meteoric rise to fame.
>
> "The world admires clean, courageous efforts, whether they be in the fight game, on the baseball diamond, the gridiron or in business.
>
> "As a game, clean, courageous fighter, you have commanded admiration in your home state and have won national notice and respect.
>
> "This letter is to commend these qualities. Voicing the suggestion of a large number of your friends in this city, I would like to add an invitation to the Stribling family to become residents of the City of Atlanta.
>
> "Very truly,
> "WALTER A. SIMS, MAYOR"

When their train arrived in Atlanta the Sunday before the Shade fight, the Striblings were welcomed to town by a Junior Chamber of Commerce reception committee. Pa met with the mayor at 10:00 Monday morning, and the next day W.L. was the guest of honor at the Atlanta Lions Club weekly luncheon. During the meal he and his father were treated to descriptions of the wonderful things that awaited them if only they moved to the capital city.

The Striblings couldn't help but be impressed by the effort being made to persuade them to move to Atlanta. They liked the city, always had, and they felt comfortable there. It was looking more and more like that could be their next home.

The fight with Billy Shade was held in the City Auditorium Tuesday night. Nearly 8,000 fans were present for the match and another 1,000 were turned away due to fire codes. The first preliminary bout would seem bizarre today, but was a fairly standard practice in 1924. Two little people, billed as Midget Boxers, fought in a comic match. But the comedy ended after that.

When Stribling and Shade entered the ring it was all business. Billy Shade was a highly regarded fighter, originally from California, but now making his home in New York. He carried the somewhat exotic title of light heavyweight champion of Australia, the result of a boxing tour of that country two years before. But Stribling, being almost a local boy, was the crowd favorite.

It was an exciting match. The crowd loved the action, and in the end Stribling won on points and took home over $3,000 as his share of the gate.

On the train back to Macon the next day, the family discussed their residential options. Pa pushed Atlanta for business reasons. Ma favored the move because she was concerned that her boys receive an education. While the whole family loved Macon and had deep roots there, the school situation was a problem. The boys weren't as much in favor of the move as their parents. After all, their friends and W.L.'s sweetheart were in Macon.

But Pa persisted. He suggested that being headquartered in a big city would boost their boxing careers, and since Atlanta boasted a number of professional teams, W.L. might find a good basketball team to join.

In the end, Pa prevailed. When they reached Macon, he made the announcement to the local paper that they would be moving to Atlanta, but didn't give a date for their departure.

For decades states and communities had struggled with the question of allowing professional boxing in their jurisdictions. Some saw it as a sport while others perceived it as a violent display of aggression, and neither side was inclined to compromise. Some locations outlawed the sport altogether. Others allowed it with various restrictions.

But a few states such as New York embraced boxing and built an entire industry around it. And Florida—Miami in particular—had recently become a thriving center for the sport. Fans flocked to the tropical city for the winter boxing season where the lifestyle was laid back and partying was encouraged.

So it was a surprise when Florida Governor Cary Hardee issued an order in late January that boxing professionalism would no longer be allowed in the state. Small contests between virtual unknowns could still go on, but there would be no more matches between "fighters of national prominence." Accordingly, the February 1 Jacksonville fight between Young Stribling and Soldier Buck was cancelled.

The governor's order sent the boxing world reeling as promoters scurried to change the venues of their scheduled Florida matches, but the cancellation of his Jacksonville bout had little effect on W.L.'s overall schedule. He had fights arranged all over the eastern half of the country for the next few months.

President Woodrow Wilson had been abroad for several months at the Paris peace conference. His absence, in a time of economic turmoil, was eliciting strong criticism in the United States. He was expected to return in February, bringing with him a treaty organizing the League of Nations, but Congressional ratification of the treaty was doubtful.

Although the country was facing uncertain times, the Stribling family's economic situation in February 1924 was good. And W.L. continued to do well professionally. In the first two weeks of the month, he won three fights. Then on February 15, the long-awaited rematch with Mike McTigue was finally scheduled. It would take place in Newark on March 31. McTigue's title was nominally on the line, but it was to be a no-decision match, meaning the only way Stribling could win the championship was to knock McTigue out.

Spirits were high in late February when they traveled to Buffalo, New York, for W.L.'s first match in that state. They stopped en route in Newark so that Pa and W.L. could sign the contract that already bore

McTigue's signature. It provided a guarantee of $15,000 for McTigue and $8,000 for W.L.

As usual, they were met by reporters. This time the newsmen wanted financial information and for once it was Ma who spoke with them. W.L. had earned, according to his mother, $22,000 in the first two months of 1924. Even though the McTigue fight would bring in at least $8,000, she estimated that they would lose about $5,000 in income because the contract specified that both fighters had to train a full month for the fight. That time off would require the cancellation of the fights W.L. had already scheduled in March.

"But we're glad to make the sacrifice," Ma said. "My boy has been anxious to get McTigue into the ring so that people around New York can judge for themselves as to whether or not he deserved the verdict in that first fight."

More than 12,000 people showed up on February 25 to see W.L. take on Jimmy Slattery, but Slattery won the six-round match on a decision. It was only Stribling's fourth career loss, but he was disheartened because he feared that the newspaper writers in that part of the country would now have another reason to disparage him. And his fears were well founded. The northern press wasn't kind in reporting his latest loss.

Pa and Ma Stribling with Herbert and W.L., Richmond, Virginia, ca. 1908. Courtesy of Billy Braswell, Pelham, Georgia.

Above, Willie Stribling and Lillie Braswell at the time of their marriage, 1904;
below, promotional postcard, 1910. Courtesy of Billy Braswell, Pelham, Georgia.

Poster of the Novelty Grahams, ca. 1909. Stribling Family Album.

Pa sparring with thirteen-year-old W.L., 1917. Courtesy of Billy Braswell, Pelham, Georgia.

Above, Herbert and W.L. in action, ca. 1912. Stribling Family Album; below, Herbert delivers "knockout" punch to W.L., ca. 1912. Stribling Family Album.

Above, Promotional postcard. Pa counts out W.L. as Herbert stands to one side, ca. 1912. Stribling Family Album; below, Pa and Ma, ca. 1917. Stribling Family Album.

W.L. and Herbert, ca. 1924. Stribling Family Album.

Ma and W.L., ca. 1922. Courtesy of Middle Georgia Archives, Washington Memorial Library, Macon, Georgia.

Lanier Poets basketball team, W.L. top center, 1922. Courtesy of Middle Georgia Archives, Washington Memorial Library, Macon, Georgia.

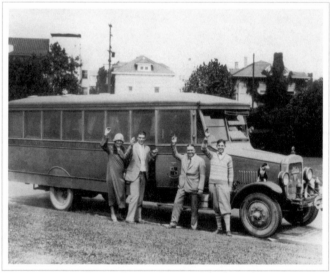

Above, W.L. beside new car, ca. 1925. Courtesy of Mrs. W. L. Stribling, III; below, Ma, W.L., Pa, and Herbert Stribling with their touring bus, 1925. Stribling Family Album.

Above, W.L. and Clara soon after their marriage, 1925. Courtesy of Billy Braswell, Pelham, Georgia; below, W.L. and Clara, ca. 1926. Stribling Family Album.

Above, training camp, Hendersonville, North Carolina, prior to Berlenbach fight, 1926. Courtesy of Special Collections Department, Pullen Library, Georgia State University; below, W.L. sparring with Jack Dempsey, Hendersonville, North Carolina, 1926. Courtesy of Special Collections Department, Pullen Library, Georgia State University.

Above, Pa and Jay Thomas, ca. 1926. Stribling Family Album; below, W.L. and Walk Miller, 1927. Stribling Family Album.

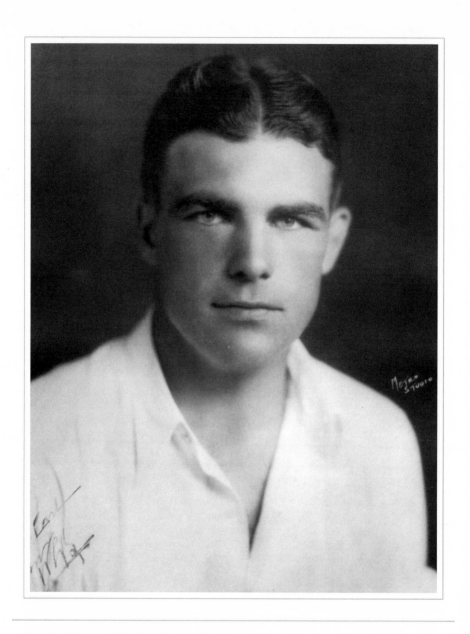

W. L. Stribling, ca. 1926. Stribling Family Album.

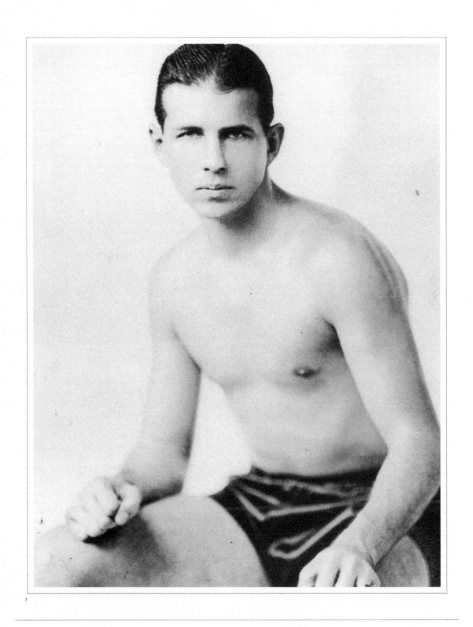

Herbert Stribling, ca. 1929. Courtesy of Billy Braswell, Pelham, Georgia.

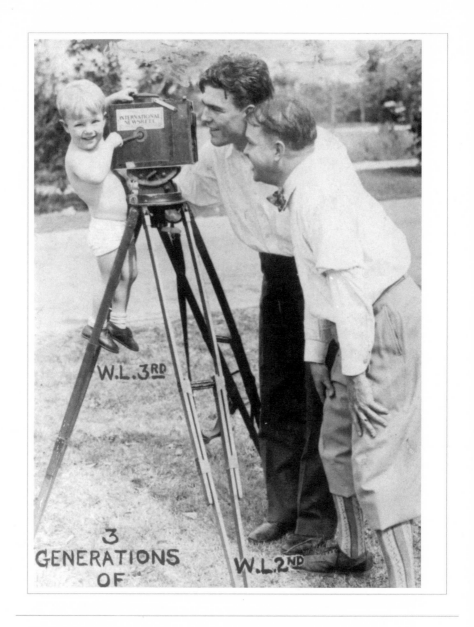

Tee, W.L., and Pa, 1928. Courtesy of Mrs. W. L. Stribling, III.

Tee Stribling, 1928. Courtesy of Mrs. W. L. Stribling, III.

W.L. in Miami, 1929. Stribling Family Album.

Above, Mary Virginia, Clara, W.L., Ma, Tee, and Pa Stribling at Miami dog race track, 1929. Stribling Family Album; below, Jack Dempsey, W.L., and Seminole tribe members, Florida, 1929. Courtesy of Middle Georgia Archives, Washington Memorial Library, Macon, Georgia.

Above, Macon welcome home parade, W.L. and Clara, after Sharkey fight, 1929. Courtesy of Middle Georgia Archives, Washington Memorial Library, Macon, Georgia; below, boating at Lakeside Park, ca. 1929. Courtesy of Middle Georgia Archives, Washington Memorial Library, Macon, Georgia.

W.L., ca. 1929. Stribling Family Album.

Second Lieutenant W. L. Stribling, 1929. Courtesy of Middle Georgia Archives, Washington Memorial Library, Macon, Georgia.

Above, Mayor Glen Toole, Michael Maurer, W.L., and Clara, Macon, Georgia, 1930. Stribling Family Album; below W.L. and Charles Moore, manager of Macon Peaches baseball team, 1930. Courtesy of Middle Georgia Archives, Washington Memorial Library, Macon, Georgia.

W.L. and Clara at Macon Terminal Station, 1930. Stribling Family Album.

Above, Rosemary Inn, Thomasville, Georgia, site of Stribling banquet, 1930. Stribling Family Album; below, W.L. and Bobby Jones at Atlanta's Capital City Club, in background are Col. Robert P. Jones, *Atlanta Journal* editor John Cohen, Robert Woodruff, and unidentified man, 1930. Courtesy of Mrs. W. L. Stribling, III.

Above, Jay Thomas, Jack Dempsey, Bert Orndoff (manager of Jefferson Hotel), and W.L., Birmingham, Alabama, 1930. Stribling Family Album; below, Pa, Stevens Luke, Jack Dempsey, Judge Roscoe Luke, E. R. Jergen, and W.L., Inman's Drug Store, Thomasville, Georgia, 1930. Courtesy of *Thomasville Times-Enterprise*.

Above, W.L., Tee, and Jack Dempsey at Ochlocknee, 1930. Courtesy of William W. McCowen, Macon, Georgia; below, Gus Stribling, Tee, Pa, W.L., and Jack Dempsey at Ochlocknee, 1930. Stribling Family Album.

W.L. and Jack Dempsey, 1930. Stribling Family Album.

Above, Tee on horseback with unidentified boy, Jack Dempsey, and Pa, with Gus Stribling in background, 1930. Stribling Family Album; below, W.L. plowing, Ochlocknee, 1930. Stribling Family Album.

Above, W.L. and Jack Dempsey, Miller Field, Macon, Georgia, 1930. Stribling Family Album; below, Pa, Clara, Mary Virginia, W.L., Ma, and Tee, ca. 1930. Stribling Family Album.

Max Schmeling and W.L., Miami, 1931. Courtesy of Middle Georgia Archives, Washington Memorial Library, Macon, Georgia.

Mary Virginia, photo appeared in *Macon Telegraph*, 1930. Courtesy of Middle Georgia Archives, Washington Memorial Library, Macon, Georgia.

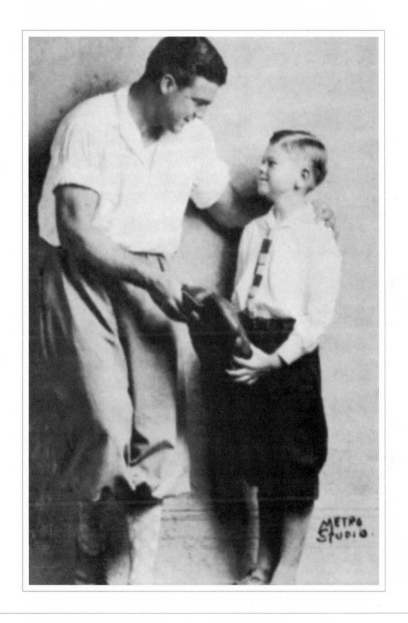

W.L. gives gloves from Phil Scott fight to C.D. Porter, 1930. Courtesy of Middle Georgia
Archives, Washington Memorial Library, Macon, Georgia.

Above, W.L. and Clara in speedboat "Socko" on Ocmulgee River, 1931. Stribling Family Album; below, motorboat races, Macon, 1931. Courtesy of Middle Georgia Archives, Washington Memorial Library, Macon, Georgia.

W.L. and Jack Dempsey, 1931. Stribling Family Album.

Tuffy Griffiths/Young Stribling fight, Chicago, 1930. Stribling Family Album.

Publicity photos of W.L., ca. 1931. Stribling Family Album.

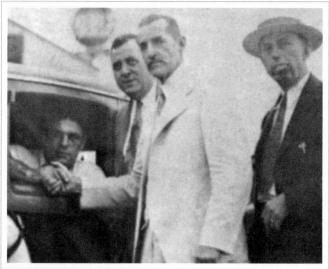

Above, W.L., Ma, and Luis Angel Firpo, New York, ca. 1930. Stribling Family Album;
below, W.L, Roland Neel, and Herbert Smart at parade in Macon after von Porat fight,
1930. Stribling Family Album.

Above, W.L. and New York Celtics at Miller Field, 1931. Stribling Family Album; below, W.L. and unidentified sparring partner, 1931. Stribling Family Album.

W.L. and Tee at Lake Geauga training camp, 1931. Stribling Family Album.

Above, Will Rogers, Leo P. Flynn, W.L., and Clara, Tulsa, Oklahoma, ca. 1931. Stribling Family Album; below, Ma, Pa, Mary Virginia, W.L., Tee, and Clara, 1933. Stribling Family Album.

W.L. and Clara at Seven Falls, Colorado Springs, Colorado, 1931. Courtesy of Mrs. W. L. Stribling, III.

Clara, W.L., Mary Virginia, and Tee, 1933. Stribling Family Album.

Clara beside Stribling Room display, Macon YMCA, 1934. Courtesy of Middle Georgia Archives, Washington Memorial Library, Macon, Georgia.

Above, Pa and Ma at W.L.'s graveside service, 1933. Courtesy of Middle Georgia Archives, Washington Memorial Library, Macon, Georgia; below, downtown Macon, ca. 1933. Courtesy of Middle Georgia Archives, Washington Memorial Library, Macon, Georgia.

Above, Pa, Maxie Rosenbloom, Bobby Norris, Ralph McGill, Primo Carnera, Johnny Risko, Nathan Gans, Robert Gamble, Frank Bachmen, and Jimmy Jones at Nottingham Drive house at the time of boxing benefit, 1934. Courtesy of Middle Georgia Archives, Washington Memorial Library, Macon, Georgia; below, Herbert with Pa and Ma, ca. 1954. Stribling Family Album.

Above, Stribling Bridge, Macon, Georgia. Photo by Dr. James Bryant; below, Tee Stribling, Jimmy Jones, Bill McCowen, and Macon mayor Ronnie Thompson with bust of W. L. Stribling, 1971. Stribling Family Album.

Stribling monument, Riverside Cemetery, Macon, Georgia. Photo by Dr. James Bryant.

Portrait of Bishop Randolph Claiborne, ca. 1965. Courtesy of Mrs. W. L. Stribling, III.

Above left, Charles Morgan, coach of Lanier Poets, ca. 1960. Courtesy of Middle Georgia Archives, Washington Memorial Library, Macon, Georgia; above right, Tee Stribling, ca. 1960. Stribling Family Album; below left, Mary Virginia Stribling, ca. 1960. Stribling Family Album; below right, Guerry Boone Stribling, ca. 1960. Stribling Family Album.

Back in Macon W.L. had a little free time before he had to begin serious training for the fight with Mike McTigue, so he decided it was time to take up golf. He had been introduced to the game in Atlanta when sportswriter O. B. Keeler had taken him to the East Lake Country Club the year before.

Keeler's main objective was to get some good photos of the young boxer on the links, but he was surprised at how quickly and naturally W.L. took to the sport. W.L. was now determined to master the game.

While his son spent hours each day on local golf courses, Pa got busy setting up W.L.'s training headquarters at the gym on Cherry Street. Everything was in order when training started in earnest on March 12.

W.L.'s routine was to do a few miles of roadwork early in the day in his North Highlands neighborhood. Then, in the late afternoon, he sparred four or five rounds at the gym. These exhibitions, which always drew an audience, were a mix of serious work and silliness. W.L. couldn't resist joking with his friends and pulling pranks.

Hoy Stribling, Pa's younger brother, had moved to Macon to join the family boxing business, and one evening W.L. competed with his uncle in a semi-serious wrestling match. The crowd thought it was great fun, but Hoy was sore and bruised for several days afterward.

McTigue was also in training. He had located his camp in Ballston Lake, New York, and predicted a quick win over the Georgia fighter. But he also told reporters that he was concerned he would be hampered by the still troublesome injury to his hand, which he said he had sustained in the earlier fight with Stribling.

When the Striblings left for Newark a week later, sparring partner Billy McGowan went with them for the long automobile trip north. Pa knew a great publicity opportunity when he saw one. Yes, W.L. was in training for an important fight, but he didn't have to stay in one place to get that training done.

As they made their way through Atlanta, Greenville, Charlotte, Richmond, Washington, D.C., and Baltimore, Pa had sparring partners waiting in gyms in each city. Fans were invited to come in and watch the training and exhibition matches.

When they finally arrived in New Jersey, W.L. began training in the Newark Athletic Club. McTigue had already set up his headquarters in the Madison Square Garden gymnasium. Both fighters were accustomed to outdoor roadwork, but the extreme cold and snow the region was experiencing that late winter made it nearly impossible. They had to make the best of the indoor tracks at the two facilities.

The press was taking considerable interest in the match. Even though McTigue was reported to be in great shape, he hadn't entered a ring since his last fight with Stribling. There was speculation that, since this would be a no-decision match, McTigue might approach the contest in a defensive mode. Since he could only lose his title by being knocked out, some predicted he would simply retreat from Stribling, cover up, and maintain his feet through the twelve rounds.

The Irishman took exception to those reports. "I'll be there to do all the fighting that's in me. There'll be a knockout and I'll take care of that part of it. I've got a lot at stake next Monday night. If I don't beat the boy decisively, then every man has a right to believe he beat me the first time."

The Striblings' vaudeville background combined with their small-town values made for great copy in the northeastern press. W.L. was interviewed on radio, and sportswriters reported him to be a soft-spoken gentleman outside the ring. But he also had his detractors.

The Irish contingent of the population was strongly behind McTigue. And the newspapers had resurrected stories of the near riot after the two men fought in Columbus, Georgia, giving rise to speculation that the Ku Klux Klan was supporting Stribling.

When he was asked about the fracas in Columbus, McTigue said, "I've nothing against the Striblings. They're fine folks and I'm not blaming them in the least for what happened down in Columbus, but it sure was a rough experience. I saw so many guns around that day I thought the war was on again."

W.L. wasn't the only member of the family to attract attention. Pa was constantly quoted about his son's condition and how they were approaching the match, but Ma Stribling emerged as the real media favorite.

Naturally she predicted her son would win the fight and echoed Pa's opinion that the boy was in great shape. But when the women writers, known at that time as sob sisters, discovered her, the resulting articles appealed to everyone, not just fight fans.

W.L.'s love life was a favorite topic, and Ma revealed that the boy received thousands of love letters each year. W.L. rarely even opened them, giving them to his mother to handle. It was clear that she didn't approve of such forward behavior.

"I want him to marry a sweet, old-fashioned girl," Ma said, turning toward W.L. who sat nearby, "and he will. Now won't you, sugar?"

The embarrassed boy blushed, but didn't answer.

"Is there anyone special in your life right now?" the reporter asked him.

Again he had nothing to say, but when the reporter pressed for an answer, Ma admitted that there was a girl—a very nice, old-fashioned one at that. Although she wouldn't give them her name, everyone in Macon knew she was speaking about Clara Kinney.

Several of the family's friends drove to New Jersey for the fight. Bob Gamble, Eddie Morgan, Mike Witman, and Mark Ethridge spent Sunday with the family. They had lunch in Newark, then piled into the Striblings' car for a ride out to see Freddie Welsh's Health Farm. On the way, a police officer stopped them because the car had no front license tag.

"Where's your tag?"

Pa, at the wheel, explained that Georgia required only a rear tag.

The officer then asked to see a title to the car, which Pa didn't have with him. "But I can establish my identity."

Upon hearing the name Stribling, the officer asked, "Do you happen to be any relation to the boy that's fighting tomorrow?"

"Only his father," Pa said, jerking his head in W.L.'s direction. "There's the boy."

After that, all thought of traffic enforcement was gone. The officer propped his foot comfortably on the running board and leaned into the car, smiling. He spent several minutes in conversation with the party chatting about the coming fight before they resumed their trip.

Advance ticket sales were heavy. One athletic club in New York bought $1,000 in ringside seats, and orders from the South kept coming. A fight fan in North Carolina ordered 100 tickets, and Southern Railway arranged a special train for fight fans so that they could travel to Newark in comfort.

McTigue was the initial favorite with the fans, but as more was written about Stribling and more people saw his workouts, that began to change. The odds, which had originally favored McTigue, gradually changed as well. By the day before the fight, they were nearly even.

When W.L. and his family arrived at the Newark Armory Monday night, a record crowd was on hand and quite a few celebrities were in evidence. Boxers Harry Greb, Gene Tunney, and Mickey Walker were at ringside. New York Senator Bill Lyons was there along with boxing promoter Tex Rickard, New York Giants owner Charles Stoneham, and Jimmy Johnson, president of the Sports Alliance of America. Boxing commissioners Bill Brower and Bill Muldoon had front-row seats, and Mrs. William Randolph Hearst had bought a block of 100 tickets for herself and her friends.

The crowd sat through several preliminary bouts before the main event started about 10:00 p.m. On the advice of Tex Rickard, the fight was not broadcast over the radio. He believed that doing so lowered sales of the cheaper seats. But the fans in Macon could still hear an ongoing description of the action as it was announced from the *Telegraph* office.

If there was any doubt that bad feelings still lingered from the Columbus match, it was erased when the two fighters joined the referee in the center of the ring for the ritual explanation of the rules and to examine the taping of each other's hands.

Stribling caught McTigue's hand in his and asked, "Is it well yet?" Before the champion could form a reply, W.L. said, "You're a big bum, you are," turned, and walked back to his corner.

It was a partisan crowd very much in favor of McTigue. As the opening bell rang, a McTigue supporter at ringside yelled, "Go after him, Mike! He's a bum."

Stribling heard him, looked around and smiled, then rushed into the center of the ring and sent a left jab to McTigue's nose. From there on, Stribling set the pace for the fight and never let up. In the third round, McTigue was almost out on his feet, and in the fourth Stribling had him up against the ropes until the referee pulled him off.

McTigue was knocked to the floor in the tenth and remained down for a count of three or four. When he was on his feet again, Stribling continued the attack. In desperation, McTigue grabbed the boy in a tight clinch. Stribling began some fierce infighting, but the referee stepped in and separated them.

The crowd, which had gradually turned from McTigue backers to Stribling fans, started shouting, "Let them fight! Let them fight!"

The same behavior continued through the final two rounds, with Stribling unable to land a knockout blow and the referee, who was now being booed, separating the two when McTigue held on.

When it was over, no one in the arena doubted that Stribling had won. Even McTigue later admitted he had been beaten. But since there had been no knockout, the champion was able to limp out of the ring with his title intact.

The next day, the newspaper decision made Stribling the winner. The only thing the writers disagreed on was how many rounds the Georgia boy had taken. Some gave Stribling ten. Others said he had won eleven. He was, in everything but name, the light heavyweight champion.

With no school to hurry back to, W.L. and his parents spent a little extra time in the Northeast. Wednesday afternoon they visited the New York Cotton Exchange where buyers were so excited to see W.L. that they crowded around him and trading was actually suspended for a short while.

That evening they were guests of Mike Witman for dinner at the famous Moulin Rouge Dinner Musicale. Almost as soon as the party was seated, the orchestra began playing a familiar song, but the orchestra leader substituted these words:

"Oh my love, there sits Young Stribling. Oh, my love, he's there all right. He won his fight with Mike last night and he's here with us tonight." Alerted to his presence, everyone turned to look, some standing up to get a better view of him. W.L. just grinned and resumed conversation with those at his table. But their night wasn't over yet. Dinner was followed by the theater where, as they made their way to their seats, an usher recognized W.L.

"It's the Georgia Peach!" he said in a loud voice.

Once again, a room full of New Yorkers twisted and turned to get a look at the young fighter.

Pa Stribling hated to turn down a match without good reason. Where other professional boxers fought fewer than a dozen times a year—and the top tier of fighters far fewer than that—W.L. was in the ring several times a month. He had been fighting professionally for just over three years and had engaged in nearly 100 matches.

So his schedule didn't slow after the McTigue fight. On April 4, he put on an exhibition match in Hartford, Connecticut. On the 11th, he fought and knocked out Joe Quinn in Appleton, Wisconsin, and did the same to Tex McEwen in Philadelphia three days later.

It was in the McEwen fight that sportswriters first noticed what came to be called Stribling's "buckshot punch." It was a fast double feint followed by a treacherous right to the jaw. Harder than the punches he usually threw, it landed with a sickening thud and laid McEwen out on the canvas as if he had been hit over the head with a shovel.

The name came from Pa shouting from W.L.'s corner, "Buckshot! Buckshot! Shoot it now!" just before the blow was struck.

The family arrived back in Macon on the evening of April 17. Pa was as eager as ever to share his thoughts with his friends at the *Telegraph*. He bragged that they had made about $10,000 on their recent trip north and declared that he had in his pocket at that very moment contracts for fights all over the country that carried guarantees of $50,000.

But W.L. wasn't interested in talking with reporters that night. He was exhausted and simply crawled into bed and went to sleep. The next day he went straight to Clara Kinney's house. The two wanted nothing more than to marry, but every time W.L. brought it up with his parents, they refused to even consider the possibility.

The minor league Macon Braves baseball team began their 1924 season with a game at Central City Park. Mayor Luther Williams fell down as he threw out the first pitch, but the honorary catcher W.L. Stribling stayed upright and caught it. After the game, he went to Kinnett's ice cream factory for a publicity appearance and was photographed eating a quart of ice cream. He joked that this was the start of his training for his next fights.

The family was back on the road a week later, and W.L. was back in the ring. From then until the end of May, he fought five times—in Connecticut, Toronto, Ohio, Virginia, and Georgia—winning four matches and fighting one no-decision. In the May issue of the *Ring Magazine*, W.L. was referred to as the "uncrowned light heavyweight champion" by virtue of his performance against Mike McTigue.

In June Pa was finally offered a Madison Square Garden fight for W.L. with Tommy Loughran, one of the most sought-after fighters in the country. It was only a six-round bout, and while the match wasn't everything Pa had hoped for, the attraction of the Garden and a nationally ranked opponent was too much to resist.

17

W.L. was training hard for his upcoming New York fight, but his fans in Macon were looking forward to the one he had scheduled a week later on the Fourth of July. It had become almost a tradition for Stribling to fight in Central City Park on the holiday. But then Pa got a better offer.

For months he had been trying to set up a match between W.L. and middleweight champion Harry Greb. Greb's manager had finally agreed, but the only date and place he would consider was July 4 in Michigan City, Indiana. With W.L. already under contract to the Macon American Legion for that day, Pa had a problem.

He met with Legion officials and eventually paid them several hundred dollars to release Stribling from the contract. W.L. was then free to fight Greb, but the episode left a bitter taste in the mouths of Macon fans.

The June 26 bout with Tommy Loughran was to benefit the New York Milk Fund, a charitable organization that provided food for poor children. There were four matches that night, but most of the 60,000 fans had come to see the Stribling–Loughran fight.

It was a furious battle. Loughran seemed to dominate at long range, but Stribling scored heavily in the close fighting. In the end, the judges gave the win to Stribling, but the decision was unpopular with the crowd. They booed W.L. along with the judges. The match with Harry Greb, which had caused some hard feelings in Macon, never took place. A smallpox quarantine in neighboring Michigan caused the open-air event to be postponed. And soon afterward, due to a disagreement about Stribling's share of the receipts, the fight was cancelled for good.

So W.L. was idle on July 4, and as it turned out, he had little to do professionally for the whole month. He was free to return to the summer pursuits he loved—swimming, golfing, and seeing his friends. And near the end of July, he joined the rest of the country in following the Leopold and Loeb murder trial.

Nathan Leopold and Richard Loeb were wealthy University of Chicago students who, in May of that year, had kidnapped and murdered fourteen-year-old Bobby Franks. It was intended to be the perfect crime, something they believed they could accomplish because of their superior intellect. However, they were soon apprehended and during police questioning they confessed.

Famed attorney Clarence Darrow was hired to defend both boys. The trial began on July 21, and Darrow shocked everyone by immediately entering guilty pleas for them. He understood that there was no way to win acquittal for his clients and chose to present his evidence during the sentencing phase of the trial to a judge rather than a jury.

But the prosecution wasn't ready to accept a life sentence. They brought in witness after witness to relate the full horror of the crime. Day after day, Americans faced the details of the brutal murder in their morning newspapers.

Darrow's summation, which lasted twelve hours and in which he attacked capital punishment and the desire for vengeance, was ultimately successful. Leopold and Loeb were sentenced to life in prison.

In Macon, the *Telegraph* ran a short piece comparing Leopold and Loeb, sons of millionaires raised in the lap of luxury, to W.L. Stribling, son of parents of modest means. Where the Chicago boys had brought shame and horror to their families, W.L. was making his parents proud and prosperous.

The Striblings spent a few days vacationing on the Georgia coast. They had always loved the water, and all four were tanned and relaxed when they returned to Macon on the first day of August. That afternoon Pa announced that W.L. would fight Paul Berlenbach in Madison Square Garden August 27.

Berlenbach was a strong contender for the light heavyweight championship and had twice agreed to fight W.L., only to cancel at the last minute due to injuries. But this time, it looked like the match, which had been arranged by Tex Rickard, would go ahead as scheduled.

With a big fight on the horizon, W.L. began training the way he liked best—in the ring against other fighters. On August 12, he fought and knocked out Leo Leonard in Charleston for the benefit of the war veterans of the army's 30th Division.

Before returning to Macon, they made a side trip to Savannah so that Pa could purchase a downtown building. He paid $45,000 for it and added it to the collection of real estate he had already started.

As the Berlenbach match approached, Pa decided that W.L. needed to spend more time in traditional training. He set up a camp at the New York spa resort of Saratoga Springs. When the Striblings arrived there on August 20, it was rumored that W.L. had a bad cough, but Pa denied there was any problem.

One week later, W.L. and Paul Berlenbach met in the New York Velodrome. Stribling was favored by bettors at 8 to 5 odds, and sportswriters pointed out that fans would be seeing the clash of opposites that night. While Berlenbach represented brute strength, Stribling was speedy and considered a "scientific" boxer.

Twenty-five thousand people were in the New York audience. In Macon some 4,000 crowded Cherry Street between Third and Broadway, waiting to hear the fight called by megaphone. There had been great anticipation about the contest in both cities, but the match itself was slow and disappointing. It ended in a draw, and there were few satisfied fans in either city.

The next day sportswriters criticized both fighters, particularly W.L. They suggested that he had fought defensively because he was afraid of Berlenbach. The truth was that he had been suffering from bronchitis, but neither he nor his father had wanted to tell anyone for fear of being accused of looking for an excuse.

On Labor Day W.L. met Bob Fitzsimmons in the ring in Central City Park. It was the first time he had fought in Macon in almost a year and helped to soothe the hurt feelings left over from July 4.

September 1 was hot and humid. The temperature was nearing 90 when the boxing program got under way at 4:30 that afternoon. The crowd sat sweltering through three preliminary bouts, including one in which Herbert Stribling beat Harry Allen, before the feature match began at 5:30.

As soon as the two fighters entered the ring, it was obvious that Fitzsimmons was no match for Stribling. But W.L. was conscious of the hometown crowd and strung out the fight through ten rounds trying to give them their money's worth.

For the Macon boxing fans, Stribling's homecoming was bittersweet. The family had been spending more and more time in Atlanta and were now referred to as being "from" there whenever written about in the national press. More than once, W.L. had been called "an Atlanta boy."

Even local sportswriters had to admit that this most recent fight demonstrated that there was little chance Stribling would appear again in a Macon ring. He was simply too good for local and regional contenders. His only real competition now lay in the higher ranks of nationally known boxers.

Clara and W.L. saw little of each other in the late summer of 1924. The Kinneys vacationed at St. Simons Island, and W.L. seemed to be in Atlanta or on the road all the time. Clara realized she wasn't looking forward to another year at Wesleyan College. Life as a day student seemed little different than life as a high school student, and she was ready for a change.

Her good friend Mary Jim Walker of Eastman attended Brenau College in Gainesville, in Northeast Georgia, and had raved about both the school and living away from home. She urged Clara to join her there as her roommate. It sounded like a wonderful adventure, and after considerable pleading, Clara convinced her parents to let her go. In the fall of 1924, she transferred to Brenau.

Although they continued to maintain their home in Macon, the Striblings were now living in a rental house in Atlanta, and W.L. was enrolled at the University School for Boys on 14th Street. Although he wasn't playing any organized sport there, his new school awarded him a letter sweater on the basis of his overall athletic talent.

Herbert had never been interested in school and, as a consequence, hadn't done well. Rather than enroll him in an Atlanta high school, his parents decided to try a more disciplined setting for him. That fall he began attending Riverside Military Academy in Gainesville.

For all the concern Pa had voiced about W.L.'s receiving an education, there was little follow-through. The boy's attendance at his new school was sporadic. With more and more fights scheduled, most of his time was spent traveling and training. One Macon sportswriter referred to him as the "Georgia schoolboy who never goes to school."

The Striblings crisscrossed the eastern half of the country that fall as W.L. fought match after match. In the last four months of 1924, he had eleven fights. Six were no-decision bouts, but he won all of those where winners were declared and took the newspaper decisions in the others.

Although W.L. and his parents were on the cover of the October issue of the *Ring* and he was once again referred to as the "uncrowned champion," not everything written about them was positive. The young boxer's demanding schedule attracted the attention of sports observers all over the country. One New York writer accused Pa of killing the goose that laid the golden egg. Another declared that W.L.'s parents were ruining the boy by overworking him, sacrificing his health and future for their own monetary gain.

Pa finally responded to the charges through an interview with *Telegraph* sports editor Jesse O. Irvin. He scoffed at the idea he had overworked W.L. by having him fight so many matches. Most of the fights, Pa insisted, were no more than light workouts for his boy.

W.L. was in excellent physical condition, he said, and there wasn't a week that went by that his son wasn't seen by a doctor. To silence critics Pa offered to make W.L. available for examination by any doctor at ringside before any fight. He guaranteed that his son's blood pressure and other vital signs would prove normal.

Of course W.L.'s life wasn't all training and fighting. A good-looking, well-built young man, he attracted attention everywhere he went, even among people with no interest in boxing. While they were traveling in the Northeast that September, the Striblings spent a few days on Long Island. One afternoon, W.L. drew a crowd of well-to-do women who mistook him for the Prince of Wales.

It wasn't as big a mistake as might be thought. The Prince was visiting the United States at the time, and W.L., dressed in a well-cut light gray suit with his hair parted in the middle, was certainly handsome enough to have been royalty.

When they returned to Georgia later that month, W.L. took a detour to Gainesville. He first stopped in to see Herbert at Riverside, then called on Clara at Brenau. It was a visit he wouldn't make again.

W.L. had visions of strolling around the campus with her, admiring the autumn leaves and catching up on their separate lives, but that didn't happen. Brenau was very particular about their girls dating. Before she was even allowed to see a young man, Clara had to have a note from her parents giving permission. The note was just the beginning.

She and W.L. weren't allowed to walk alone on campus. They weren't, in fact, allowed to be alone at all. Instead they had to stay in a parlor with two chaperones where the only available seating was hard chairs separated by small tables.

It wasn't like any date W.L. had ever been on, sitting on an uncomfortable chair "with a hawk at one end and a dragon at the other" as he put it later. After that one experience he declared he would never go back. They would just have to find another way to get together.

The family spent the week before Christmas in Macon, the place that still felt like home to them. Although his friends were happy to see him, they were a little surprised to observe W.L. wearing a letter sweater with a big "U" on it.

On Christmas Eve, the Striblings traveled to Ochlocknee, but W.L. was back in Macon by the 26th to celebrate his 20th birthday with Clara and his friends.

Financially 1924 was a banner year for W.L. and his parents. As it came to a close, his earnings neared $250,000. In a time when men's ties cost $1.00, a full dinner in a first-class restaurant was $3.00, and a brand-new Ford touring car could be purchased for less than $300, it was a remarkable income for a twenty-year-old boy.

18

Macon welcomed 1925 with church bells and factory whistles. Celebrants crowded the downtown streets, shouting "Happy New Year," some secretly sipping illegal beverages, until the early morning hours. At daylight, special masses were said at St Joseph's Catholic Church, and the Vineville churches—Baptist, Methodist, and Presby-terian—joined together for a sunrise service at Vineville Presbyterian.

Once the sun set on New Year's Day, revelers swayed to romantic tunes like "What'll I Do?" and "It Had to be You" at several dances around town. But W.L. and Clara didn't attend any of those celebrations. Their holiday time together was over, and it was time for him to go back to work.

That evening he left for Miami where his parents and brother were waiting for him. Pa had already set up training quarters in South Florida, and W.L. would spend the next couple of weeks there preparing for a fight with Hugh Walker on January 12. The Florida authorities had relaxed their earlier stand on professional boxing, and nationally known fighters were again taking part in matches there.

The day before the fight, the first international ranking of boxers was released. Compiled by Tex Rickard for the *Ring*, fighters in each weight classification, from flyweight to heavyweight, were ranked. In all divisions but one, the current champion was rated first.

The exception was Mike McTigue, who had been so discredited in his matches with Stribling. He still held the title of light heavyweight champion, but was in the fourth spot in Rickard's rankings. Gene Tunney was first in that category and Young Stribling second.

The Walker fight was a no-decision bout, but the newspapers gave W.L. the win. Two days later he fought Mike Wallace in St. Petersburg,

Florida, with the same result, then finished January with a third newspaper decision over Jimmy Delaney in Grand Rapids, Michigan.

Although W.L. was taking on what many people saw as a string of second-rate boxers, Pa's strategy was to keep him in shape until he could be matched with some nationally ranked contenders. W.L. continued to be in demand for advertising endorsements. Sometimes the other members of his family were included. In January, all four of the Striblings were featured in an ad for the United American Life Insurance Company. The caption under their photo was "Georgia Family 100% For a Georgia Company."

Thanks to the moving pictures that now played in every little town in the country, W.L.'s fame was spreading across the nation. Nationally known sportswriter Grantland Rice produced a series of short films called *Sportlights* and in early 1925 W.L. was featured along with Ty Cobb, Cy Williams, and Babe Ruth in one of these features dedicated to the importance of rhythm in sports.

There were two major occurrences in the Stribling family in February. W.L. made his debut as a heavyweight boxer on February 2, taking on Joe Burke in Columbus, knocking him out in the third round.

The second was Pa's purchase of a new vehicle—a $10,000 bus he had bought from the Leonhardt Company in Baltimore. Deep brown in color, it was billed as a combination limousine and Pullman car.

Pa decorated it with what he called the Stribling coat of arms—a picture of a ripe peach and a pair of boxing gloves against a field of blue with the motto *Amino et fide*—roughly translated, "courage and loyalty."

He loved showing off his new acquisition and would conduct a tour of the vehicle for anyone who was interested, happily pointing out all of its special features. There were sleeping compartments for seven and a day coach that could accommodate twenty-five passengers. Pa boasted it had all the conveniences of a Pullman train car without the bother of having to tip the porter.

Although they planned to take the bus on a few quick trips around the Southeast to some of W.L.'s next matches, the primary reason for purchasing the huge vehicle was to stage a barnstorming tour of the country later that summer.

W.L. liked the bus just fine, but preferred driving his new blue roadster. He had two more fights in February and two in the first two weeks of March, winning them all. Then it was back home to Atlanta where he could climb behind the wheel of his new car.

He loved the roadster and he loved going fast. It was that combination that brought him into conflict with two Atlanta motorcycle officers the next night. He was stopped for speeding and taken to police headquarters. But the famous Stribling charm asserted itself, and the charge was later dismissed in Recorders Court.

The third week of March the Striblings took a train to San Francisco. It was the farthest they had ever traveled for a fight. While they weren't strangers to the city, having performed there numerous times during their vaudeville years, this was the first time W.L. had fought professionally on the West Coast.

His opponent for the March 28 fight was no stranger. W.L. had defeated Tommy Loughran in a six-round match in New York only nine months before. But the decision had been unpopular with the New York fans, and Loughran had been vocal in voicing his own disagreement. This match was an opportunity to settle the question of who was the superior fighter once and for all.

The boxing world was still shaken by the recent news that Jack Dempsey, who had failed to act on an ultimatum issued by the New York State Athletic Commission to immediately defend his title, had been declared ineligible to fight in New York. Accordingly, any boxer who chose to fight Dempsey anywhere in the country would also be ruled ineligible to fight in New York. There was rampant speculation as to where the champ would go from here.

But on that cool, cloudy Saturday afternoon in Recreation Park, the attention of 22,000 San Francisco fans was focused on the match at hand. Loughran was popular in the state and favored to win. But when the tenth round ended, the referee's decision went to Stribling and the crowd agreed.

W.L. attended school when he was in Atlanta and was also able to see Clara from time to time. After that first unpleasant experience at Brenau, they searched for a way to see each other away from the college. With the help of Clara's mother, the two concocted a scheme that allowed them some time together away from the fierce Brenau chaperones.

Even though she had no dental problems, Clara occasionally left school that spring to visit an Atlanta dentist. Mrs. Kinney arranged for her release from the campus and transportation to the dentist's office, W.L. taking over from there. The two young people would have lunch, go for a drive, and just enjoy being together before Clara had to return to school several hours later.

They were sure that their future was together and were determined to marry. Clara's parents were in favor of the match, but the Striblings were still opposed. The young couple knew that W.L.'s parents would never give permission for their minor son to marry, so they made the best of the time spent in each other's company and planned for a happy time they both knew would come.

19

May 1925 was mostly training and travel for W.L. He fought and won in Boston, Kansas City, and Hutchinson, Kansas, that month. Once again, sportswriters criticized Pa for scheduling so many fights for his son.

What they didn't know was that W.L. hated training. He didn't mind skipping rope, but he really disliked sparring and roadwork, believing that his best workout was fighting. He actually encouraged his father to schedule the fights rather than keep him in the gym.

And there was another advantage to the arrangement, as Pa occasionally pointed out. "We get paid for fighting, not training."

Pa traveled to Florida in May to negotiate some matches with other promoters and also found time to purchase some land in Fort Lauderdale. When the Florida press asked him about it, Pa declared that his family loved the area and hinted that they might some day live there.

This was too much for Macon sportswriter Wilton E. Cobb. In a May 3 column, he poked a little fun at the senior Stribling, observing that he had a habit of buying property in different places and then announcing that the Stribling family would move there. He declared that W.L. needed to be triplets in order to fulfill his father's promises to live in so many different towns.

Pa was first and foremost a showman. He knew that the most successful performers were the ones who were best known, and what better way to get Young Stribling's name out there than to take him to the heartland so that people all over the country could see him in action? And that was exactly what he hoped to accomplish with their bus tour that summer.

Pa planned the trip as a sort of extended mobile training camp. W.L. wouldn't take on any top-notch contenders along the way, just "good, strong local boys" who would be able to give him a good workout. The hope was, Pa told reporters, that after three months or so W.L. would be in such good shape he would be ready for a run at Dempsey or whoever might hold the heavyweight title at the time.

The publicity generated by the proposed trip brought forth hundreds of letters and telegrams. People all over the United States wanted W.L. Stribling to visit their town or fight their local tough guy.

The Striblings had grown up on tour, so the idea of such a trip wasn't foreign to them. And this time they would be far more comfortable than they had been during their vaudeville years. They would be traveling in style. There would be no second-rate hotels and no dictatorial theater managers to please. The bus was not only equipped with sleeping and coach quarters, there was a bathroom, an area where Ma could cook and wash clothes, and even a section in which W.L. could work out.

Of course such a trip required planning and preparation. Pa spent hours working out the itinerary, but it fell to Ma to decide what they needed to take with them. One afternoon in late May reporters found her at the Nottingham Drive house, furiously sorting and packing W.L.'s clothes.

As she added suit after suit to the stack that would be loaded onto the bus, she joked, "My, I wish somebody would give my poor boy another suit of clothes."

On June 1 the cross-country tour began. In addition to the bus, the Striblings brought along their automobile, a roomy Chrysler. Ma and the boys took turns driving the car. The activity broke up the boredom of riding on the bus hour after hour.

Like any good barnstorming tour, the Striblings had an advance man. Jay J. Thomas was still a young man, but in his short career he had been a fight manager, a machinist, and a barber. The Striblings had hired him as their publicity manager, but in reality he served as everything from press agent to advance man to sparring partner.

Thomas brought his nephew Harold Thomas along with him. The two traveled by car and were usually several days ahead of the Striblings. They would roar into a small town, put out the word that Young Stribling was coming, and then drum up publicity as they searched for likely contenders to fight him.

Thomas was good at his job, and by the time the tour was half over, the family's pictures had appeared in papers all over the country. W.L. fought for either a flat $1,000 or 40 percent of the gate. As the tour progressed and his popularity grew, they usually chose the percentage.

The Striblings were welcomed wherever they went and showered with good wishes and sometimes gifts. One of the most elaborate was a brand-new bright red motorcycle presented to W.L. by the Indian Motorcycle Company and shipped to his Macon home where it would be waiting for him when the tour ended.

In June and July they traveled through a number of states in the East and Midwest. W.L. fought at least once a week, usually winning in the early rounds.

Then they headed for the West Coast. Crossing the Rockies was an ordeal in the unwieldy vehicle, but they managed it, and on August 4 W.L. fought and knocked out Johnny Lee in the second round of a match in Salt Lake City.

The fight wasn't particularly memorable, but the time they spent in that city made quite an impression on all of them. They were offered rides in a small airplane, and Pa, Herbert, and W.L. eagerly accepted the invitation.

It was a defining moment for W.L. Flying was the most exciting thing he had ever experienced. He planned to repeat it as soon as he could.

Pa's first flight wasn't as pleasant. After the plane was airborne the motor died and couldn't be restarted. The pilot did an admirable job of bringing the craft down, but they dropped the last 150 feet or so and landed hard on the runway. The airplane was seriously damaged, and Pa's knee was fractured and his side wrenched. Surprisingly, the experience didn't ruin flying for him. Like his son, he had loved it.

Two weeks later they were in Los Angeles where Stribling beat Jimmy Delaney before the largest indoor crowd in that city's history. Afterward a young fighter named Red Fitzsimmons approached them. He lived in Texas and was trying to get home. He had heard the Striblings were going to be driving through his home state and asked if he could travel with them. He was a likable fellow, and they were happy to take him along.

The trip back across the country wasn't without mishaps. Jay and Harold Thomas were hit head-on by another car just outside Oakland, California. Although the driver and occupants of the other vehicle were injured, neither of the Thomases was hurt. But their car was so badly damaged that they had to lay over in Oakland for ten days while it was being repaired.

Crossing the Mojave Desert from California to Arizona was a nerve-wracking experience for everyone. The road across the desert was constructed of small logs, arranged end to end, and was only wide enough for one vehicle at a time. Pull-offs, constructed of the same logs, were situated about every mile so that if one driver saw another coming, he could pull his car over out of the way and allow the other to safely pass.

Staying on the logs was important. Any vehicle venturing off the sides of the road immediately sank into the soft sand and was stuck there until a wrecker could come to pull it out.

The Striblings crossed the Mojave without incident, but just outside Tucson Ma was driving the Chrysler ahead of the bus. She hit a culvert and flipped the car. Her passenger Red Fitzsimmons was unhurt, but Ma was rushed to a nearby hospital where 30 stitches were needed to close the gash in her head. The accident made the local newspaper and was picked up on the wires.

A week later Jay Thomas was traveling ahead of the main party once again. He arranged a match for W.L. in El Paso, then moved on. But when the Striblings arrived there they learned that the scheduled opponent couldn't appear. The local promoter had been frantically looking for a substitute, but without success.

He asked for a postponement, but Pa explained that wasn't possible. They already had fights scheduled for two weeks ahead. The promoter finally suggested that Red Fitzsimmons appear in the ring with W.L.

Pa didn't think it was a good suggestion. Although Fitzsimmons had no connection to the tour other than catching a ride with them, such a match could appear questionable. But the El Paso man insisted. He had spent a lot of money setting up the Stribling appearance and stood to lose what, for him, was a fortune if there was no boxing that night. So, against his better judgment, Pa agreed and W.L. and Red Fitzsimmons fought in El Paso on August 25. Stribling knocked him out in the third round.

Unfortunately, Pa's misgivings were well founded, and the match did cause trouble. The newspapers had picked up the story of Fitzsimmons accompanying the Striblings from California when he was involved in the wreck with Ma. After the El Paso fight, reporters accused Stribling of fighting his own chauffeur. They even suggested that he had been fighting the same man over and over in all the towns in which they had appeared.

It was unjust criticism. W.L. never fought the same man twice during the time they were on the road. But the suspicions lingered.

During their three-month journey across America, the family traveled through 34 states and covered more than 11,000 miles. W.L. fought in fourteen matches, winning them all, and Herbert appeared in five.

The trip was a success on two levels. They had made a good amount of money in that three months. More important, the tour planted W.L.'s name and face firmly into the public consciousness, not only in the big prize-fighting centers, but also all over the country. People were taken with the handsome, clean-cut young man and his colorful, nomadic family.

But three months was a long time. Everyone in the group was glad to leave the bus and get back to their normal routines that first week of September when they arrived in Macon.

W.L. couldn't wait to get his hands on his newest toy. The Indian Motorcycle Company had shipped it to Macon unassembled in a crate, but it only took Stribling an afternoon to put it together. He rode it for hours the next day, delighting in speeding along the road with the wind in his face.

Pa wasn't interested in the motorcycle. His focus was expanding the family's business holdings. In early October, he purchased 1,100 acres in Thomas County, which, he told friends, he hoped to turn into a stock farm.

The Striblings were back on the road in October, but they left the big bus at home this time, opting for train travel. W.L. won a match in Los Angeles on the 10th and another in Columbus, Georgia, on the 22nd. In early November they were in Memphis. The fight there with Soldier Buck was scheduled as an eight-round event, but it didn't last nearly that long. W.L. knocked him out in the third, and a few hours later the family was on a southbound train, heading home.

After a night in a Pullman car, the three had breakfast in the dining car. Yesterday's fight was forgotten. Their attention was now on the new Thomasville property. W.L. was lobbying hard for raising horses while his father leaned more toward cattle.

The Striblings weren't the only celebrities on the train that morning. Across from them, sipping his morning coffee and reading the newspaper was internationally known humorist Will Rogers. They didn't recognize him nor did he know who they were, but he certainly noticed them.

In a column he wrote the next month for the McNaught Syndicate, Rogers said that he was first attracted to the group because of their accents. Having spent so many years in the North, it was a pleasure for him to hear genuine southern speech.

The second thing he noticed was their good humor. They were affectionate with each other, polite, and upbeat. They were, in fact, a pleasure to observe. The only thing that puzzled Rogers was their relationship.

The woman was lovely. In her mid-thirties, she looked far too young to have a grown son. At first, Rogers thought the younger of the two men might have been her husband, but soon realized that the interaction between the two wasn't right for that relationship. The second man's position in the group puzzled him as well since he appeared much too young for the role of father.

Rogers was still undecided about that when the Striblings left the dining car. He was enjoying another cup of coffee when the conductor approached him.

"Have you ever heard of Young Stribling?" he asked.

"Well, I know of him," Rogers said, "but I never met him."

"Would you like to?"

The conductor took Rogers back to one of the day coaches and introduced him to the family he had seen only a short while before at breakfast. They greeted him like an old friend, and he spent the next few hours chatting away with them. They discovered their vaudeville connection almost immediately. Although they had never toured with Rogers, the Striblings had played many of the same theaters and had a number of acquaintances in common.

Rogers soon learned the Striblings' history and how W.L. had grown into a nationally known boxer. Although Rogers would have enjoyed hearing more about the prizefighting aspect of their lives, the Striblings preferred talking about their new farm. And basketball.

Basketball was W.L.'s favorite conversational topic. He proudly showed Rogers the two medals he had won playing the game at Lanier High School.

The only boxing story W.L. related that morning concerned a fight he had had early in his career when the drawstring in his opponent's shorts had broken and the referee, not wanting to interrupt the fight, had grabbed the back of the man's shorts and held them up as the match continued. W.L. laughed so hard at the memory that he could hardly speak.

Rogers concluded that the Striblings were the happiest family he had ever encountered.

Later that month, Macon opened its new City Auditorium, a building that could accommodate 4,000 people. Promoters boasted it was so large that it could host three conventions at one time. Sweeping stairways and columns adorned the outside of the building. Inside were red velvet curtains, plush seating, and a lobby decorated with five murals of Italian garden scenes.

Macon was proud of this new addition, but W.L.'s mind was on love, not architecture. In the free time he had between fights and training in November, he and Clara managed to meet several times when she was in Atlanta for her "dentist appointments."

It was on one of these visits that he formally proposed. He asked Clara to marry him on his 21st birthday. It would, he said, be the best birthday present he would ever have. Clara responded with a gloriously happy "yes!"

The Kinneys were thrilled when Clara called home with the news. Since it was to take place in a few weeks, the wedding would have to be a small ceremony, and they decided to hold it in the Kinneys' home.

Even though it wouldn't be a big affair, there were still many things to consider—attendants, flowers, what the bride would wear! Clara and her parents were swept up in an exciting flurry of planning.

The reaction in the Stribling household was another story. Pa and Ma were adamantly opposed to W.L. marrying Clara Kinney or anyone else. They argued with their son for days, but he refused to bend his will to theirs. W.L. had lived his whole life doing what his parents told him to do, but he loved Clara Kinney, she loved him, and they were going to marry.

He finally put an end to the discussion by pointing out that, on December 26, he would be twenty-one years old—a legal adult—and able to do anything he wanted, including marry.

To emphasize that new freedom, he made another declaration. He would honor his commitment to the two fights already scheduled for the remainder of 1925, but he warned Pa not to schedule any more until he was given the go-ahead.

"I don't know what I'm going to do," he told his parents. "I may not fight anymore."

W.L. kept his word about the upcoming matches. On November 27 he knocked out Billy Britton in the first round in New Orleans. A week later, he fought Tony Burns to a no-decision in Grand Rapids, Michigan. With those bouts behind him, he felt that he had done what he had to and could now concentrate on Clara and their upcoming marriage.

In public Pa acted as if W.L. had never spoken about marriage. He told the press that his son would graduate from the University School for Boys that month and begin classes at the University of Georgia some time in 1926. No mention was made of the impending wedding.

By December 10, Pa, Ma, and Herbert were in Miami, but W.L. stayed behind in Macon. He and Clara were swept up in a swirl of celebration. It seemed like everyone they knew wanted to honor them with a dinner or a party.

He also worked out with the newly formed Right Way Athletic Club basketball team when time permitted. Made up of former Lanier and Mercer players, it was a talented squad, and W.L. was excited to hit the court with the team when they played their first home game on the 12th against the Waycross Y Five. With W.L. at forward, Right Way won 37-24.

On December 20, the announcement of Clara and W.L.'s engagement appeared in the *Telegraph*. The match had overtones of a royal wedding in Macon. W.L. was young, handsome, and the most famous athlete the city had ever produced. And his parents were nearly as famous as he was.

Beautiful young Clara Kinney was as close to a princess as anyone could find in Middle Georgia, and her family was socially prominent. Her father was a successful businessman and had recently been elected Chairman of the County Board of Commissioners. Her mother was a civic and political leader in her own right. And Clara's maternal grandfather, Dupont Guerry, had been a judge, served as president of Wesleyan College, and at one time was a candidate for governor of Georgia.

Newspaper reporters rushed to find the happy couple. They weren't available, but Clara's mother was happy to talk with them. She spoke in glowing terms of her future son-in-law and declared that her daughter couldn't have chosen a better husband.

A few days before Christmas, W.L. traveled to Savannah to do some hunting, but reporters tracked him down. He didn't have much to say about the wedding except that he was marrying "the prettiest girl in Middle Georgia," but his response to their questions about his future made headlines on sports pages all over the state.

"I won't do any more fighting after I'm married," he told them, "not for a long while anyhow."

When they asked how his father felt about that decision, W.L. just shrugged. "I can't say how he feels."

Pa and Ma returned to Macon on December 22. They brought a wedding cake with them, perhaps as a peace offering. It had been made by Mr. Winter of Miami—a famous baker who regularly produced cakes for celebrities, including the president of the United States. It was a multilayered creation, all white, embossed by white sugar roses, cupids, and lovebirds.

But when they arrived, W.L. wasn't at the Nottingham Drive house. They hadn't spoken to him since leaving town and now were surprised to learn he was in Savannah. When questioned by the press they admitted they had no idea when the wedding was to take place, but planned to be present.

Pa acknowledged that W.L. had told him a month before not to book any more fights for a while since he was getting married, but he couldn't resist letting them know that he was still negotiating with Gene Tunney's management for a future bout. Pa didn't give up easily.

20

Saturday, December 26, was a cloudy winter day, quite cold by Georgia standards. The temperature had dipped into the 20s the night before and wasn't expected to venture far into the 40s that afternoon. There had even been snow flurries in parts of the state.

But the weather didn't bother Clara and W.L. The two were married at noon in the flower-filled parlor of the Kinneys' house on Cherokee Avenue. The bride's whole family was there, and her great uncle, Methodist clergyman Tom Ed Davenport of Reynolds, Georgia, performed the ceremony.

Mary Jim Oliver and Viola McNeil were Clara's attendants. Herbert Stribling stood up with W.L. and his best man, his boyhood friend J.T. Bridges. The beautiful wedding cake from Miami was set in a place of honor in the dining room, but Pa and Ma weren't there. They just couldn't bring themselves to celebrate what they believed was the biggest mistake their son had ever made.

After the ceremony, the couple accepted quick congratulations from the assembled guests, then dashed out the rear of the house where W.L. had parked his roadster. Within minutes, they were on their way to Terminal Station for the train to Atlanta, unseen by the reporters and photographers who had set up on the Kinneys' front lawn.

But the couple couldn't avoid the press for long. When they arrived in Atlanta a group of reporters was waiting for them. Being surrounded by flashing cameras and people shouting questions was almost routine for W.L., but it was Clara's first time attracting that sort of attention. Surprisingly, she was just as much at ease as her new husband in answering their questions.

"No," she told them, "I don't have any objection to my husband fighting in the ring."

When they asked the two to face each other and strike boxing poses, W.L. hesitated, but Clara laughed.

"Snap into it," she told him. "I don't know a thing about boxing, but if the news boys want to see how I stack up against you, I'm willing to take a chance."

So W.L. obliged his wife and the next morning a picture of the newlyweds squared off against each other, fists up and broad smiles on their faces, appeared in papers all over the country.

Several newsmen followed them to an Atlanta restaurant. When they entered, the orchestra broke into *The Wedding March* and the other patrons applauded. They were seated and quickly served. One reporter noticed that W.L. had quite a lot of food on his plate and commented on it.

Stribling grinned. "I don't believe in undertraining for a honeymoon."

Just before 5:00 they boarded the Birmingham Special train. Two days later they rolled into New York City and checked into the Cumberland Hotel at Broadway and 54th Street. Both had spent time in the city before and loved the excitement, the constant activity, the food, and the shows. But this time it was even better because they could enjoy it all together.

One of their first stops was a visit to Tex Rickard, the flamboyant boxing promoter. They entered his office at the new Madison Square Garden trailed by a group of reporters. After he got the preliminary pleasantries out of the way, Rickard zeroed in on what was most important to him.

He fixed both of them with a steady stare and asked, "When are you going to fight?"

Clara wasn't just a pretty southern belle. She had a quick wit and a fine sense of humor. Assuming an innocent tone, she fluttered her eyelashes and said, "Why, we don't ever expect to fight, Mr. Rickard."

The promoter was flustered for a moment, and W.L. smilingly got things back on track.

"I'll be ready to fight in six weeks," W.L. said, "and I'll fight anybody you select for me—Dempsey or Tunney or Tom Gibbons. I'd especially like a rematch with Jimmy Slattery."

The six-round loss to Slattery two years before still stung the young fighter. He wanted a chance to prove the judges wrong.

Not only did the print reporters and photographers follow them around, men with big motion picture cameras were often nearby, filming everything they did. Later that month, a Kinogram newsreel featuring the couple on their New York honeymoon appeared in theaters all over the country. Their friends in Macon saw it at the Grand Theater on January 7.

The Striblings were recognized wherever they went. They dined in fine restaurants and visited nightclubs where jazz was played. If the young couple knew that some religious leaders were condemning it as the devil's music, they didn't let on. They were young and in love and life was grand.

On Saturday afternoon, January 16, the couple boarded the steamship *City of Chattanooga* for the trip south. When the ship arrived at Savannah on Wednesday morning a number of friends and relatives met them on the dock, along with the usual contingent of reporters.

Once again they were showered with a barrage of questions, but this time the experience was more relaxed. They were home now, and the reporters seemed more like neighbors than professional newsmen.

As always there were questions about his future, and that morning W.L. told them he wouldn't be going to the University of Georgia that year. The attendance problem couldn't be resolved, he said, and the commercial course in which he was interested would take three years to complete, not the two he had anticipated. Besides that, it was hard to picture this famous young man and new husband as a freshman wearing the required red beanie hat.

Clara described their honeymoon in New York as "glorious," but admitted she had been overwhelmed by all the attention. "I didn't know whether to feel like the Queen of England or Ellin Mackay Berlin," she said, referring to a well-known debutante recently disowned by her father for marrying songwriter Irving Berlin.

The couple spent a few days in Savannah, then went on to Macon. Clara visited with her parents, and W.L. played a couple of games with the Right Way basketball team.

As the first month of 1926 came to a close Clara and W.L. left for the farm in Ochlocknee for an impromptu family reunion. Pa and Ma were resigned to the fact that their son had married. They didn't approve, but had no choice but to accept it.

Pa was sort of absentmindedly pleasant to Clara. Now that the riff between him and his son seemed to have healed and he still called the shots in W.L.'s career, she really made little impact on his life.

Pa and W.L. had an informal 60/40 financial arrangement, with the elder Stribling making all the financial decisions for the family. Their business interests were burgeoning. W.L. was bringing in thousands of dollars a month, and Pa was making some astute investments with that money.

He had purchased property in Savannah, Macon, and other parts of Georgia, in South Florida, South Carolina, and Texas. He had been named vice president of the United American Life Insurance Company and had bought stock in two Britling's Cafeterias, a southern restaurant chain.

As a result of that last purchase, W.L. was now a vice president of that company, and a new Britling's opened in Miami where one of the features of the menu was produce fresh from the Young Stribling "plantation" in Thomasville. They also served "Knockout Syrup" made from the farm's sugar cane.

In order to streamline his operation, Pa formed Stribling Realty in 1926 and assumed the role of president. Headquartered in Miami the company was involved in general real estate brokerage, but also managed all of the Stribling holdings. He and Ma began spending much of their time in South Florida.

Even though Pa had become quite a businessman, his abiding interest was still boxing and his son's career. On February 8 he finalized arrangements for the long-awaited rematch between W.L. and Jimmy Slattery. It would take place in Madison Square Garden on March 25.

W.L. easily slipped back into a training schedule. And it soon became routine for his new wife. It was her husband's job. While other young men dressed in suits and tight collars and left their houses bound for offices early in the morning, her husband pulled on a sweat suit and athletic shoes and left the house to run five miles.

Young Stribling wasn't the only Georgia boxer making news in early 1926. Tiger Flowers was part of Walk Miller's Atlanta organization, and on February 26 he met Harry Greb in a fifteen-round match in Madison Square Garden before 18,000 people.

When the fight was over, Flowers was the new middleweight champ, the first African American man to hold a national boxing title since Jack Johnson reigned as heavyweight champion from 1908 to 1915.

On February 20 W.L. and Clara joined his parents in Miami where he would continue training for the Slattery fight. The elder Striblings weren't especially happy to see their daughter-in-law—they believed she was a distraction for W.L.—but the newlyweds were determined to stay together.

Pa was quiet in his disapproval, but Ma was direct. Clara tried hard, but she seemed unable to please the older woman. Determined to solve the problem herself, she never complained to W.L. about his mother's constant criticism. But one afternoon he walked into a room when Ma was berating Clara for some minor thing.

"You'll have to watch your tongue," he told his mother with barely controlled anger. "No one can talk to Clara like that."

The tirades ended, and after that incident Ma left Clara alone. Most of the time she simply ignored her.

Gene Tunney, a leading contender for a national title, was also in Miami preparing for a match, and he and W.L. often worked out together at the same gym. But that was as close as the two fighters would get. In spite of the best efforts of managers, promoters, and financial backers, money disputes and Florida's complicated prizefighting laws couldn't be overcome. A bout between Stribling and Tunney never took place.

W.L. wouldn't have minded fighting Tunney, but right then all his concentration was focused on Jimmy Slattery. He, Clara, and his parents took a steamer ship out of Miami and arrived in New York City on

March 24. Clara and Ma were at ringside in Madison Square Garden the next night for the fight.

Nearly 20,000 people watched the ten-round Stribling–Slattery contest. Stribling was impressive, and they cheered when he won the judges' decision. The next morning sportswriters raved about his "comeback" as if he were a broken-down fighter approaching middle age rather than a young man who had only recently turned twenty-one.

The elder Striblings returned to Miami soon after the fight, and W.L. and Clara were back in Macon by the last day of the month. They were living in the Nottingham Drive house, but they had little time to settle into a routine. On April 10 W.L. left Macon with his father for a three-week Midwest tour, and Clara remained at home.

W.L. fought four matches during April, winning three and getting a no-decision in one. Then it was back to Georgia to begin training for his next fights. Two were booked for May, but the really important one—a rematch with Paul Berlenbach—was scheduled for June in Yankee Stadium. In that one, the light heavyweight championship would be on the line.

The Striblings might have been preoccupied with prizefighting, but the rest of America had other concerns, both serious and frivolous. There was disturbing news from Europe where Mussolini had just had himself crowned Emperor of Italy and the Germans were bringing back the Kaiser to reestablish their military superiority. The United States had declared it was staying out of it all.

On the lighter side, the Charleston, a dance that was already wildly popular in the Northeast and Midwest, was working its way south. In 1926 the craze was sweeping Georgia. Macon's Rialto Theater sponsored a three-day Charleston competition in May with contests held every afternoon and evening. On the final night so many people showed up to watch the last event that crowds spilled out of the theater and blocked streetcars.

On May 24 W.L. faced Ray Neuman in Atlanta. Minutes before the match, R. D. White, president of Atlanta's University School for Boys, awarded W.L. his high school diploma. White and Stribling posed for pictures, then White took his ringside seat and W.L. entered the ring, ready for battle.

It wasn't much of a fight. Neuman connected only a few times and Stribling won every round, but Neuman had done some real damage with one of those lucky punches—he had knocked out Stribling's front teeth.

That night after the fight, W.L. and his parents drove to Hendersonville, North Carolina, where Jack Dempsey had established a training camp. Pa wanted a secluded place with no distractions where W.L. could prepare for the Berlenbach fight. But before any training could begin, a dentist had to be called in to make a bridge for W.L.'s mouth.

It wasn't a quick process. The bridge took time to construct and couldn't be installed until the swelling went down. In the meantime W.L. took all his nourishment through a straw. It was a less than ideal situation for a young man training for a championship bout. But neither Pa nor W.L. mentioned the injury to the press and never considered canceling the upcoming fight.

On Saturday, June 5, the Stribling party left North Carolina for New York where they were joined by Clara and her mother. Going into the match on Thursday night, the odds on Stribling and Berlenbach were being quoted as even.

Promoters expected about 50,000 spectators for the Yankee Stadium match with proceeds anticipated at $200,000. Berlenbach, the champion, would receive 37½ percent or $75,000. W.L. could expect $25,000 for his 12½ percent.

On Thursday, the day W.L. was to fight Paul Berlenbach for the light heavyweight championship, Clara awoke feeling ill. Thinking she must be coming down with something, she decided to stay at the hotel and rest that night rather than attend the fight. She didn't feel like being buffeted by crowds and annoyed by reporters and photographers. Besides, she knew that W.L. didn't much like her watching him fight.

Yankee Stadium was crowded by the time the Striblings arrived. Pa took his place in W.L.'s corner and Ma had her usual ringside seat. They were both anticipating a win. But any hope they had that W.L. would be the next light heavyweight champion lasted only a short time. He broke a knuckle on his right hand in the first round and the injury grew more painful with each passing minute. By the tenth round, his hand was all but useless.

Pa wanted to throw in the towel, but W.L. wouldn't hear of it. He knew the sportswriters in that part of the country weren't admirers of his and was afraid they would call him a quitter. So he returned to the ring, round after round, even when it became apparent that he couldn't combat the battering being handed out by Berlenbach.

The young Georgian managed to stay in the fight through all fifteen rounds, but everyone watching knew that it was a feat accomplished through strength of will alone. The fight belonged to Berlenbach, and everyone, Stribling included, understood it. When the match was over and the referee raised Berlenbach's hand, W.L. went forward to congratulate him.

Afterward the consensus was that, even disregarding his injured hand, Stribling had overtrained. People who saw him hours before the fight noticed that his usual high energy was missing. The doctor who was standing by as the two fighters weighed in recognized that he was exhausted and whispered to another bystander that Stribling wouldn't make it through ten rounds.

Whether he had been overtrained or his low energy was the result of being on a forced liquid diet for part of the previous two weeks, the fact remained that W.L. had been convincingly defeated.

W.L. accepted the defeat gracefully. There were no excuses, no alibis, and no complaints from the Striblings.

W.L., Clara, and Mrs. Kinney had had enough of New York and went home to Macon. The boxer looked tired and unusually thin when he got off the 10:30 train in Terminal Station the next night. Pa had always been proud that his son was nearly unmarked by his years of boxing, but that wasn't the case now. There were visible bruises on his face. His right hand was bandaged, and he had a deep cut on his lip.

Still W.L. was willing to discuss the loss with *Telegraph* reporter Gordon Allen.

"I lost," he said simply, "and that's all there is to it."

When asked if he thought he had trained too hard before the match, W.L. shrugged. "Maybe. I think I trained down to too fine a point and my old-time vitality was lacking." But he gave Berlenbach the respect he was due, describing him as a great fighter. "Even if I'd been in my top form, the decision might still have been as it was."

The only time bitterness crept into his voice was when he recalled the eastern sportswriters calling him a coward for clinching in the last rounds. "They said I was yellow. I believe they were unfair. I gave it all I had that night."

Noted columnist Damon Runyon rubbed a bit more salt into that wound a few months later when, referring to all the rural fights W.L. had had with unknown opponents over the years, he derisively called him "The King of the Canebrakes." His conclusion was that Stribling might do well in rural America but had no business trying to compete in New York.

Pa and Ma stayed on in New York for several days. One of the people they saw there was Tex Rickard, and Pa asked his opinion of W.L.'s future in the ring.

"Don't worry," Rickard said, slapping the elder Stribling on the back. "We'll bring him back, and your son will be a champion yet."

21

W.L. and Clara got wonderful news in July 1926. She was pregnant with their first child, and they began setting up one of the bedrooms in the Nottingham Drive house as a nursery. The summer passed pleasantly. There were Saturday night dances at the Idle Hour Club, dinners with friends, tennis games and boating at Lakeside, but W.L. was careful to see that Clara did not overdo it.

In July the couple hosted a bridge party for twenty friends in Clara's parents' home. Crockett Odom presented a musical program, and with her mother's help, Clara served a late supper after the card games.

Clara was almost as much of a sports lover as her husband, and she had never been content being just a spectator. She especially enjoyed playing tennis, but in 1926 it would have been considered improper for a pregnant woman to be seen playing on a public court. W.L. solved that problem by having a court built on their Nottingham Drive property. There Clara and her friends could indulge in their favorite exercise in privacy any time they chose.

But there were a few clouds in Clara's life. From the beginning, Pa had controlled their money. He rarely refused W.L. anything, but he kept a close eye on what Clara spent. It was he who decided how much money she got for household expenses every month. If she needed anything over the amount he doled out, she had to go to Pa and ask for it.

She went to him once that summer to ask for additional funds.

"Why do you need more money?" he asked. "I gave you $50 last month."

She was so angry and embarrassed that she made up her mind she would never ask him for anything again. She was determined not to worry W.L. with her problem, but at first she couldn't figure out how to solve it.

After some thought she realized there was another avenue open to her. Macon was a small town, and she knew the officers at the bank where W.L. and his father had accounts. So she went to see one of them and asked for help. The banker never hesitated.

"Of course," he told her. "How much do you want?'

"Well, I'm not sure. . . ." She had been hoping for as much as a hundred dollars but was now nervous about asking for that much.

"Two thousand?" he prompted. "Three?"

Clara was so surprised she could hardly speak. After that she was never again forced to go to Pa for money.

In July, rumors began circulating that W.L. was going to fire his father as manager and sign with someone else. The tales were helped along by an article in *Collyer's Eye*, a national sports publication that reported "close friends of Stribling" stated that W.L. was unhappy with Pa's management. W.L. denied the reports soon afterward.

"Pa and I are getting along all right," he told reporters. "I don't see how it would be any advantage to me to quit him."

Pa kept W.L. out of the ring that summer to give his knuckle sufficient time to heal after the Berlenbach loss, but W.L. was still interested in the boxing scene. On July 12 he traveled to New York to see Paul Berlenbach take on Jack Delaney.

It wasn't the best time for a visit to the big city. The transit system's switchmen and motormen had walked off the job on July 6. Although replacement workers had been brought in, service levels dropped. Mobs of people crowded subway platforms vying for seats on the few trains that were running, and emergency fleets of buses were brought into the city.

Like everyone else, W.L. had some difficulty getting around during his visit, but he managed to get to Ebbets Field in Brooklyn on July 16 to be present when Jack Delaney surprised the critics and defeated Paul Berlenbach for the light heavyweight title.

Initially W.L. enjoyed having time off, but as the months passed he grew bored with the life of leisure. He continued the light daily workouts he had done for years and spent hours on the golf course. But he was ready for more. By September W.L. was pushing Pa to get him back into the ring, and his father agreed.

His first match since the New York loss came on September 17 when he fought Buck Ashton in Tampa and won by a knockout. But Ashton wasn't considered a serious contender. The real test of whether Stribling was back, whether he was ready to once again start the climb toward the title, came against Chuck Burns on September 21.

Clara chose not to travel, so only Pa and W.L. drove to Atlanta the Sunday before the fight. They went to a downtown hotel, parked outside, and went in to register. When they returned to the car they discovered their luggage had been stolen.

Ordinarily there wouldn't have been a rush to buy new clothing, but they weren't going home after the match. Instead they planned to leave as soon as the fight was over for Philadelphia. So the two spent Monday shopping to replace what they had lost.

Their concerns about clothing seemed trivial the next day when they learned that a huge hurricane had swept up from the West Indies over South Florida and left unbelievable devastation in its path. Thirty-eight thousand people had lost their homes, and the death toll stood at over 1,000 by Sunday night.

Fort Lauderdale and Miami Beach were the hardest hit. Property damage was in the hundreds of millions of dollars, and the worst had occurred in the area where the real estate boom was taking place.

The hurricane was yet another blow to the South Florida economy. Earlier in the year a number of banks in the state had failed, and there were still ongoing investigations into land fraud schemes. The Striblings, along with other investors, had been hit hard, and the hurricane increased their losses.

On Tuesday evening, W.L. fought Chuck Burns in the Atlanta auditorium and won the decision, but the sportswriters were disappointed with his performance. They had expected him to come out of a three-month rest like a lion. Instead they got ten rather tame rounds in which excitement was at a minimum.

But it was a win and the Striblings were satisfied with it. By the next evening they were in Philadelphia at the SesquiCentennial Stadium for the Dempsey–Tunney match. Tex Rickard saw them as they were making their way to their seats on the 28th row. He hurried over to them.

"What kind of seats do you have?"

Pa showed him their tickets, and Rickard shook his head.

"I can get you closer to the ring than that."

Minutes later they were settled in excellent seats in the 12th row. From there they watched as Gene Tunney defeated Jack Dempsey and was crowned the new heavyweight champion.

Gracious in defeat, Dempsey declared, "It's the old story. The best man won. I have no alibis."

Macon's new airport officially opened on September 26 and was christened Miller Field in honor of the city's mayor, Wallace Miller. Macon immediately became an official stop on the Atlanta to Florida airmail route, and many people predicted that the city would soon become an aviation center.

However, W.L.'s mode of transportation was still the automobile when he went to Memphis for a fight on the 29th of the month where he knocked out Frankie Busch in the sixth round. Then he and Clara headed for Ochlocknee for a rest.

Clara loved the farm and the people there. The Braswells always made her feel welcome, and she especially looked forward to Annie Braswell's cooking. Aunt Annie was a sweet, plump little woman who was said to be the best cook in Thomas County.

W.L. was back in Atlanta on October 5, but this time he was there to speak rather than fight. Billed as a pugilist, world traveler, and owner of a chain of cafeterias, he gave a speech at the National Restaurant Association's eighth annual convention. His topic was "A Traveler's Observation of Restaurants," and his soft-spoken manner and self-deprecating wit made him an instant hit.

W.L. and Clara stayed busy that fall redoing the house on Nottingham Drive, hoping to finish the renovations before the baby arrived. Clara supervised all the work, keeping an especially close watch on anything taking place at one end of the house where a beautiful climbing rose grew. She was so vigilant that the job superintendent finally started doing any work near the rose himself to avoid problems.

When the job was finally done, the house had four bedrooms, a dining room, living room, and two bathrooms. Two bathrooms in one house was the height of extravagance in that time.

Changes were taking place in Ochlocknee, too. Pa had decided that it would make a wonderful training camp. In the slack time after the harvest, a ring was constructed near the house and work was started on several other buildings. By the first of November, W.L. was able to train there for an upcoming fight in Des Moines, Iowa.

He won a newspaper decision over Battling Levinsky in Des Moines on Armistice Day. On the 18th, he defeated Ed Smith in Miami and, eight days later, knocked out Big Boy Peterson in Tampa. Then it was back to Macon.

Now that they were about to start a family, Clara was determined that she and W.L. would become active in a church. She had no real preference as to where they went. Growing up she had attended both Methodist and Episcopalian churches, and they went to the Baptist church when they were in Ochlocknee. She just wanted them to become involved.

W.L. agreed to go anywhere she wished, and the first church they attended in Macon happened to be having a revival on the day they attended. Halfway through the service, Clara realized she had made a terrible mistake. The preacher's tirade on hellfire and damnation was making her uncomfortable, and she feared that W.L. would never set foot in a church again.

"Let's go," she whispered to him as the ranting continued.

But W.L. was unperturbed. "No, we'll stick this out."

Neither enjoyed the service, but the experience didn't sour W.L. on religion. He was still willing to try other churches, and they soon regularly began attending Mulberry Street Methodist Church.

Walk Miller had wanted to handle W.L.'s career for several years. That fall he met with Pa Stribling to discuss taking over W.L.'s management. With Tiger Flowers in his stable, Miller already had one champion. He declared that he could make W.L. a champion, too, and offered $100,000 for a three-quarters interest in him. It was a great deal of money, and Pa agreed to consider it.

W.L. fought and won once more in December, but his horizons were broadening far beyond the boxing ring. He was enjoying married life and excited about becoming a father. In one year he had made the transition from boy to adult.

When Tex Rickard was interviewed by sportswriters on December 28 about serious contenders for the heavyweight title, he didn't mention Stribling's name. But W.L. wasn't finished yet.

22

Pa and Walk Miller finally reached an agreement, and on Monday morning, January 3, 1927, they announced that Miller had purchased controlling interest of W.L. Stribling's contract for one year. Walker would call the shots—deciding how and where W.L. would train and whom he would fight—and Pa would have no say in any of it.

A large sum of money had changed hands, but the determining factor for Pa was Miller's assurance that he could get W.L. a shot at Tunney and the title.

"I think it'll be a shorter cut to the championship for him," Pa explained when people asked him why. "I know W.L. can beat Tunney."

W.L. accepted the change without much comment. He was a boxer, and he wanted to fight the best in the world. Miller promised him that chance. He was the man who had taken Tiger Flowers to a national title, and it seemed reasonable that he might do the same for Stribling.

Miller began immediate negotiations to arrange a big match for Stribling. He wanted him to face Paul Berlenbach again or take on Jack Sharkey or Jim Maloney. All were top contenders, but the decision of whom W.L. would or wouldn't fight in New York was ultimately Tex Rickard's.

Rickard was conducting what he called a heavyweight elimination tournament that would stretch over several months. Whoever emerged as the ultimate winner would get a shot at titleholder Gene Tunney. At Walker's insistence, he agreed to include W.L. in the tournament. The match would probably take place in late February, but Rickard wasn't ready to name his opponent just yet.

W.L. picked up the pace of his workouts in anticipation of the February bout. He was in the gym in Macon most days, and Herbert, still under Pa's management, trained with him when he was in town.

On January 24 Tex Rickard's annual ranking of boxers was released. In the heavyweight division, which Rickard called "the finest lot in history," he divided contenders into three tiers.

The first group was led, not surprisingly, by Gene Tunney, followed by Jack Dempsey and Jack Sharkey. The second tier consisted of Jack Delaney, Paul Berlenbach, Jim Maloney, and Paolino Uzcundun. It wasn't until the third and last group that W.L.'s name appeared with Monte Munn and Jack Renault.

That announcement demonstrated that Rickard was less than impressed by Stribling, and fight fans knew then it might take a long time for W.L. to work his way up through the ranks. And to do so he would have to win at every level.

But the Striblings weren't thinking about boxing that day. At Macon's Oglethorpe Sanitarium in the early morning hours of January 24, Clara gave birth to an eight-and-a-half-pound boy. They named the baby William Lawrence Stribling III.

W.L. had never been so excited. He called everyone he could think of all over the country and sent telegrams to those he couldn't reach by telephone. With the help of a local florist, he filled Clara's hospital room with flowers and ordered more for the house in anticipation of her and the baby coming home.

Pa, too, was enthralled by the baby. That night he was in Herbert's corner at the Macon Auditorium. Herbert won his fight with Jordan Shepherd, but many of the congratulations voiced were for the new grandfather. The man who had been known as Pa Stribling for so many years now declared he should be called Grandpa.

While W.L.'s attention was focused on his wife and new son, Walk Miller was concentrating on getting him into a ring with nationally ranked boxers. He hired Dr. Carl Studer, a chiropractor and veteran trainer, to work with W.L., and Studer confidently declared he would make a heavyweight contender of him. Where Pa had concentrated on teaching W.L. defensive fighting and how to score points, Studer planned to transform him into a power puncher.

"Strib is a brainy boxer and should be easy to handle if they'll give me a free rein," he told reporters when he arrived in Macon. "But he has never proven that he possesses the one thing that will take him up to the big time—the power to hit and take one to give two."

Studer only had one week to work with W.L. before his February 7 fight with Eddie Huffman in Madison Square Garden. His workouts had been attracting the usual crowd of fans and sightseers in Macon, but his new trainer put an end to that. Studer excluded spectators from the workouts, not wanting W.L. to have any distractions.

W.L., his parents, Walk Miller, and Carl Studer all traveled to New York a couple of days before the fight. Clara and the baby remained in Macon with her parents.

Even though his match with Huffman was part of Rickard's elimination contest and billed as the heavyweight test for Stribling, it wasn't a big draw at the Garden. In fact it attracted the smallest crowd of the season.

W.L. concentrated so hard on what Studer had been teaching him that he showed no initiative of his own. He won the ten-round decision, but the fight was so slow, boring, and punctuated by frequent clinching that, at one point, the crowd booed the fighters. Stribling easily outhit, outwitted, and outboxed Huffman, but lacked the knockout punch the fans and his management were hoping to see. New York sportswriters were merciless in their comments. The overall opinion was that W.L. might have won the fight, but had no future in big-time boxing.

But Miller and Studer weren't ready to give up just yet. They booked a couple of local fights for him and he did well, knocking out both his opponents. Observers noted that, just as his trainers had predicted, Stribling was changing his style. He had always had a dangerous left hand, but reserved his right for infighting. Now his right was much more in evidence.

Miller decided it was time for W.L. to move up the ladder a bit. He arranged a March 17 match for him with Spanish heavyweight contender Paolino Uzcundun in Boston. But a week before it was to occur, the Spaniard backed out and a last-minute replacement had to be found. Maxie Rosenbloom was brought in from New York.

There was still plenty of antisouthern sentiment in the Northeast. That was apparent when a local sportswriter declared, "This marks the first time a Jew was ever matched against a Ku Kluxer on St. Patrick's Day in a stronghold of Irishmen."

It was a partisan crowd that saw the fight in Boston that night, but Stribling beat Rosenbloom convincingly. Then he went on to Buffalo where he took on Art Weigand. With his newly energized right hand, he knocked Weigand through the ropes in the sixth round and the referee stopped the fight.

Stribling won two more fights and no one could argue with his success, but it was still on a fairly small scale. Walk Miller knew that better than anyone. His contract with Pa had originally seemed an advantageous one, but now he was having second thoughts.

The contract provided that Miller got 75 percent of Stribling's earnings—but only on those fights where the boxer made more than $5,000. With the caliber of opponents he was facing, W.L. seemed unlikely to make more than $5,000 a fight for months to come. He was slowly working his way back to the top, but wouldn't be commanding the big money until he got there. Meanwhile, Miller was paying Studer's salary as well as all expenses for publicity, training, and negotiation and getting nothing in return.

But things were slowly changing. Miller succeeded in getting W.L. a May 3 bout with light heavyweight champion Tommy Loughran. Although Stribling had beaten Loughran twice in the past, there were no guarantees he would win this match. Loughran was a tough opponent, and there would be additional pressure on him with the title on the line.

On April 21 W.L. and Studer left Macon for Newark where Miller set up a training camp on the rooftop of a large hotel. W.L. had never trained in such a place before, but soon discovered that sparring, skipping rope, and roadwork were pretty much the same wherever he happened to be.

Miller was well aware of how the eastern press had treated W.L. over the years and set about trying to change Stribling's image. He went out of his way to tell anyone who asked that he had never lost faith in the young Georgia boxer.

"Billy's only a baby," he would say. "But he's growing bigger and stronger and better all the time. He'll be the heavyweight champion of the world."

While his manager believed in him, W.L. still chafed under the criticism the sportswriters heaped on him. Finally he had to do something to let his side be heard and, on April 29, wrote an open letter to the fans and the press. In the letter, which was published in the New York papers, he acknowledged the criticism he had received in the past and asked that they withhold their judgment until the fight with Loughran. "I will abide by their decision on that showing," W.L. concluded.

Once again, the bad luck that seemed to stalk Stribling every time he neared a title fight intervened. A few days before the match, he hurt his neck during a hard workout. Miller and Studer were concerned and wanted to postpone the fight, but W.L. wouldn't hear of it.

He had already been hurt enough by the press. He knew that they would call him a coward if he asked for a postponement, so he told Miller he wanted to go ahead with the match.

Back in Macon, the *Telegraph* had set up the usual wire communication for calling the fight, and they were also in constant telephone communication with an announcer at WMAZ radio who would broadcast the blow-by-blow details to the whole town. Clara had a radio in her home, but she didn't want even a few seconds' delay in hearing the action. She was in the *Telegraph* office that evening, anxiously waiting as the details came over the wire.

Tuesday, May 3, wasn't an ideal day for outdoor boxing. It was cool and cloudy, and by fight time that evening, a light drizzle fell intermittently. Pa was in W.L.'s corner along with Studer when the first bell rang. Stribling rushed Loughran, delivered a left hook to his stomach, and then drove him into the ropes.

It was a good, strong start, but it didn't last. W.L. was soon overwhelmed by Loughran's smashing and slamming. In the end, Loughran won seven out of 10 rounds and W.L. had, once again, lost before a New York audience.

Clara listened quietly to the whole fight, never grimacing or showing any emotion. When it was over, she just smiled and said, "W.L. is coming home Thursday, and that interests me most of all."

Stribling left New York while the unfavorable press write-ups were still being published there. He arrived in Macon the same day, and when his hometown newsmen asked him about future plans, he had little to say except that he already had two fights booked and in a week he would be in the ring in Kentucky.

He was discouraged and disappointed, but all those feelings evaporated as soon as he was back with Clara and their new son. William Lawrence Stribling III, who was called "Three" by his parents, completely charmed his father out of his depression.

W.L. started training his own son very early just as his parents had done with him. With the baby lying on his back on the bed, W.L. would put out his thumb and Three would grasp it. Then his father would begin to gently pull away. By the time he was only a few months old, Three would hold on, lifting his upper body a few inches off the mattress. Once that move was perfected, W.L. used two thumbs to provide grips for both of the baby's hands. Within a few months, Three was holding up his entire weight with his hands.

There were still fights scheduled, but news of W.L.'s winning his remaining matches in May received little notice from the press or the public. The bouts were with insignificant opponents, and the country had a new hero that month. A virtually unknown U.S. Air Mail pilot named Charles Lindbergh crossed the vast Atlantic in a nonstop solo flight from New York to Paris and became an overnight sensation. Soon everyone was talking about "Lucky Lindy."

W.L. took special note of Lindbergh's adventure. Although he already owned several fast cars and had added a motorcycle to his fleet, he was fascinated by airplanes. He had already been a passenger in a plane and now began to consider flying one himself.

As the halfway point neared in his yearlong agreement with the Striblings, Walk Miller was far from satisfied. The boxer he had expected to swiftly scale the ladder to the championship had, for the most part, disappointed him. In June he effectively cut his losses by calling Carl Studer back to Atlanta to work with his other fighters and turning W.L.'s day-to-day management back over to Pa.

While little fanfare accompanied the decision, there were immediate changes. Ma was once more in charge of her son's diet and training schedule. And the workouts in both Macon and Ochlocknee were again open to the public.

Beginning with a July 4 match in Macon, W.L. put together a string of ten wins, one draw, and a no-contest in a six-month period. He didn't venture back to New York in 1927. Instead he returned to the heartland—Indiana, Nebraska, Washington, Oregon, and Kansas.

It was while he was in Kansas that W.L. was finally able to indulge his latest interest. He began taking lessons under Charles Laundree at the Wichita Flying School. He crowded as many flight hours as he could into the time they had there and vowed to return as soon as possible to finish his training.

He didn't tell his mother what he was doing until he had clocked eight hours in the air, but Clara knew of his plans from the beginning. The whole idea scared her. What if he were hurt? But she hid her fear because she understood it was something W.L. really wanted to do. It wasn't right to make him unhappy just because she was afraid.

Stribling kept fighting and winning, but the second half of the year wasn't without controversy. On September 7 he appeared in a match against Leo Diebel in Omaha. The fight was slow and the referee stopped it in the sixth round, declaring that the boxers weren't giving the fans their money's worth. He hustled both men from the ring and declared the bout "no contest."

Minutes later, the surprised fighters were arrested and charged with participating in a sham fight. After being held in the local jail overnight, they were brought before a police judge for arraignment the next morning.

W.L. and his father were furious. Pa told the judge that neither he nor his son had ever met Diebel before and would never take part in such a thing.

"W.L. hurt his right hand in the third round," he told the court, "and couldn't use it thereafter. He did his best with his left hand."

When the judge demanded to know why W.L. hadn't told anyone he had been injured, Pa explained as patiently as his temper would let him that unless a fighter threw in the towel, he never wanted to let his opponent know he was hurt. It would give the other man a distinct advantage.

But the arresting officer Ben Danbaum was adamant that the fight had been a sham. His opinion seemed to have been colored by the rumors that began during the family's 1925 barnstorming tour.

"They've staged hippodromes all over the country," Danbaum said, "but they can't get away with it here."

The judge imposed a $100 fine on both men. Diebel paid his, wanting nothing more at that point than to get out of Omaha. But Pa refused to pay. Neither he nor his son were about to admit guilt when they hadn't done anything. Instead, he posted a $500 bond and demanded that the criminal charge be scheduled for trial.

But Pa wasn't going to sit and wait for the slow-moving legal machinery to grind out justice. Two days later he appealed the referee's decision to the Nebraska State Boxing Commission.

When word of the situation reached Macon, scores of telegrams were fired off to Nebraska, attesting to W.L.'s high morals, clean living, and excellent standing in the community. Among those sending wires were the chief of police, presidents of several civic clubs, business leaders, and the entire membership of the Chamber of Commerce.

The State Boxing Commission acted quickly. On September 10 the matter went before Judge Lincoln Frost, head of the Nebraska State Department of Public Welfare. After the testimony of the fight participants, referee, and arresting officer, it became apparent that Stribling and Diebel hadn't staged a sham fight. They were victims of ignorance and confusion.

The referee, who couldn't really articulate a specific reason for his claim, admitted he had never before officiated at anything but third-rate, quasi-amateur bouts. The arresting officer was equally unconvincing.

Four physicians testified that W.L.'s hand was, indeed, injured. The doctor who had examined both fighters prior to the match declared that the hand had been fine before the fight and that he was convinced the injury occurred during the match.

At the end of the hearing, the fighters were exonerated. And Boxing Commissioner Ira Vorhees announced that the State Boxing Department had not charged nor had it any intention of charging either fighter for participating in a sham match.

Within a week the criminal charges were also dropped, and the purse, which had been withheld by the authorities, was distributed to the fighters. The Striblings' share of the gate was $3,200. They deducted expenses and donated the rest to an Omaha charity. Diebel and his manager did the same.

Neither boxer ever fought in Nebraska again.

In late September, Jack Dempsey made one last run on the heavyweight title in a rematch with Gene Tunney. Although Dempsey made a good showing, the decision went to Tunney in the "Long Count" fight. After the fight, Dempsey officially retired from the sport.

23

Riverside Military Academy and Herbert Stribling hadn't been a good match, primarily because he was absent so much of the time. But the Striblings weren't yet ready to give up on their younger son's education. In the fall of 1927 he was enrolled in high school in Ochlocknee.

At twenty years old, Herbert was not known for applying himself to his studies, but he was very popular. He played drums and drove his Baby Overland convertible all over the unpaved roads of Thomas County. That alone would have been enough to impress his classmates since no other boy in town had a car. But Herbert could have done so without the vehicle. He was handsome and witty and able to charm almost anyone he met.

Herbert was now a welterweight, and Pa booked regular fights for him. He and his dog were a common sight around town, running mile after mile of roadwork. He possessed a winning record, but he and his father both knew he would never reach the same level in the sport as his older brother. The youngest Stribling boy also showed more independence that W.L. and often chafed under Pa's strict supervision.

In November the boxing world was saddened by the sudden death of Tiger Flowers, the Atlanta boxer who had won the middleweight championship from Harry Greb in 1926. Although he had lost the crown ten months later to Mickey Walker on a controversial decision, he was by no means finished in the ring. His manager, mentor, and friend Walk Miller had been grooming him for a comeback.

Flowers had just won his fourteenth fight of the year when, on November 16, he entered a New York City hospital to have scar tissue removed from around his eyes. It was a simple procedure, but complications from the surgery caused his death. It was eerily similar to the way Harry Greb had died a year before of complications from surgery to repair his broken nose.

Flowers had been a good man—soft-spoken, easygoing, and deeply religious, called the "Georgia Deacon." Atlanta welcomed him home on November 18 with a procession down Decatur Street, and seven thousand people, black and white alike, jammed the city auditorium for his funeral.

W. L. Stribling turned twenty-three years old on December 26. He was a husband, a father, and a businessman holding positions in at least two companies. He had fought 193 matches and earned hundreds of thousands of dollars over a short, seven-year career. But did he have the drive and the skill to attempt another try for the championship?

The end of the year brought the official end of Walk Miller's management of Young Stribling. Most critics believed that W.L.'s best years of fighting were behind him, but Pa was still hopeful and in December again predicted his son would claim the championship.

W.L.'s first fight back under his father's full management was in Wichita, Kansas, on January 9, 1928, where he won a ten-round match with Chuck Wiggins. He had been eager to get back to Kansas. The fight was only part of the reason he had traveled there.

He continued the flying lessons he had begun months before, moving ever closer to earning his pilot's license. He also ordered a Waco monoplane from the factory in Wichita. Once it was built, it would be flown to Macon and delivered to him.

W.L. wanted the airplane because he loved to fly, but Pa saw greater potential there. A boxer who was also a pilot would garner more newspaper space than one who simply boxed. What could be more dramatic than having one of the contestants fly into town and swoop low over the stadium only hours before a fight?

Stribling was so excited about his new purchase that he hardly noticed when Tex Rickard's *Ring* ranking of boxers came out the next day and he had moved up a bit from the previous year. He was now ranked number two in the second tier of light heavyweights. But the news made little impression on him. After all, he had just bought an airplane. He could hardly wait for it to be delivered.

But Pa never stopped working. He continued scheduling matches for his fighters, and a week later he and W.L. traveled to Miami. It was the height of the Miami boxing season, and W.L. was scheduled to fight Martin Burke.

Tex Rickard and Gene Tunney were at ringside that Monday night in late January. Just before the match started, Tunney climbed into the ring, greeted Burke, and slapped him on the back. He completely ignored Stribling who was standing only a few feet away.

Some people later suggested that the slight had been intentional, something to arouse W.L.'s anger. It worked. Stribling was furious, and when the bell sounded he came out of his corner with fierce determination. Forty-five seconds later, he knocked Burke out.

Rickard was surprised and impressed by his performance. He later told reporters, "Two more fights like that will place Stribling back in the elimination picture."

But a writer from Burke's hometown of New Orleans had another opinion. Still stinging from his favorite's defeat, he hinted in his next day's column that Stribling had used a "gimmick" in his glove. Gimmick was boxing slang for a foreign object, such as a piece of iron.

When he heard the accusation, Stribling was so angry that he threatened to punch the writer. He didn't do that, of course, but he did make his father promise to schedule a rematch with Burke as soon as possible.

Left alone while her husband traveled all over the country, Clara filled her time caring for the baby, who was now almost a year old, and volunteering with the Junior League. It was an association that brought her great satisfaction, but it almost didn't happen.

She had been invited to join the Junior League just before marrying W.L., but had declined. The membership was shocked. No one ever turned down an invitation to join them. But Clara had been concerned that her future husband's profession wouldn't be acceptable to the society ladies in the organization. Nothing could have been further from the truth. W.L. was very popular with everyone in Macon, even the ladies of the Junior League.

When she was approached again after her marriage, Clara quickly joined and soon found herself doing volunteer work at the Well Baby Clinic under the guidance of Dr. Benjamin Bashinski.

Of course, there was also a social side to the Junior League. Teas, balls, parties, and dances were held throughout the year, and many of them were very fancy functions. Clara thought W.L. might resist donning a tuxedo to attend a society affair, but she needn't have worried. He was as comfortable in formal dress as he was in hunting clothes. And he looked like a movie star. Witty, gallant, and an expert dancer, he charmed the ladies, all of whom wanted to dance with him.

W.L. had matches scheduled every week during the winter and spring of 1928, but still managed to continue his flying lessons. His new plane had been delivered right on schedule. He had hired a local instructor and his lessons were progressing well, but he kept asking to be taught more exciting things than simply taking off and landing.

He had watched stunt flyers for years, trying to be on hand every time they would come to Macon to perform their dives and loops. That was what *he* wanted to do, but his instructor in Macon steadfastly refused to teach him such risky moves. He knew Pa Stribling would have his hide if he did.

In February, W.L. made his first flight to a boxing match. Although his instructor was in the copilot's seat on the trip to Jacksonville, W.L. handled the flying duties himself. They also had a passenger for the trip—Ma Stribling was with them.

W.L.'s mother had once declared, "I'll never ride in one of those things," but she was persuaded to go and, by all accounts, enjoyed the experience.

W.L. made numerous flights that spring, and Ma wasn't his only passenger. Pa and Herbert joined him on occasion, and he and his instructor flew Clara to Thomasville several times.

The Southeastern Air Derby came to Macon in February, and W.L. was looking forward to seeing some state-of-the-art aerial stunts. The Derby opened at Miller Field on Saturday, February 18. To drum up interest, a local flying school was hired to fly over downtown Macon that morning and toss out large firecrackers and leaflets advertising the event. Samuel L. "Buck" Steele piloted the small plane that day. His only passenger was Francis Ashcraft, brother of one of the owners of the flying school.

The publicity stunt worked well for the first few minutes. While the noise and sight of the airplane drew some notice on its own, the firecrackers guaranteed that everyone's attention was directed skyward. Once alerted, people saw the leaflets fluttering to the ground and picked them up and read them.

The first two explosions took place as planned, but something went very wrong with the third. It appeared to observers that the firecracker detonated while it was still beside the plane. The aircraft's wing shot up in the air. The plane spun over, then plummeted to the ground 2,500 feet below, burying the nose in the sidewalk outside a Cherry Street pharmacy.

The pilot and his passenger were killed immediately, as was thirty-four-year-old C. E. Murphy, who had been standing in that spot watching the plane. Horrified crowds rushed into the street and ran to the site. So many people jammed onto the already-damaged sidewalk that it collapsed, plunging a number of them into a cellar below. Twelve people were injured in the fall.

The Air Derby continued in spite of the crash, and the following afternoon the contestants flew over the city in formation and dropped flowers over the crash site. Most flyers, including Stribling, took the news of the accident philosophically. Crashes were a part of flying that they all accepted.

Soon after the Cherry Street crash, speculation began that the Crader-Steele-Ashcraft Flying School would shut down. One of the owners had been killed, along with a relative of another, and word was that the remaining operators had no interest in continuing.

If the school did close its doors, it would leave a void in Macon's aviation industry. And W. L. Stribling, who had just purchased his second airplane—a Swallow biplane—wanted to be the one to fill that void.

On the evening of February 21 he appeared before the Macon City Council to apply for exclusive privileges to conduct a flying school at

Miller Field. Even though he hadn't yet earned his pilot's license, he did have pilot and instructor Jimmy Northcutt in his employ, and he told the council that he expected to shortly earn his own license. A few weeks later the council granted him the permission he had asked for, and the Stribling Aerial School was born.

Two days after meeting with the council, W.L. was back in the ring, this time in Montgomery. Then it was on to Miami and Cleveland for more matches. He won those fights. In fact he had won all eight matches he had fought that year, but it wasn't just his winning way that made headlines.

On March 6 the *Cleveland Plain Dealer* carried a front-page story of the Striblings' arrival in that city. The article was accompanied by a large photo of W.L., Pa, and their pilot standing with their plane, smiling their delight at being in Ohio. There was almost no mention of his opponent in the whole article. Pa's latest promotional idea was working well.

W.L. continued to fight several times a month, and in spite of having torn a ligament in his left hand, he continued to win. As the year progressed, the critics once again began to take notice, and talk of his burnout soon changed to talk of a comeback.

Even when W.L. was in Macon, he made the papers. Willie Snow Etheridge, a reporter for the *Telegraph*, interviewed him in his East Macon home for a feature story. At first the interview progressed in the usual way, but W.L. was never one to sit quietly and answer questions. As he and the reporter talked, fourteen-month-old Three wandered into the room and the fighter began playing with him.

At one point, he threw Three into the air, then held his hands out and the baby landed with one little foot in each of his father's hands, perfectly balanced. Three grinned and stood there, just as his father had taught him to do.

Next W.L. grasped the child's feet and swung him in a slow arc toward the floor. The baby remained absolutely rigid. When he was extended sideways over the floor, he raised himself back up to stand again in his father's hands and balanced on one foot. W.L. then knocked that foot out from under him and caught the child in both hands as he fell.

The reporter was struck speechless at this display, but both father and son laughed with delight. Clara, sitting nearby, just smiled serenely. Stribling explained he had been working with the baby all his life and, for Three, being tossed around by his father was normal—just as it had been normal for W.L. at that age.

The flight school expanded in early summer. In addition to teaching flying, the Striblings were now official sales agents of Swallow Airplanes. To promote their business, they put on exhibitions at the airfield and brought in stunt flyers and parachutists.

Clara Stribling learned in May that she was pregnant again. W.L. was thrilled that they had another baby on the way. Whenever his fight schedule permitted, he was at home with his wife that spring.

There was plenty to do in Macon. Radio had come into its own, and the town now had a number of stations with programs available from mid-morning until after eleven at night. Dances were held at Idle Hour most weekends, and in April the first talking pictures arrived. Al Jolson in *The Jazz Singer* was an immediate hit there and all over the country.

By the first week of May, W.L. had earned his pilot's license and flew Clara and Three to Florida. Ma and Pa were already there, having set up training facilities for W.L. He had a May 8 match scheduled with Andres Castano.

But the week in Florida wasn't all work. He took time off to enjoy the resort with his family and also managed to fly every few days.

One afternoon he took his mother up for a ride. It was a wonderful afternoon for flying, and the two enjoyed having the time together. But as they were returning to the airfield, the engine began missing and soon stopped altogether. W.L. had to set the craft down in a field. Neither of them were injured, but one of the plane's wings was damaged by contact with a fence.

After winning the Castano fight, W.L. and his family had to return to Macon by car. His plane was left behind in Miami for repairs.

The airplane mishap might have made some people think twice about flying again, but W.L. took it in stride. Once the craft was fixed he returned to Miami to retrieve it. He then flew alone to his next fight in Tampa.

He knocked out Marcello Gubinelli in the May 18 fight, but W.L. wasn't ready to return home just yet. He wanted to do something he could never have done at home.

The next day he located a stunt pilot at an airfield just outside of town and hired him on the spot. The two spent the afternoon in the air, and W.L. soaked up everything he could about stunt flying.

The following afternoon people in Macon noticed a plane above the city executing a series of amazing stunts—sharp climbs, free falls, and enough loops to make the spectators on the ground dizzy. There was speculation that a famous stunt pilot had come to town unannounced, but it was only W. L. Stribling practicing his new tricks.

Less than a week later W.L. was back in Florida to take on Charles Rammell in Pensacola. But that wasn't his only fight of the evening. From the time he entered the ring, he was heckled by a taxi driver who was seated at ringside. Smoker called the Georgia fighter every name he could think of, cursing him, questioning his lineage, and belittling his boxing ability. W.L. did his best to ignore the hostile spectator and went on with the match.

He knocked out Rammell in the second round, was declared the winner, and left the ring. But Smoker would not let it go. He continued to shout at W.L., cursing him, and getting right in his face in the aisle. Finally Stribling lost his temper and punched him.

Smoker wasn't visibly hurt, but that didn't stop him from filing assault charges against W.L. and the boxer was arrested. Stribling promptly filed countercharges against Smoker for cursing.

W.L. paid his fine and made a public apology, but it wasn't enough for the other man. The next day Smoker told reporters he was going to file suit against Stribling for $25,000. But it was all bluster. No record of such a case exists in Pensacola court records.

24

Pa continued to schedule matches for W.L. throughout the summer of 1928, and he won every one. But W.L.'s real interest that year was aviation. Miller Field needed a hangar, and on June 1, W.L. joined with the Junior Chamber of Commerce to jointly purchase one. A regulation steel army hangar would be installed at Miller Field in July and would be capable of housing twelve planes.

W.L. never missed a chance to fly, whether it was a jaunt to another city or just a few leisurely passes over Middle Georgia. It was even more fun if he could take friends with him.

One summer morning he made a quick flight around the area with his brother Herbert and friend Roy Barrow. When they landed back at Miller Field, young mechanic and pilot-in-training Jack Banks was there to help.

W.L. greeted him by name and invited him home for lunch.

Banks, self-conscious about his greasy overalls, was hesitant. "I better not, Strib."

"Sure you can," W.L. told him. "Let me call my wife and see if she has enough."

When he returned from the office he told Banks, "She's cooking meatloaf and she has plenty. Come on."

The young man climbed into W.L.'s big car with him and the others. Clara served them a delicious lunch and treated Banks as a valued guest in her home. When Stribling later dropped him off at Miller Field, he had made a lifelong friend. Banks went on to become a pilot with Delta Air Lines, but he never forgot the kindness shown to him by W. L. Stribling.

There was more aviation news that summer. Amelia Earhart, the first woman to make a transatlantic flight, piloted her plane from New

York to Burry Port, Wales. And dirigibles—buoyant, engine-driven airships filled with light gas—also had caught the public's imagination.

Dr. Hugo Eckner had built and been flying the luxury craft Zeppelin for some time. That year it had crossed the Atlantic from Germany to Lakehurst, New Jersey, and Eckner was now considering a flight from Germany to California.

On the Fourth of July W.L. once again fought in the main boxing event in Macon. Fans were excited to see him in action again. They were also relieved that the fight would be held inside that evening. They had spent too many holiday afternoons baking under the July sun.

Three thousand spectators crowded into the auditorium that night, hoping to see a battle of equals. W.L.'s opponent Bucky Harris was nicknamed the Kansas Killer, but he didn't live up to the billing. Stribling did his best to prolong the match for the fans, but when he finally administered the knockout punch in the third round it seemed almost merciful.

The American public's interest in boxing hadn't lessened, and the Striblings were listening on the radio along with thousands of fight fans across the country when Gene Tunney crushed Tom Heeney in the heavyweight title fight on July 26. But Tunney's announcement a few days later that he was retiring undefeated threw the boxing world into turmoil.

With no champion at the helm, anyone and everyone believed they were eligible for a shot at the crown. Tex Rickard stepped in with a solution that was typical for the promoter. There had be an elimination process where, by virtue of a win, each participant could move up the ladder to the next fight until one stood alone at the top. That person would then be crowned the champion.

And Rickard, of course, was the one who would decide which contenders would be included in the elimination matches. Pa immediately began negotiations to make sure W.L. was one of those contestants.

Throughout the hot summer months W.L. continued racking up wins. The northeastern sportswriters took notice, but they didn't hesitate to criticize. He wasn't fighting title contenders, they complained, and his father had him scheduled for too many bouts. They predicted he would soon be burned out.

One of his fights that summer was more important to W.L. than the others. It was the rematch he had wanted with Martin Burke. It took place in Mobile on August 13, and once again Stribling knocked him out—this time in the first round. And, again, the New Orleans sportswriter was at ringside.

When the short match ended, Stribling walked to where the writer sat and dropped his gloves in his lap.

"Here are my gloves.... Nothing in them but my fists. Now what are you going to say in your column tomorrow morning?"

Every word written about Stribling in the next day's column was complimentary.

Rickard included W.L. in the first round of his elimination tournament. On September 6, Stribling fought Johnny Squires, the heavyweight champion of South Africa, in Madison Square Garden.

W.L. hadn't fared well the previous times he had fought in New York, losing fights he had been expected to win. Even when he had won his last match with Jimmy Slattery, the press and fans hadn't been kind, questioning his courage and the decision itself. But this time it was different.

Before a crowd that began as hostile but ended as supportive, Stribling proved he was the clean, hard-hitting fighter his backers always said he was. He came out swinging, and from the time the first blow landed, the fight was his.

The South African made it through the first round only because he was saved by the bell. When the second round began, Squires was virtually out on his feet. The few punches he threw were ineffective and Stribling never relented. Gone was the boxer known for having no killer instinct. He pursued Squires until he knocked him down and the referee counted him out. The entire match lasted three minutes and 44 seconds.

Finally the newspaper writers gave Stribling the respect he felt he deserved. Even while they pointed out that Squires wasn't much of a boxer, they had to acknowledge W.L.'s relentless attack. Rickard was so impressed that he immediately signed W.L. for three more matches.

His performance hadn't gone unnoticed in Macon either. To show him that they were squarely behind him, the Macon American Legion produced a boxing program of five matches at the City Auditorium on September 17 in honor of W. L. Stribling.

Everyone entering the building received a photo of him, and the boxer himself sat near the door and autographed the pictures. He had a friendly greeting for everyone who came in and signed his name hundreds of times during the first half hour.

When the preliminary matches were over, W.L. climbed into the ring. He had agreed to referee the two main bouts. It was a surprise to the young man when Alderman Charlie Bowden joined him there. When the politician introduced W.L. as the next heavyweight champion of the world, the crowd broke into thunderous applause.

"It matters not whether you win or lose, W.L., Macon, your hometown, will always greet you with open arms."

He presented W.L. with a cake from Barker's Bakery and a toilet kit in a small case. Then he, and the rest of the crowd, wished him luck in his upcoming fight with Frankie Wine.

W.L. thanked them with his usual modesty, then went on to referee the two fights.

The same day he was honored by his hometown, W.L. received the disturbing news that Walk Miller, who had taken Tiger Flowers to the title and had managed Stribling for a year, was dead. The promoter had shot and killed himself at his training camp in Kingston, New York. No one could provide a reason for his actions.

Wrapped in the good wishes of his hometown fans and friends, W.L. and Pa traveled to Grand Rapids, Michigan, where he fought and beat Frankie Wine on September 20.

Stribling was soon ready for another fight, but Tex Rickard was having difficulty finding anyone willing to fight him. Knute Hansen, Jack Sharkey, and Jack Delaney all said they wanted a warm-up fight before facing him. The same sentiment was echoed by Johnny Risko,

Tommy Loughran, and several others. W.L.'s showing against Johnny Squires seemed to have unnerved the best boxers in the business.

Rickard continued to book fights for his elimination tournament, but he was also involved in another project. Pleased with the way his Madison Square Garden was producing, he was ready to expand.

In late September he announced that he would be opening a new sporting club in Miami Beach. The complex would have a dog racing track, an arena, and an exclusive clubhouse. It should be ready sometime during the coming winter, and Rickard believed it was going to offer a fine winter alternative to Madison Square Garden.

And when Tex Rickard finally found an opponent for Stribling—he signed Jack Sharkey to fight him in February—it would be the first match in his new Miami open-air stadium. Sharkey had recently won the title of heavyweight champion of North America. He was a tough opponent, and Rickard knew he would provide a real test for the young fighter.

On November 6 Republican Herbert Hoover was elected president. He had supported Prohibition and run on a ticket calling for improving the country's efficiency and maintaining America's isolationist foreign policy.

The Striblings were firm Democrats, but they weren't overly concerned with the election that year. Their thoughts were closer to home. Three days after the election Clara gave birth to their second child, a girl they named Mary Virginia.

W.L. had five more fights in 1928 and knocked out every opponent he met. The longest match lasted only six rounds. Pa had scheduled fewer fights than usual for him that winter, and the change was a welcome one, giving him more time to spend with his family. They divided their time between Macon and Ochlocknee.

It was a wonderful place for the family to get away, but now it was more than a retreat. The farm had become quite a large concern. They raised hogs and cattle and grew cotton, corn, and sugar cane on the 1,500 acres.

W.L. still flew every chance he got. In early December he helped the Rialto Theater promote the new movie *Wings* starring Clara Bow and Gary Cooper by flying over the city and dropping 75 free tickets.

For once his schedule allowed him to enjoy the holiday season with his family. The Junior Chamber of Commerce and Retail Merchants Bureau teamed up to decorate the Macon streets for the Christmas season. The brightly colored lights were turned on for the first time on December 14, and on Christmas Eve a mass choir sang carols on the steps of the Municipal Auditorium.

On December 26 W.L. turned twenty-four years old. He was a man and a boxer in his prime. It had been a remarkable year. He had had thirty-eight matches and won every one, thirty-four by knockout. He started the new year the way he had finished the old one. On January 1 he fought Jack League in Kansas City, winning by a knockout in the first round.

Tex Rickard's new Miami sporting facility opened right on schedule on New Year's Day. The first event was a greyhound race attended by some 13,000 people, followed by a reception at the elegant new clubhouse. The reception and race went as planned, but the host was absent.

Rickard, his wife, and three-year-old daughter had been in Miami for several days preparing for the big debut, but the promoter hadn't felt well for several days. About 7:30 p.m. on New Year's Day he was admitted to the Allison Hospital in Miami Beach and diagnosed with acute appendicitis. Doctors operated and were initially optimistic about his recovery, but he developed a severe infection. He died in the early morning hours of January 6.

His close friend Jack Dempsey was shocked by Rickard's death. "I've lost the best pal I ever had," he said that afternoon.

The Stribling family also felt the loss deeply.

"The passing of Tex Rickard is sad news to us," Pa told the press the next day. "We never went to New York without calling on Rickard. He was on the square. He was one of our best friends."

Rickard's sudden death created questions about the future of his sports facility and the upcoming match between Stribling and Sharkey. But cancellation of the fight was never a real possibility. The Madison Square Garden Corporation and the city of Miami had put too much planning and money into the match to cancel it. On January 7 it was announced that the fight would go on as planned, and boxing great Jack Dempsey had agreed to assume the role of promoter.

Stribling fought five matches in January and won them all with knockouts—his version of light training. He had planned to fly to Miami in early February to start training for the Sharkey match, but Dempsey put a stop to that plan. W.L. was to stay out of airplanes, his and anyone else's, until the Sharkey fight was over. He wasn't going to chance losing one of the contestants in a crash, and the contract W.L. had signed gave him the right to lay down the law.

So W.L., Clara, Three, and two-month-old Mary Virginia left Macon by auto on the morning of January 28. They traveled first to Jacksonville to meet W.L.'s parents and brother, arriving there in time to see Herbert defeat Billy Edwards in a ten-round match. Then the whole party headed south for Miami.

25

The Stribling–Sharkey fight in Miami was more than a boxing match. Scheduled during the height of the Miami social season, it was the event that would establish Madison Square Garden's place in the winter season in South Florida and quickly took on the characteristic of a carnival.

Rickard's Miami Kennel Club was just as glamorous and exciting as predicted. Both fighters had established training camps on the grounds, which was where Rickard had planned to stage the fight. But as anticipation of the attendance climbed—in early February it was predicted that 50,000 people would be there—the event was moved to a larger arena being constructed in Flamingo Park, a small community north of Fort Lauderdale.

Dempsey oversaw every facet of the event with an eye to detail that verged on obsessive. He was determined that everything associated with the fight would be first class. The training facilities were equipped with everything that the fighters could ever want, and he set up the participants and their staffs in beautiful houses on the beach.

He rented the Carl Fisher mansion and invited engaging sports personalities and writers to be his guests there. Under his direction the George Washington Hotel on the beach was named the official press headquarters with a twenty-four-hour open bar and restaurant. Prohibition might still be the law, but this was Miami.

With the fight nearly a month away, neither boxer trained hard the first week of February. Sharkey spent Saturday golfing while W.L. went to the beach and swam for several hours. Reporters who had followed him asked when he would start serious training.

W.L. grinned. "I plan to get a substantial tan before I get active."

Both men believed that they were in great shape and didn't really need to do much heavy training before the fight. W.L. had fought in five matches in January, and Sharkey had trained hard for his recent win over K. O. Christner.

By the second week in February Sharkey had established a routine of light training, and Stribling was only doing three miles of roadwork a day. So relaxed was the Georgia fighter that, on February 12, he left for an overnight fishing trip in the Everglades.

Dempsey worried about what he saw as their lackadaisical preparation for the fight. He was so concerned that on February 14 he declared that both of them had to step up their efforts. His suggestion, which had the weight of Madison Square Garden behind it, produced immediate results. The next day both camps issued statements that they had decided to train more heavily.

But doing so wasn't easy. The atmosphere in Miami that winter wasn't conducive to serious training. There were parties and dinners every night, and celebrities were everywhere. Every hostess wanted to include Stribling and Sharkey on her guest list.

Even the training camps seemed more like entertainment venues than gyms.

Both were open to the public, and visitors streamed in and out all day to watch the daily sparring matches and workouts. Reporters followed the fighters and their managers around, taking notes and peppering them with endless questions. Photographers snapped pictures of the boxers and any celebrities who happened by.

The circus atmosphere was only intensified by the arrival of Hughie Henry, who had made a name for himself as a clown in Kansas City ballparks and boxing rings. Pa hired him to entertain the people who came to watch W.L. train. And the clown wasn't the only entertainer there.

The elder Stribling loved showing off his grandson's talents. Tee, as the boy had named himself when he was unable to say Three, was as smiling and compliant as ever. Pa threw him in the air, had him balance on one foot in his hand, and swung him in arcs, holding only his feet. Through it all the child's parents, grandmother, and uncle looked on placidly. The fans were fascinated by W.L.'s son, and the baby often received the day's biggest round of applause.

The demand for fight tickets was skyrocketing. By Valentine's Day, sales had reached $250,000. Although seating at the arena was expected to accommodate 40,000 to 50,000 people, the Miami area expected upward of 70,000 visitors the week of the fight. Railroads planned special trains from all over the South, and in Macon the Junior Chamber of Commerce had arranged a delegation of over 100 people to travel to Miami to cheer on their hometown hero.

Northerners weren't as quick to climb on a train as people across the South. They had heard wild stories of how dangerous things were in that section of the country. The Klan was supposed to be running rampant, and southerners had an undeserved reputation for violence. However, one trip to the region generally won over the doubters.

Jack Sharkey, apprehensive at first, fell in love with the South after being there only a short time.

"All that stuff I heard and read about what would happen when I came down here has turned out to be bunk," he told *New York Sun* sportswriter Wilbur Wood. "I left my children in Boston because I was persuaded there might be some unpleasantness here. Now I wish I had brought them along."

Among the notables in Miami that February was the notorious gangster Al Capone. He owned an ostentatious, fortress-like home on Star Island, and the town was abuzz about the lavish parties he hosted. Champagne smuggled in from Bimini was said to flow like water, and some of the biggest names in crime reportedly acted as waiters and doormen.

One afternoon at the dog track, Capone recognized W.L. in the crowd and sent him a note. It was an invitation to come to his home to talk business. W.L. had no interest in that and began his refusal to the messenger, but Pa stepped in.

"What's going on?"

"Something we don't want to have anything to do with," W.L. said.

But Pa took the note. "I'll be the judge of that."

The result was that the next day W.L., Clara, Pa, and Ma went to visit Capone. They were picked up and taken to his house in a chauffeured limousine. After passing through a security check at the front gate, they were shown inside to a large room.

The living room was beautifully and conventionally furnished except for four men sitting on straight-backed chairs in the corners. Dressed in black suits and wearing fedora hats, each man had a newspaper in front of his face that he appeared to be reading and a gun resting on his knees. It made it difficult for the Striblings to relax in their opulent surroundings.

Then Capone himself walked in. He was full of energy and looked younger than he appeared in newspaper photos. He didn't waste time on small talk.

Capone announced that he wanted to manage W.L.'s career. By way of persuasion, he guaranteed that Stribling would be the world champion in six weeks. If not, he would pay Pa a great deal of money for his time and trouble.

While Pa didn't accept the offer, he didn't refuse it either. And when Capone asked them to return for dinner that evening when the contract would be ready to sign, Pa agreed that they would be there.

No one spoke about the offer during the limousine ride back to Coral Gables, but once they were inside the house, W.L. announced he wasn't going back to dinner at the gangster's home.

"You have to," Pa told him. "I gave my word we would be there."

For once, Clara intervened. She was terrified of Capone and insisted that W.L. refuse. "I'll pack my bags and be on the next train back to Macon with the children if you sign a contract with that man."

"Honey, I believe you mean it," W.L. said, surprised at her unusual show of will.

She assured him she did.

But he didn't need Clara to persuade him that associating with a criminal was a bad idea. Once again, he told his father he wasn't going to dinner.

"Tell Capone I don't play that way."

So Pa and Ma went to dinner without them. They came back raving about the three-inch steaks and French champagne they had been served. But in the end Pa had regretfully refused Capone's offer. He knew his son wouldn't change his mind on this matter.

Dempsey continued to keep a close eye on the preparations for the fight. He worried about everything from Sharkey's sore thumb to W.L.'s problems placing his left jab. And then came word that W.L. was also injured. But everything went forward as scheduled.

Although he had reportedly dislocated a rib several days before, W.L. appeared relaxed and upbeat the day of the fight. In fact, he had shown no sign of stress during the whole training period although he must have been aware of the importance of the fight. If he didn't defeat Sharkey, it would be nearly impossible for him to ever make another attempt at the world championship.

The press had been after Pa for days asking about W.L.'s injured rib and the neuritis that was rumored to have developed in his left arm. He finally admitted there had been an injury, but insisted that his son was much better. He had kept quiet, he said, because he didn't want to give the northern papers anything they could use against W.L.

"We took this fight at a gamble. We let them pick a northern referee and we agreed to take a chance on a low-percentage basis, anything for a fight with Jack Sharkey. Now, boys, if I come out with a statement that my boy is hurt, the wolves will be howling 'alibi and yellow.' My boy will fight Jack Sharkey Wednesday night if he has to fight with one hand."

What Pa didn't tell the press was that W.L. was also suffering from a severe toothache. Two of his molars were inflamed and terribly painful. In the last few days eating had become such a miserable experience that he often skipped meals rather than endure it. But neither he nor his father wanted to have the teeth treated until after the fight.

All the drama in Miami Beach that week didn't come from boxing alone. Jack Dempsey provided quite a lot of it himself when he reported that an armed intruder entered his bedroom and fired a shot at him.

Dempsey shared a room with fight promoter Floyd Fitzsimmons at the home of hotel magnate Henry C. Moir. The two had spent Sunday evening socializing with friends, then retired some time after midnight. They were awakened about 5:00 a.m. by a man entering their room with a gun. Dempsey jumped out of bed and rushed the stranger. He fled, but not before firing the gun in Dempsey's direction. The bullet lodged in the wall some four feet away from him.

The incident was reported to the police, but no one was ever arrested. When Dempsey talked with newspapermen that afternoon he showed them the flattened bullet that he had dug out of the wall.

"I don't know what it was about, but the fellow didn't seem to want money," he said. "He didn't demand anything, and he didn't take any of the money that was on the dresser. All I can think is that he might have thought he could take me for a ride."

He did acknowledge that it was a bizarre story. "If this wasn't an actual fact, it would sound like the bunk or the old ballyhoo, but that bird gave me a scare when I first saw his head poked through the doorway and what looked like a gun in his hand."

No more shots were fired during the next couple of days, but there were fireworks. Jack Sharkey showed his temperamental side a couple of days before the match when Dempsey announced he had purchased special white gloves and custom-made trunks for the fighters for the match.

Sharkey's were black with a wide red stripe around the waist. Stribling's were bright red with a black waistband. It seemed as if everything was set for a color-coordinated fight, but Sharkey flatly refused to use either the gloves or the trunks.

"Dempsey's not the man to tell me what to wear," he declared. "I'll fight in my old trunks. They've given me good luck in most of my fights."

As for the gloves, Sharkey said he would just wear the regulation brown ones, and Dempsey didn't force the issue.

Tempers also flared at the weighing-in ceremony on the day of the fight. The Sharkey camp was annoyed when the Striblings were late. Snide remarks were made and equally unpleasant answers given, but the weigh-in progressed as planned. When it was finished, the fighters shook hands and left the building, but just outside the door Sharkey's trainer Tony Palozzolo grabbed Pa's arm and got in one last jibe.

"I'll bet you $500 that Jack knocks that punk of yours out tonight."

Pa pulled away, but the other man grabbed him again. Patience gone, Pa's answer was a fist to Palozzolo's chin that sent him stumbling backward. Both groups rushed each other.

Although the fighters and their managers quickly removed themselves from the fracas, supporters of both sides waded in with enthusiasm and a near free-for-all developed. Jim Downing, one of Dempsey's assistants, finally broke it up. No one was seriously hurt, but there were a number of bruised faces, swollen noses, and black eyes at ringside that night.

Spectators began arriving at the Flamingo Park Arena in mid-afternoon to get the best seats. People streamed in all day and kept coming through the preliminary matches that started after 8:00.

It was a perfect South Florida night. Palm trees towered above the scene, and the air was warm and balmy. The stars and quarter moon shining above were all but blotted out by thirty-five huge electric lights blazing down on the center of the arena.

No one could remember seeing a gathering such as this in Florida before. Dress for the evening ran a gamut of styles. Men in evening clothes and women in revealing tropically hued gowns sat shoulder to shoulder with people in street dress.

There were plenty of millionaires in the crowd, but those folks who worked for hourly wages were also well represented. There were actors, producers, playwrights, sports figures, songwriters, and novelists. Jockeys and racetrack owners rubbed shoulders with gangsters. Seven governors were in the audience along with thirty-two congressmen, twelve federal judges, eighteen U.S. senators, bankers, and business tycoons. And at ringside 300 sportswriters were ready to record the action.

W.L. mingled with the crowd in the arena before the match. Hundreds of celebrities and notables surrounded him, all wanting to meet and talk to him, but through the hubbub he noticed a familiar face at the edge of the crowd. An old friend from the flying service stood there, dressed in a crumpled mechanic's outfit.

W.L. extricated himself from the group, made his way through the milling crowd, and went over to shake the man's hand and talk for a bit. He wasn't a man who forgot his friends.

The main event started about 10:00 p.m. and W.L. started off as the aggressor, knocking Sharkey to his knees with a hard right in the first round. But Sharkey recovered quickly and returned W.L.'s punches blow for blow. The first rounds were either won by Stribling or were thought to be even, but by the fifth, W.L. appeared to be tiring.

Sharkey opened a cut in W.L.'s lip, and a bruise soon appeared under one eye. The neuritis he had developed earlier in the week made his left arm all but unusable in the later rounds, but the most punishing blows were those to his ribs. It was obvious that the injury there hadn't healed.

As the fight neared its end, Stribling's supporters realized the best they could hope for was a draw. But after ten rounds, Referee Lou Magnolia gave the decision to Jack Sharkey, and most of the experts and newsmen attending the fight agreed.

The Stribling supporters in the crowd were stunned by the decision, and at ringside, Ma Stribling was furious. She argued vehemently with anyone who would listen that her son had been robbed.

But Pa was more philosophical. He believed that W.L. had acquitted himself well. He had proved that he was a heavyweight fighter who could go the distance with anyone, even when injured.

And W.L. refused to dwell on the loss. He was already looking toward the future. "All I want is another chance at that fellow. He's a good fighter but he didn't hurt me any. Next time he won't get away from my right hand. I'll be in better shape then. That bad rib had my left arm dead after two rounds."

Sharkey was generous in victory. "Anybody that walks into that fellow will get killed," he said. "Stribling is the kind of fighter who can murder you with a right-hand punch if you come into him. I was hitting him harder than I ever hit anyone before in my life. That boy can take it."

The fight was a great success for Jack Dempsey and the Madison Square Garden Corporation. The gate was $405,000, of which Sharkey received $100,000 and Stribling $63,500. More important, the event came off without a problem.

"It was a great fight," Dempsey declared. "I liked the fight. I liked the crowd, and I liked the experience. I am very happy to have seen the dream of my old pal Tex Rickard come true in such a way as this." He then summed up the experience in one word. "Lovely."

Although a certain element of the sporting public was ready to write off Stribling and his hopes of a championship, the fighter himself wasn't discouraged. He had lost his match with Sharkey, it was true, but it was only his seventh loss out of 237 fights. His confidence was intact, but his body had some healing to do before getting back to work.

W.L. stayed in Miami after the fight, and Dr. Cecil B. Ferguson, who had treated him for his injuries during training, was called back in to help with his recovery.

While his rib and arm were healing, dentists checked the teeth that had been bothering him. They were abscessed and had to be removed, and, after he had healed, another bridge was installed in his mouth.

While W.L. recuperated in Miami, Herbert Hoover was inaugurated in Washington. In his inaugural address, he promised to dedicate his administration to law and order at home and peace throughout the world.

W.L. might have lost the Sharkey bout, but he had shown by his efforts that he was still considered to be a contender. Few promoters were ready to count him out of the ongoing heavyweight elimination.

Pa's first order of business was to arrange a rematch with Sharkey, and he met with representatives of Madison Square Garden to get the ball rolling. In the meantime he received numerous offers of fights from all over the country and Europe, but none of the matches materialized. The money didn't meet with Pa's approval, and W.L. was still not a hundred percent.

While he was content to take his time getting back into the ring, W.L. had no intention of retreating from his other interests. He arrived back in Macon on March 30, the same day it was announced that he had applied for a commission as a second lieutenant in the United States Army Air Corps Reserves.

The new baby was almost five months old now and was quickly becoming her father's little girl. When he wasn't spending time with Tee and Mary Virginia, W.L. played golf and rode his motorcycle, and he and Clara both made good use of the tennis court on Nottingham Drive.

He flew his airplane when he could and on the 27th completed his examination for an army pilot's license. W.L. was looking forward to flying with the Army Air Corps, but he wasn't the only member of his family involved in aviation that spring. Herbert was spending some time in Indianapolis, where, enrolled in a flying school, he expected to earn his pilot's license in a few months.

26

On the first day of May, doctors announced that W.L. ought to be ready to fight within 30 days. But he had another spell of bad health soon afterward—his tonsils had to be removed—and that added a bit more time to his recovery.

He was feeling well enough, however, to take part in a Shriners parade down Cherry Street on May 23. There were bands, clowns, and even chorus girls on elephants to celebrate the Al Sihah ceremonial. W.L. marched in the back of the parade with the other initiates.

In addition to the Shriners, W.L. had joined numerous civic and social organizations, including Kiwanis, Junior Chamber of Commerce, the Idle Hour Country Club, the Elks, the Outboard Motor Club, the Tennis Club, and Pi Chi Fraternity.

Pa had been working with New York promoters for a couple of months trying to arrange another fight for W.L. in that city, but there seemed to be some problem with every match proposed. When negotiations slowed to the point of stopping, he fell back on a familiar formula and began scheduling fights for his son in cities across the Midwest and the South.

W.L.'s first match after the Sharkey loss was against Babe Hunt in Wichita on June 17. His parents and Herbert went with him to Kansas, and while they were there, they visited the Travel Air Company.

The whole family was impressed with the quality of airplane manufactured there. W.L. liked the planes so much that he purchased one himself. It was faster and bigger than his other aircraft, and he named it Little Ginger after his baby daughter.

Soon after the Striblings arrived in Wichita they had a surprise visitor. Seventeen-year-old James Barfield, now known to his friends as "Ears" for obvious reasons, showed up at their hotel room after having spent six days hitchhiking across the country.

"I caught 37 rides to get here!" he told them proudly.

The son of the Striblings' longtime friends Ernest and Hettie Barfield had always idolized W.L. That summer he decided he wanted to see him fight again and made his own way across the country to do so.

They took him in, gave him a place to sleep, and took him along with them to the match on Monday night. Barfield was right there at ringside as W.L. won a ten-round newspaper decision over Hunt.

After the fight Ma, Herbert, and Barfield took the train back to Macon, but W.L. and Pa picked up the new airplane on Wednesday and flew to Flint, Michigan, where W.L. fought and defeated Jack Lee four days later.

On their flight home they ran into bad weather and had to land in Kentucky. It was June 28 before they were in Macon again.

As soon as they landed, Pa headed for Terminal Station for a train back to Ochlocknee. He and Ma were now spending most of their time at the farm.

But W.L. didn't even set foot in his house. He simply refueled his new airplane, took friends Roy Barrow and Harry Kendall aboard, and took off again. His destination this time was a barrier island off the Georgia coast. Clara, the children, and members of her family had been vacationing on St. Simons Island, and he and his friends joined them there for a few days of relaxation.

W.L. had five more fights in July. He won the first four easily, then flew to Tulsa, Oklahoma, on July 25 for the fifth. The next day the Macon papers reported that Stribling had been jailed in Tulsa for reckless flying and disturbing the peace.

The charge reportedly resulted from his flying low over the city with a siren blaring from his plane. Johnny Husong, a Kansas boxing promoter, was arrested at the same time for speeding in his car through the Tulsa business district.

W.L. posted a $250 bond. Husong put up $20. The wire story of their dual arrests appeared on nearly every sports page across the country, even making the front page in some papers.

But *Telegraph* sports columnist Jimmy Jones had his doubts about the validity of the reckless flying charge, based on his knowledge of Pa

Stribling. In a July 30 column Jones suggested that the whole incident was a publicity stunt, but admitted it was a further tribute to Pa's genius in keeping Stribling in the public eye.

By the time W.L.'s bond was returned to him without explanation and the charges dropped, the story of the arrest had raised so much interest in his upcoming Tulsa match with Babe Hunt that it was a near sellout.

However, it wasn't the contest the fans had hoped to see. Although it was an aggressive fight from the start and Stribling knocked the other man down twice, Hunt was declared the winner by a foul in the sixth round. The referee said that one of W.L.'s powerful right-hand blows had landed below his opponent's belt and he was disqualified.

W.L. was at home for a while after the Hunt fight. His business interests kept him occupied in Macon and out of the pilot's seat, but there was aviation news in the papers. On August 4, the huge German dirigible *Graf Zeppelin* docked at Lakehurst, New Jersey, completing its second Atlantic crossing. A week later, it left the United States to begin an around-the-world voyage.

W.L. fought around the country in August and September. His winning streak continued, and his appearances set attendance records in Missouri, Kansas, Oklahoma, and Arkansas. However, he reinjured his left hand in an August 29 fight against Joe Packo in Evansville, Indiana.

As usual, he worked through the injury with few complaints, but one challenge he encountered that summer proved almost too stressful for the young boxer. While in Kansas City, he was persuaded by his friend and fight promoter Gabe Kaufman to judge a bathing beauty contest at the Winnwood Beach resort.

As nearly 10,000 people looked on, W.L. stood uncomfortably on a stage as twenty fetching young women in swimsuits paraded before him. He made his decision quickly, endured the winner's thanks, and left Winnwood as soon as he could.

"That's about as tough a job as I ever tackled," W.L. joked later. "About the only harder job is judging a baby show where every mother's baby is the prettiest and the healthiest and you take your life in your hand when you pick out any one baby."

In September, Pa put the final touches to plans he had been making for a European tour. When everything was in place he announced to the press that the family would sail for France at the end of the month.

W.L. had an obligation to fulfill before leaving the country. He had received his commission as a second lieutenant in the Army Air Corps Reserves in June, and in September he was required to spend two weeks in aviation training at Maxwell Field in Montgomery, Alabama.

When the Striblings left Macon for New York on the last Thursday of September 1929, the only member of the family not making the trip was Mary Virginia. Still less than a year old, she stayed with her maternal grandmother in Macon.

The group appeared happy and excited when they boarded the ship in New York, but reporters noticed that W.L.'s left hand was encased in a plaster cast. It hadn't healed after the August 29 injury as the doctors had hoped it would. They decided the best thing to do was keep it immobile for a while. His first scheduled European bout wasn't until November 6, and they had assured him that the hand would be fine by then.

The Striblings traveled to France on the *Ile de France*. The grandest vessel afloat, it carried over 1,700 passengers. The first-class dining room was three decks high with a grand staircase on which diners could make dramatic entrances. The cabins had beds instead of bunks. There was a fully equipped gymnasium and even a merry-go-round for the children. Traveling on the *Ile de France* was synonymous with traveling in the lap of luxury.

Autumn in Paris was a beautiful season, and with plenty of time before he had to fight, W.L. and Clara were free to enjoy the romantic city. They visited museums, saw historic sights, ate in fine restaurants, and went to clubs and the horse races.

The only member of the group who was less than content during this trip was Tee. At nearly three years old, he had very definite likes and dislikes in the area of food and drink. And one of those likes was chocolate milk. He loved it and was given it regularly at home. But people in France had never heard of such a thing and it wasn't on any menu. Tee was not at all happy with the situation.

As the month drew to a close, disturbing news about the American economic situation reached Europe. On October 29, after days of frantic buying and selling, the bottom fell out of the stock market. Several million shares were sold in the first thirty minutes, and prices fell so fast that, by the end of the day, many stocks had lost all their value. It was the worst trading day in the market's history and began the most devastating financial disaster the United States had ever seen.

In Paris, there was concern, but no panic. The Striblings, while keep-ing watch on the situation at home, saw no reason for serious worry at that moment. They were more concerned about W.L.'s up-coming fight with Maurice Griselle than domestic economics.

On the evening of November 6, a crowd of 6,000 people began arriving at the Cirque de Paris. Even though the feature fight between Griselle and Stribling wasn't scheduled until 10:00 p.m., spectators were there early. Sandwiches and red wine were sold. Three musicians—two with accordions and one with a mandolin—formed an impromptu trio in one corner of the audience and entertained those sitting nearby. Parisians knew how to make a party of almost any event.

When W.L. and his opponent finally entered the ring and were introduced, each was given polite applause. They were about the same weight, although Griselle was a bit taller. The first round was full of excitement with W.L. taking the fight to Griselle and even knocking the Frenchman off his feet once. But after that, the match settled into a points battle.

Much of the blame for W.L.'s lackluster performance may have been Pa's. Between each round, he cautioned W.L. to take it slow and be careful. And W.L. did as he asked. In the end, Stribling was the winner, but the audience had expected more action from the famous American fighter.

After the Griselle fight, the Striblings left Paris for London, where W.L. would meet Primo Carnera on November 18. Carnera was a giant of a man, standing six and a half feet tall and weighing 260 pounds. From the day the Italian boxer had first set foot in England that October, he captured the attention of the English public. After his first win in

London newspapers there were so impressed that they predicted some day he would become the world's champion.

Stribling might have beaten Griselle in Paris, but the English fight fans and sportswriters expected little from him. His loss to Sharkey earlier in the year had been well reported, and the prevailing belief was that the American was on a downward path.

There was little interest in seeing Stribling fight. Jeff Dickson, the European fight promoter who had arranged the Stribling–Carnera bout, was initially concerned that attendance would be small. But then came word that His Royal Highness the Prince of Wales had purchased seats for himself and a large party of friends for the fight at Royal Albert Hall. Overnight, the match was a sellout.

Although they might have been predisposed to dismiss him, it didn't take the British press long to discover W.L.'s charm and that of his family. Pa opened his son's daily workouts at Dyer's Gymnasium to the public. Observers there not only got to see the handsome fighter training, they also witnessed him joking around with his family and playing with Tee. Within a week, W.L. had had so much favorable press coverage that he could hardly move about the city without attracting a crowd of admirers.

Attendance by the Prince of Wales turned any performance into a social event. The preliminary bouts were already under way when His Royal Highness and party arrived at Albert Hall. As the prince walked to his seat, the crowd stood and the organ played "God Bless the Prince of Wales." This was followed by a rousing chorus of "For He's a Jolly Good Fellow."

But Clara and Ma also garnered a good bit of attention when they came into the arena just before the match started and took their seats at ringside. With them, smiling and happy, was Tee. He looked around the huge hall with benign interest from his vantage point on his mother's lap.

Stribling and Carnera entered the ring at the same time, and the comparison between the two was almost comical. Carnera looked enormous, towering over Stribling. Most sportswriters had predicted that the fight would be short and the victory would go to the Italian.

But W.L. was the one forcing the action that night. Time and again, he moved in on Carnera, striking blow after blow. Although the punches seemed to hardly affect the bigger man, W.L. did manage to knock Carnera off his feet once with a violent right uppercut.

It was the first time Carnera had ever been sent to the canvas, and it enraged him. He took a count of seven, but then rushed Stribling, running into him, and hitting him on the chin at the same time. More a tackle than a punch, Carnera's attack put W.L. on the floor.

Tee had been watching the action in the ring with great interest. When W.L. hit the floor, his eyes grew huge and his face lost color. He put his little hands together in front of him and held tight. While he had seen his father fight several times before, he had never seen him knocked down.

But W.L. didn't stay down long and the fight progressed, looking more and more like a Stribling victory. In the fourth round while W.L. was delivering a battery of punches, Carnera went down again. The first thought was that W.L. had knocked him out, but then the referee declared Carnera the winner on the basis of a low-blow foul.

W.L. was confused and the audience angry. They had seen no foul and believed that, if there had been one, it was certainly unintentional. But Stribling didn't argue. He went to Carnera and shook his hand, congratulating him. While Carnera was applauded for his victory, the loudest and longest ovation that night was for Stribling.

There was a dinner party for the Striblings at the Queen's Hotel after the fight. The diners spent little time rehashing the night's loss. Instead talk centered on the rematch with Carnera that everyone was sure would come. Four days later it was scheduled.

So the Striblings crossed the English Channel once again and returned to Paris. There in the Vélodrome d'Hiver, an indoor arena for boxing matches and bicycle races, W.L. and Carnera met for a second time on December 7.

"I'll go for his jaw this time," W.L. predicted. "He can't claim to have been hit lower if I hit him on the button."

Everyone agreed it was a good match. Stribling easily outboxed Carnera in the first two rounds, but then his opponent seemed to settle down and the fight was more even. In the seventh, W.L. got in several good punches, but seconds after the bell rang ending the round, Carnera delivered a hard blow to W.L.'s head that sent him reeling to the canvas. The Italian was booed by the audience and immediately disqualified by the referee for hitting after the bell. So this time Stribling won on a foul.

The Carnera fight was W.L.'s final match on his European tour and his last in 1929.

The Striblings returned to Georgia on December 19 and were met at Terminal Station in Macon by Clara's parents and several friends. It was good to be home, and the family was especially pleased to learn that Mrs. Kinney had a hot meal waiting for them at her house. They had grown weary of European food and were ready for familiar Georgian cooking. And Tee, of course, wanted chocolate milk.

W.L. brought a curious souvenir home from his travels abroad—the boxing gloves worn by Primo Carnera in their last fight. The folks at the Herbert Smart Clothing Store on Cherry Street put the gloves on display. A pair of Stribling's gloves hung beside them, looking like baby's mittens in comparison.

W.L. and Clara were in Macon for the holidays, happy to have their young family all together again. Pa, Herbert, and Ma spent Christmas in Ochlocknee on their farm—or, as the papers had taken to calling it, their "country estate."

27

The stock market had crashed in October, but it was perceived by many as a rich man's problem. And as 1930 began, the country's leaders were forecasting a bright economic future.

W.L. was now the only fighter in Pa Stribling's stable. Herbert had broken with his father after the European trip. He was still fighting, but he spent a good deal of his time in the Midwest where he attended flight school between matches.

But the situation was temporary. Pa had also acquired a European souvenir. He had signed an agreement to manage a German fighter named Michael Maurer who would be arriving in the United States later that month.

Since the officials from Madison Square Garden were in Miami in January for the beginning of the winter boxing season, Pa knew he should be there, too. He met with the boxing moguls several times trying to get W.L. a rematch with Jack Sharkey, but met refusals at every turn.

Sharkey didn't want to fight Stribling again. He was also reluctant to take on other contenders including Tuffy Griffiths, a highly rated heavyweight. Sportswriters were reporting that it looked like Sharkey didn't want to fight anyone.

W.L. occasionally served as referee in matches around the region and was in Atlanta on January 7 in that capacity for the American Legion boxing program. Jack Dempsey, now a promoter in Chicago, had also agreed to act as a referee on the card. When reporters interviewed him after the matches, he had quite a lot to say on a lot of subjects.

He was unimpressed with the way the top contenders were handling the heavyweight elimination. "The boys are ducking the issue. A champion should meet and beat them all or shouldn't be champion."

Inevitably someone asked his opinion of Young Stribling, and Dempsey answered honestly. Stribling had a good chance of wearing the crown, he said "if he could eliminate some of his cautiousness and just go into the ring to knock his opponent out."

He also recommended that Stribling train away from his family. "When a fellow's mother, wife and, kids are around, he simply can't give the fans that knock-down-and-drag-out stuff that they like in fighters."

While boxing was W.L.'s business, his passion was flying, and he signed up to participate in the Second All-American Air Meet in Miami, January 13–15. It would be the first test of his new Travel Air plane.

He took part in several of the contests, but W.L. didn't do as well as he had hoped in Miami. His best showing was in the dead-stick landing test where he placed third by setting his plane down 15 feet and 10 inches from the mark. The Travel Air, which he had believed was such a fast craft, hadn't lived up to its reputation. He was so disappointed that he immediately put it up for sale and began looking for a replacement.

He didn't have any matches scheduled in Florida, but no fighter of Stribling's stature could be in Miami during the boxing season and not become a little involved in the activities there. When he attended the Tom Sharky–Pat McGuire match, W.L. was introduced from the ring along with Lou Magnolia, Babe Ruth, and Jack Sharkey.

Afterward he had his first informal chat with Jack Sharkey since their match the year before.

"You almost had me in the ninth round," Sharkey told him. "You had me groggy, boy, and if you had only known it and followed up you might have got me right there."

When W.L. returned to Macon, it was time to put flying on hold and get back to work. On January 22 he knocked out Jack Demave in Atlanta in the first round and the Dutchman had to be carried from the ring. He fought and won two more matches in February, but reinjured his left hand and was again forced to take time off to recover. With W.L. idle, Pa was free to concentrate on Michael Maurer. The German boxer had already won two fights, and Pa was feeling as if he had made a good investment.

As his recovery progressed, W.L. found ways to keep himself entertained. He bought a new Cord automobile and on March 12 was invited to be a guest pilot with an air circus in St. Petersburg, Florida.

It sounded like so much fun that W.L. never even considered turning it down, but the invitation was very nearly fatal. Attempting to take off in one of the circus's planes, he failed to gain the necessary altitude. It appeared a bad crash was unavoidable, but he managed to leapfrog over two other aircraft and come to a stop, right side up.

In spite of repeated governmental reassurances, the country's economic problems were now affecting a good portion of the population. Unemployment was skyrocketing. In New York 1,000 jobless men left a bread line and rushed two trucks loaded with bakery products, tearing open the doors and pulling out the goods. Soon it became an all-out riot, and police had to be called in to stop it. While Macon had no riots, there were plenty of out-of-work people on the streets there, too.

Pa thought that conditions might be better in Europe. In a move that surprised the whole family, he agreed to a fight at Royal Albert Hall between W.L. and England's Phil Scott. The first date agreed on was April 10, but then London promoter Jeff Dickson cabled that Scott wanted a longer rest before facing Stribling. He wouldn't be ready to fight until some time in late May. However, Dickson offered to arrange other bouts for W.L. in Paris and London to fill the time before fighting Scott.

Pa and W.L. sailed from New York on the SS *Majestic* at midnight, Friday, April 4. They were the only members of the Stribling family to make the trip, but W.L.'s friend Foy Boone and *Miami Herald* sports editor Jack Bell traveled with them. While not as large or as luxurious as the *Ile de France*, the *Majestic* was still a comfortable liner with all the amenities the four could have asked for.

W.L.'s popularity in London had not diminished. He was greeted and encouraged wherever he went. His first match was with Hans Schoenrath. To the delight of his London fans, W.L. knocked out the German fighter in the second round.

The next scheduled fight was against Pierre Charles in Paris on May 22, but as the Striblings were preparing to travel back to that city, word reached them that Phil Scott was sick in bed and might not be able to face W.L. later in the month.

The one purpose of their trip had been the Scott fight. He was the only heavyweight contender whose defeat Pa believed would advance W.L. another step toward a title match. The other fights that Dickson had scheduled for him were simply ways to pass the time and make a little money.

Now with Scott wavering, the Striblings decided spending more time in Europe wouldn't benefit them. They were concerned that Scott would continue to come up with excuses and the match might never take place. So they set sail for home on the *Leviathan* in the middle of May.

Back home his friends noticed that W.L. looked a bit heavier than when he left. At 201 pounds, he now looked like a real heavyweight.

"W.L. set some kind of record for eating at sea," Pa told them. "They put plenty of good groceries to him, and I've never seen the boy eat so heartily. The rest and plenty of good food put the weight on him."

Only days after arriving home, Dickson cabled Pa with the news that Scott had recovered and agreed to reschedule the match for July 28. They knew the Englishman could still back out, but this time there was a good chance that the fight would actually take place since Scott had deposited 1,000 pounds of forfeit money to guarantee his appearance. After some brief discussion the Striblings agreed to return to England the next month.

W.L. fought twice more before leaving the country. In the first match he defeated Frankie Wine in Birmingham. While he reinjured his left hand, neither he nor Pa thought it was serious.

On June 10 they traveled to Chicago where W.L. began training for a match with Otto von Porat, one of the leading contenders for the heavyweight crown. If W.L. defeated him and then beat Scott in London, he would have a sure route to a championship try.

However, it only took a short time in the gym for W.L. to realize his hand hadn't healed. But he kept working, hoping it would improve by fight time.

On June 12 W.L. and Pa took a short break from training and traveled to New York. Jack Sharkey had agreed to face a young German named Max Schmeling, the winner to be crowned the world heavyweight champion.

It was during that trip that W.L. realized he could no longer pretend that the injury to his hand was minor. The pain increased every hour and had grown bad enough that by the time they reached New York, their first stop was not Yankee Stadium but a doctor's office. The physician put his hand in a cast and ordered him to keep it immobile.

They went on to Yankee Stadium after that and were present for the big fight between Sharkey and Schmeling. Sharkey was in command from the beginning. He was leading the points until the fourth round when he landed a crashing blow to Schmeling's body and the German collapsed.

The punch was low. There was no dispute, since it took place directly in front of the judges. Managers, seconds, and handlers rushed into the ring, and Schmeling was picked up and taken, groaning in pain, to his corner. The referee consulted with the judges, and moments later Schmeling was proclaimed the winner, and the world champion, due to a foul.

While Schmeling celebrated his victory, W.L. was growing more concerned about his hand. On the train trip back to Chicago, he wrote a letter to the Illinois Boxing Commission, advising them of his injury.

"I don't think I will be able to fight von Porat June 18," he wrote, "but please don't make any mention of it for I'll try to go through with the bout if it is possible."

And try he did. Back in Chicago they removed the cast and bandaged his hand. He resumed training at Kid Howard's Gymnasium, but the pain continued. The day before the fight W.L. had to ask for a short delay. Von Porat and the Boxing Commission agreed, and the match was rescheduled for June 20.

Not everyone believed that Stribling was hurt. There was speculation that he was trying to avoid the match, and State Boxing Commission officials arranged to keep a close watch on him, concerned he might try to leave town before the fight.

When W.L. and his father were told about reports they might run out on the fight, they laughed.

"My son will be there, and he'll give von Porat a licking he'll remember," Pa said.

But Stribling didn't laugh when, the day before the fight, he received a letter from a man in Savannah who accused him of being "yellow" and declared he would never be a champion. That someone in his home state would write such a letter infuriated him.

That anger was still with him when he and von Porat clashed in Chicago Stadium the next night. The audience of 21,000, which set a Chicago record for indoor attendance at a boxing match, was stunned by W.L.'s attack on his opponent. With his left fist injected with a local anesthetic, he stopped von Porat in the first round, knocking him out after only two minutes and fifty seconds of fighting.

His anger vanished as soon as the fight was over. When he was interviewed on the radio minutes later, he was smiling and upbeat.

"Hello, Ma. Hello, Clara," he said. "I just finished von Porat in the first. Home Tuesday."

It was a fine way to start what many people were calling Stribling's comeback, but the next day he learned he had run afoul of the law. Observers at the Federal Radio Commission noted that W.L.'s sending a personal message out on the airways had violated the international radiotelegraph rules. However, they didn't expect that any complaints would be lodged. W.L. probably wouldn't be held accountable due to his excitement right after winning the fight.

During the match, W.L. had made good use of his left hand, but the exertion damaged it further. By the next day he was in serious pain, and doctors once again encased his hand in a cast.

28

His doctors forbade W.L. to fight for at least a month, but taking a break from the ring wasn't a hardship. It gave him more time with Clara and the children. Tee was now three years old, and Mary Virginia was coming up on two. They delighted in his company. He wasn't just their father, he was also a great playmate. He loved going with them to the local playground and taking part in the games they played with other children.

The whole country seemed fascinated with children that summer—actually with one child in particular. Aviator Charles Lindbergh and his wife Anne Morrow Lindbergh became first-time parents on June 22. Even though no information about the baby, not even his name, had been released, overnight he became the most famous baby in America.

There always seemed to be people eager to honor and entertain the Striblings that year. In early June the Macon American Legion gave W.L. a banquet and a few days later W.L., his wife, and parents were guests at a Kiwanis Club luncheon.

But the perhaps most heartwarming function they attended was a dinner given in their honor by the city of Thomasville on June 27. There were speeches and wishes for good luck. Stories about the old days when Pa and Ma were growing up in the area evoked laughter and more than a few tears in the room, which was jammed with relatives and old friends. Even the chefs got in the spirit of things; the banquet's menu included such delicacies as Novocaine Punch, Fighting Irish Potatoes, and Whipped Beans.

W.L. and Pa sailed from New York harbor on July 5 for their third European trip in two years. Although his hand was still in a cast, doctors had assured W.L. it would be healed in time for the Phil Scott fight in three weeks.

Ma had stayed home to oversee Mike Maurer's training, and soon after her husband left for Europe, Clara took the children and joined her parents on St. Simons Island. But she kept in touch with W.L. through frequent letters.

On the trip across the Atlantic W.L. was befriended by two young women—two young socialites, one of whom went by the nickname of Peanuts. He was happy to make friends and continued seeing them even after arriving in Europe. And he faithfully wrote Clara all the details of his new friendships.

W.L. had no idea how his letters were being received by his wife. Clara was a little jealous at first, but then she started worrying that her husband might be losing interest in her. She discussed the matter with friends and decided to do something daring, something to make him notice her all over again. She screwed up her courage and had her long dark hair cut and styled in a short bob, just like all the movie stars wore.

Herbert Stribling had not gone to Europe this time. As his father and brother made their slow way across the Atlantic, Herbert was in the air. A student at the Braley School of Aviation at Wichita, he and five of his fellow student pilots were engaged in a cross-country aerial tour.

The first photo of Charles Augustus Lindbergh Jr. appeared in papers on July 11. The same day another child's picture was featured in the *Telegraph*. Young Mary Virginia Stribling had been photographed a few months earlier by Georgia photographer Hillyer C. Warlick. He entered the picture in the National Photographers Association of America contest and won third place out of 20,000 entries.

W.L. and Pa landed in Cherbourg on July 10. They met with Jeff Dickson in Paris, then went on to London. Pa chose Windsor, a village about 20 miles west of London, as the place to set up W.L.'s training camp. They had rooms at the Harte and Garter Hotel on High Street, right in the shadow of Windsor Castle.

Wimbledon Stadium was the site of the Stribling–Scott fight on July 28. Thirty-five thousand lively fans were in attendance, and numerous small ruckuses broke out all over the stadium in the hour before the match. The disturbances weren't serious, generally having to do with hats and obstructed views or whether those spectators in the standing room spaces were taking up too much room.

While police hurried to break up the disturbances, they didn't notice the scores of fans who had dragged ladders to the outside walls of the arena. The gatecrashers quickly climbed to the top where they had a fine view of the ring.

W.L. was at a disadvantage that night. Although the information hadn't been shared with the press, his hand was still unhealed. The long days of training—both bag work and sparring—had turned the discomfort into a constant, throbbing ache. So just before the fight, a doctor injected Novocain into his joints. The drug didn't remove the pain; it only dulled it.

Stribling knew he had to end the fight as soon as possible to avoid further injury to his hand. So when the clang of the bell signaled the beginning of the first round, he went on the attack. He landed a hard right to Scott's chin, followed by several lefts to his head. Scott went down for a count of six.

As soon as Scott was back on his feet, W.L. sent a punishing left to his stomach and put him on the canvas again. This time the referee reached seven before Scott got back up. The British fighter was knocked down a third time in the first, but the round ended before he could be counted out.

Scott rallied a bit in the beginning of the second, but Stribling soon overpowered him. A right to the chin, followed by a left to his ribs finally put him down for the count and the fight ended.

It was an impressive win, but not without cost. W.L. reinjured his hand, and the next day a doctor ordered him to take a sixty-day rest from boxing.

Just as Pa expected, Stribling's win over Scott catapulted him right back into the ranks of prominent heavyweight contenders. Even before the Striblings were back on U.S. soil, there was talk about W.L. facing Sharkey, Carnera, or even Schmeling.

After the Scott fight, the Striblings traveled to Paris for more meetings with Jeff Dickson. He and Pa were determined to arrange a match between W.L. and Max Schmeling in Berlin later that year and were soon deep in discussions with German promoters. However, the champion and his manager were in New York at the time.

The Striblings had planned to return home on the *Acquitania*, but Pa and Dickson were anxious to continue their negotiations and booked passage on the *Paris*, a faster ocean liner that would put them in New York two days earlier. They had arranged to meet with Schmeling's manager Joe Jacobs and believed that time was of the essence.

Jacobs was no stranger to Pa Stribling. He had managed Mike McTigue at the time W.L. fought the Irishman in Columbus. Soon afterwards he and McTigue had had a falling out and Jacobs moved on to Schmeling.

When the ship docked at New York, Jacobs was waiting on the pier for them, right beside Ma. After meeting with Schmeling's manager for hours but reaching no conclusion, the Striblings retired to their hotel room.

There they found a table piled with telegrams, all containing offers from promoters. It seemed that everybody wanted W.L. that summer. Although there were some attractive invitations in the bunch, Pa wasn't tempted. He knew W.L. needed time to recover. Besides, he had his sights set on Schmeling and the title.

W.L. boarded the *Acquitania* alone and his crossing was more leisurely than his father's. He, too, had a welcoming committee in New York on August 15. Clara, her brother Billy, and Foy and Merle Boone had driven up from Macon to meet him.

Although she had changed her hairstyle specifically to impress him, Clara had suddenly grown nervous that morning, wondering how W.L. would react to the change. Just before leaving the hotel she had put on a cloche hat with an elaborate egret feather that circled her head and partially concealed her hair.

W.L. spotted Clara as soon as he started down the gangplank and hurried to greet her. They embraced, and it wasn't until he stepped back from her that he got a good look at her.

"What have you done to your hair?" he asked, sounding horrified.

She stuttered, trying to explain, certain now that she had done something terrible. But as the surprise wore off, W.L. admitted he liked the new look.

The group of friends spent several days enjoying New York. They attended a game at Yankee Stadium where W.L. posed for pictures with Babe Ruth and received a big ovation from the crowd, then went up to Saratoga Springs for several days of horse racing.

Foy Boone had requested that W.L. bring him a special gift from London, but it wasn't one he intended to keep. Before leaving Macon, Boone had visited C. D. Porter, a young boy who was dangerously ill with diphtheria. He told the child that if he obeyed the doctors and nurses, took all his medicine, and got well, he would ask Stribling to bring him the gloves he wore when he defeated Scott. After leaving the hospital, Boone cabled the request to his friend.

When W.L. and his party left New York on August 20 for the drive back to Macon, the gloves were safely tucked away in their luggage. Several days later, Boone and W.L. went to see the now recovered C.D. and gave him the gloves.

W.L. followed his doctor's orders to the letter. He didn't fight again for more than two months and took care not to do anything that might re-injure his hand. In the meantime, he pursued other interests. He became more involved in the flying business and even had a miniature golf course built on a vacant lot beside his Nottingham Drive home. It became a popular diversion for the folks in Macon, and W.L. and his family often played there as well.

Even though he couldn't fight, W.L. didn't stay out of the ring. He refereed several matches in Macon and Atlanta. And in late August he agreed to officiate a bout in Waycross dedicated to the memory of Sammy Buchanan. Buchanan, a promising young welterweight from that city, had collapsed in the ring in Kentucky the previous month and died from a cerebral hemorrhage.

Stribling planned to fly to Waycross. Since he had recently sold his last plane, he arranged for an Atlanta company to fly an enclosed-cabin, six-passenger, 300-horsepower Travel Air to Macon for his conside-ration. It was waiting for him at Miller Field on the day of the memorial.

It was Stribling's plan to test fly it to Waycross and back and then decide whether he was interested in buying it. But he liked the plane with its powerful Wright Whirlwind engine so well that before they were halfway to Waycross he decided to purchase it.

Soon after signing the papers and taking possession of the airplane, he named it *The King of the Canebrakes*, taking sportswriter Damon Runyon's derisive title and turning it into his own.

On August 26 W.L. and Clara left Macon at dawn in his new plane. After a stop in Atlanta to pick up pilot George Shealy and his wife, they continued on to Chicago and the National Air Races. This time W.L. would be a spectator rather than a participant in the events.

They landed at an airport about 28 miles outside of Chicago. Because of heavy traffic, the trip from there to their hotel lasted three hours—a fact they found amusing since their flight from Atlanta had taken only six hours.

Jack Dempsey was no longer the heavyweight champion, but he was still a popular figure and in great demand for personal appearances all over the country. When he agreed to referee an American Legion fight in Macon on September 15, W.L. volunteered to meet him in Birmingham the week before and fly him to Georgia.

Ma and Tee went along with him to pick up the famous fighter, then they all flew to Thomasville for a weekend at the Ochlocknee farm. They feasted on farm produce that night and discussed doing some bird hunting. The next morning W.L. and Dempsey drove to the nearby town of Pelham for shotgun shells.

The two men enjoyed each other's company. Early in their acquaintance, they had discovered they shared the same sense of humor. They both loved practical jokes and often pulled pranks together.

Minutes after walking into Chisholm's Store in Pelham, the two began cutting up.

"Put up your dukes, W.L.," Dempsey said with mock ferocity.

For the next couple of minutes, the fighters sparred right there in the middle of the store. More than one customer turned around at the door and left rather than get in the middle of something that looked dangerous. Then the two men broke into laughter, bought the shotgun shells, and left.

Sunday night they flew to Macon, and W.L. spent most of Monday showing Dempsey around town. Everyone wanted to meet the champ. He shook hundreds of hands and posed for countless photographs. He was a guest on the WMAZ noon radio show, where he promoted the upcoming boxing program.

Dempsey cut quite a figure in the ring at the auditorium that night. Dressed in gray flannel trousers and a blue silk polo shirt, he would have been right at home in Madison Square Garden, but he seemed to fit in Macon, too. A man of tremendous charm, he laughed and joked and chatted with all those around him.

But when the match started, Dempsey took his obligation seriously. He watched every move of the two young fighters in the ring, taking as much care officiating the regional middleweight bout as he would have a title fight.

W.L. was away for much of September for his annual Army Air Corps Reserves training at Maxwell Field. He flew his big plane to Montgomery with some unexpected cargo. Tucked into the passenger cabin was W.L.'s Indian motorcycle. After all, he explained, he had to have some way to get around when he was on the ground.

That fall the National Boxing Association officially recognized Max Schmeling as the world heavyweight champion, filling the vacancy left by Tunney's retirement. W.L. was ranked as the number-one contender. Sharkey was second, and Carnera third. Suddenly Stribling was more in demand than he had ever been before.

Even though negotiations for a Schmeling fight went on, Pa did book a few more matches for his son. But he wouldn't agree to a fight with Jack Sharkey, even when Madison Square Garden offered W.L. $50,000 to do so. Sharkey had refused numerous offers for rematches after their first fight and Pa saw no reason to accommodate him now. Besides, he reasoned it would do W.L. no good to fight a man who was ranked behind him.

That fall, Pa hired Edith Nolan as his secretary. She was a quiet young woman, but he told people she was the most efficient stenographer he ever had. "In fact, she's the most efficient anybody ever had."

In October W.L. started light training, and by the time he headed north to face Meyer "K.O." Christner in Boston, he was in great condition. He won the fight by a technical knockout in the third round.

On November 8 W.L. and Clara attended the Georgia Tech–Vanderbilt game in Atlanta, then returned to Macon the next day for a very special event—Mary Virginia's second birthday party.

Pa and Joe Jacobs reached a tentative agreement in November for Stribling and Schmeling to fight within a few months. But Sharkey still hadn't given up hope of a match with W.L. If he could beat Stribling, he would be right back up there in the number-one-contender position.

The Striblings continued to refuse, but in late November the Sharkey camp tried a different approach. They again offered Stribling $50,000 to fight, but this time they wanted to make it a benefit match with the proceeds going to New York's unemployed.

Although some recognized it for the grandstanding it was, it was an effective gambit. The economic crisis in the country continued. Every day more businesses were closing and more people were out of work. Bread lines were familiar sights in the big cities, and a benefit for the unemployed was hard to turn down.

But Pa did refuse. He wouldn't give in to the publicity stunt, knowing it wouldn't help W.L. in his quest for the heavyweight crown. However, some New York sportswriters fell for the ploy and criticized Stribling for refusing the challenge. One writer made Sharkey sound like a saint for offering to fight for charity.

W.L. had one last fight in November, which he won, then he and Clara went to South Georgia for a few days of hunting. Although she couldn't bear the thought of shooting a deer, Clara did hunt birds.

They joined Pa and Ma in Miami for Thanksgiving and, while they were there, W.L. took part in a speed program at Pompano Beach—he raced several automobiles with his airplane.

And his flying adventures didn't end there. When he and Clara left Miami a few days later, they stopped in Orlando to refuel. On the approach to the airport, W.L. sighted a glider floating on a nearby lake.

As soon as they were on the ground he went to investigate. He had never flown a glider, but always wanted to try it. The owner of the craft invited Stribling to take it up, and W.L. was soon at the controls as the glider was pulled into the air by a powerful motorboat. Seconds later the ropes were released and he was soaring by himself. It was great fun until the landing.

His approach onto the lake was perfect, but at the last minute a sudden crosswind flipped the aircraft over. The glider wasn't damaged, but W.L. was dumped into the chilly water. His heavy clothes and parachute were soon soaked, and the weight was pulling him under.

The motorboat driver got to him quickly, but it took considerable effort to hoist him and his sodden clothes into the boat. He suffered a mild case of hypothermia as a result of his time in the water, but after a night's rest at a local hotel he completely recovered.

Stribling's last fight of the year was in Chicago. The Illinois Boxing Commission requested that he not fly to the match as planned because of bad weather, so he, his parents, Tee, and Foy Boone traveled north by train.

On December 12 he faced Tuffy Griffiths at Chicago Stadium. Griffiths was one of the top five contenders for the heavyweight crown and it was something of a risk for Stribling to fight him, but Pa was confident his son would win the match.

It was a hard-fought contest with nonstop action for all ten rounds, but in the end W.L. was given the unanimous decision by the two judges and referee. Foy Boone later said it was the "prettiest exhibition of boxing skill I've even seen."

After the fight, W.L. was interviewed on radio with Tee in his lap.

"I tried to finish him in the first three rounds," he explained. "That's why I didn't beat him more decisively."

Griffiths sat beside him at the microphone. "I lost squarely," he said. "It was the best fight I ever fought."

Both boxers were on their best behavior while on the air, but young Tee Stribling had never heard anything about international communication rules. As soon as the interviewer turned to him, the little boy remembered that his mother would be listening.

"Hello, Ma," he said in a loud voice. "I'm going to bring you some chewing gum!"

W.L. fought ten times in 1930 and won every match. It was a smaller number of bouts than he was accustomed to fighting in a year, but he had been plagued by injuries and his problems weren't over yet.

The hand that had caused him so much trouble over the summer had healed, but he had dislocated a vertebra in his neck just before the Griffiths fight. The jostling train trip back to Macon was agony for him. While his injury gradually improved, the stiffness and soreness remained for some time.

Clara and W.L. had planned to fly to California for the holidays and attend the Rose Bowl on New Year's Day, but they canceled that plan, spending a quiet Christmas at home instead.

29

Passenger air service came to Macon in 1931. Beginning New Year's Day, Eastern Air Transport landed two passenger planes at Miller Field every day. One flew north, the other south. The flight to Atlanta took about fifty minutes and cost $5.39, and passengers could fly from there to New York.

In January Max Schmeling and his manager found themselves at odds with the New York Boxing Commission over when and where the champion would defend his title. Fed up with trying to work things out, Jacobs announced that Schmeling would meet W.L. Stribling in June somewhere in the Midwest, neatly removing the New York organization from the equation.

Pa applauded the decision, having had problems of his own with the New Yorkers in the past. "I never knew how easy it was to buck that New York bunch until I tried it," he said. "They didn't think we southerners could put over a fight without their help, and they didn't think we could play football down here until Georgia beat Yale and N.Y.U. and Alabama mopped up the Coast teams. Well, we're showing them new tricks every day."

W.L. agreed with the sentiment, but he had other things on his mind. The match with Schmeling was still six months away, but the All American Air Meet was in Miami the next week. He flew to South Florida with the hope of taking part in some of the events.

Before the meet a newsreel photographer persuaded him to perform a few stunts over that city in his plane. The resulting newsreel was a great success, but not everyone was pleased with the performance. A Commerce Department inspector grounded Stribling for ten days for violating the federal rule against flying low and stunting over an airport. So W.L. had to be content with just watching the action in Miami.

On January 22 the New York Celtics, a barnstorming basketball team generally considered to be the best in the country, came to Macon to take on the Mercer Ramblers. W.L. liked anything that got him onto a basketball court, so when he was asked to referee the match he quickly agreed.

The Thursday night game was part basketball match and part comedy performance with the Celtics running circles around the Mercer players. W.L. had great fun acting as referee. He liked the visiting players so much that he invited them to join him for some flying.

The next morning he took every member of the team up in his plane, one by one. They had all flown before and it was nothing new to them, but W.L. didn't just give them rides. He amazed and terrified his passengers by flying a series of stunts that left them shaken, relieved to get back on the ground.

But they had so much fun with him that they asked W.L. to accompany them to Atlanta where they had another game scheduled that night. Stribling couldn't resist—after all, that would combine flying *and* basketball—so he made the short trip, and two of the team members, Davey Banks and Dutch Dehnert, chose to fly up with him rather than join the rest of the team on the train.

W.L. was in the stands when the Celtics took on the Atlanta Junior Chamber of Commerce team that night. As the evening progressed he became more than just a spectator. At halftime he joined the team in their dressing room and learned that one of them had been slightly injured. So W.L. donned a Celtics uniform and took the court with them.

Some in the crowd cheered when he appeared, but others thought it was a joke. What was a prizefighter doing on a basketball court? But the laughter faded away when W.L. scored the first two goals of the half. He easily fit into the Celtics' complicated passing routines and played the rest of the game looking as if that were right where he belonged.

The nation's economy continued its downward spiral. In Washington, the Senate passed a bill giving the Red Cross $25,000,000 to aid the hungry. And in Macon Mayor Toole announced a new program for creating jobs. For one dollar, citizens could have a decorative tree—dogwood, holly, mimosa, or magnolia—planted in their yards. The city workers hired for the purpose would retrieve the trees from nearby woods with the landowners' permission and plant them. The Macon Civic Employment Exchange was also formed that year. It was a networking service that out-of-work men and women could join. Macon residents could go to the exchange to find workers for cleaning, painting, and repair jobs.

Max Schmeling had returned to his native Germany after winning the championship. When he returned months later on January 29, he was met by the usual collection of reporters. At their prompting, he predicted he would easily beat Stribling.

When reporters told W.L. about Schmeling's statement in Charleston where he and Clara were visiting, the fighter just grinned. "What do you expect him to say?"

But he wouldn't make any predictions of his own. "I'll do my talking in the ring with the mitts."

In late March Pa decided it was time for W.L. to start light training for the Schmeling fight. So on the March 26 he, W.L., Jack Bell, William Blanchard, and J. McCord climbed aboard the *King of the Canebrakes* and flew to Dallas. Three days later they were in Matamoros, Mexico, where W.L. fought a four-round exhibition match with Texas heavyweight Champ Clark.

The mood was optimistic when they left Mexico the next day. The match had been a good workout for W.L., and he was glad to be heading home to his family.

As they neared Houston, they were enveloped in a blinding rainstorm. W.L. tried to fly through the bad weather, but soon realized he would have to put the plane down. He spotted a clearing of sorts and calmly told his passengers, "Hold on tight."

The forced landing was rough. The wings of the plane were smashed, but no one was hurt.

"Well," W.L. said cheerfully as they climbed out into a pasture in the middle of nowhere, "here we are. Nobody knows where it is, but at least it's some place we've never seen before."

They arranged for the wrecked plane to be shipped north to the factory for repairs, then made their way home by train.

W.L. continued his light training by working out for a few days with the Brooklyn Dodgers baseball team that made Macon its spring training home. Then he and Clara spent a week at Warm Springs in West Georgia. W.L. golfed, rode horses, and swam in the spring-fed pools there.

Warm Springs was an internationally known treatment center for polio victims, and W.L. spent hours at the hospital, visiting with the children. One afternoon he put on an impromptu exhibition for them, shadow boxing and skipping rope, all the while whistling "Life Is Just a Bowl of Cherries."

Pa and Joe Jacobs had spent countless hours hammering out the details of the Schmeling–Stribling match. Ironically, after months of dealing with promoters in the Midwest, they finally agreed that officials of Madison Square Garden would promote the fight. When the contracts were signed, it was announced that the fight would be held in Cleveland, Ohio, on July 3.

With the Schmeling fight settled, W.L. went back to light training. He played 18 holes of golf on April 15, and the next day he and Clara attended the season-opening baseball game between the Atlanta Crackers and the Chattanooga Lookouts. Governor-elect Richard Russell threw out the first pitch, and Stribling served as his catcher.

Before buckling down to real training, W.L. decided to try his luck in another sporting contest. He entered the second annual Southeastern Sand Greens Golf Tournament in Macon with players from all over Georgia.

W.L. teed off Thursday morning, April 23, at 11:15. He shot 101, which was considerably above par, but low enough to qualify him for the rest of the tournament.

While Stribling didn't come anywhere close to winning the tournament, he had a respectable showing, winning the fifth flight trophy, and spent the weekend doing something he loved.

No sooner was the golf tournament over than another sport caught his attention. Motorboats were being raced at Lakeside. He bought a fast Century outboard racing boat that he christened *Socko*. He moored it in a boathouse on the Ocmulgee River close to his house where it was convenient to him whenever he chose to zoom up and down the waterway.

Clara tried to match her husband's love of adventure and usually kept up with him pretty well. She knew W.L. hated to see people lose their nerve, so she went with him when he invited her for a ride in the new speedboat.

He didn't make any concessions to her presence, driving it just as fast as he did when he was alone. The bumping of the boat on the water was jarring, and Clara bounced around so hard that she could hardly walk for a week, but she never complained to W.L. However, after that first experience she tried to have something else to do whenever a boat ride was offered.

Pa was more than happy to join his son for a ride. The two scooted around the river for a while, then W.L. brought him back to the boathouse.

"It's the stuff," Pa declared, grinning broadly as he stepped back on shore. "And more thrilling to me than the airplane."

On Saturday afternoon, May 9, boaters from four states gathered at Lakeside Park for the Southeastern Outboard Motorboat Regatta, and W.L. was right there with them. There were more than 25 professional drivers entered in the races, although he entered as an amateur. Clara and the children joined the elder Striblings to watch the action and cheered when W.L. placed fourth overall in his event.

But the day was marred by several spectacular crashes, and although no one was hurt, Pa realized just how dangerous the sport could be. As a result W.L. attended the races on Sunday as a spectator. His parents had decided it was much too risky for him to participate again. An injury could cause a cancellation in the Schmeling fight.

It seemed to W.L. that everyone was trying to restrict his activities that spring. First his parents forbade any more boat racing. Then days later the fight promoters asked him not to fly until after the Schmeling bout.

But Stribling bowed to their requests. On Tuesday, May 19, a caravan of three cars headed north from Georgia. Pa and Ma took his secretary Edith Nolan and a cook/housekeeper in their car. W.L. left his luxurious new Cord auto at home and drove the larger family Ford.

With him were Clara, Tee, and the children's nurse. Mary Virginia had again been left behind with her grandmother.

In the third car were three men who would serve as W.L.'s sparring partners. Battling Mims of Milledgeville was at the wheel, and Bobby Hooks and Curtis Hambright—the newest member of the Stribling stable known as Battling Bozo—were with him.

The group reached Ohio on Thursday. The Lake Geauga Resort, some twenty miles outside of Cleveland, would be home as well as training camp for the next month-and-a-half. The resort offered boating, swimming, and nightly dances, and Pa had come to a special arrangement with the owner. In exchange for the use of the facility, W.L. would box at least six public exhibition rounds every day. The owner was sure this would attract more customers to the park.

The training camp was set up beside the lake where a number of rental cabins were scattered in a grove of trees. A ring had been constructed in the center of the area with plenty of room for spectators. Most of the cabins were reserved as sleeping quarters for the party, their guests, and the press. However, one two-room structure filled a dual purpose: One half was equipped as a training center with a shower, punching bags, weights, and a rubdown table. The other was furnished with tables and typewriters for reporters.

The Striblings wanted to make the camp as much like home for W.L. as possible. They had shipped several boxes of food to Ohio, and when the party arrived they found country ham, bacon, cane syrup, pecans, and a variety of vegetables waiting for them.

On Friday evening both fighters attended a banquet in Cleveland held for them. It was hosted by the newly formed Madison Square Garden Corporation of Ohio. The two men couldn't have been more polite when they met there that night. They shook hands and greeted each other like long time friends.

After the meal, each of them was asked to say a few words and that's just what they did. Schmeling spoke for 35 seconds, but W.L. bested him. His speech lasted only 15 seconds. It was probably just as well that the speeches were short. With W.L.'s thick southern drawl and Schmeling's heavy German accent, it's doubtful many of the midwestern and northern sportswriters assembled there would have understood them anyway.

After a few days W.L. had settled into his new quarters and begun preliminary training. Clara, Tee, and the nurse returned to Macon, but more familiar faces soon appeared when Foy Boone and Lake Russell arrived. Boone, of course, was a close friend of the family. Pa had hired Russell, head football coach at Mercer, as W.L.'s trainer. The coach also brought Nate Lewis and Bob Smith to the camp. They would work with Russell and act as W.L.'s seconds during the fight.

One of the first things Russell did was suggest that W.L. keep more regular hours and cut out a lot of the socializing that was going on. But that was easier said than done.

There was a constant flow of people through both fighters' camps. Newsreels of the training were shown in theaters across the country, and sportswriters nearly outnumbered boxing fans during the sparring. This was the biggest fight of the year, and story after story was filed.

No incident was too small to report. When Pa ordered W.L. to cut down his time on local golf courses, it made headlines on sports pages across the country. Herbert Stribling's arrival later in the month was duly chronicled as well.

While Schmeling's camp had been established in the cool western mountains just over the Pennsylvania border, it was the hottest July on record at Lake Geauga. The daytime heat made training difficult, and Pa soon called in a team of electricians to install outdoor lighting around the ring. After that W.L. was able to work out and spar after dark, avoiding the punishing afternoon sun.

One evening Pa was refereeing a sparring match when W.L. playfully threw a punch at him. It was intended to be a light tap, but it landed with unexpected force and laid the older man out. He had to sit down for several minutes to recover. W.L. apologized and tried to make light of the incident, but Pa wasn't inclined to laugh it off.

"The kid's idea of playing may be fine for him," he said, "but it's not so hot for me."

While there was a lot of hard training being done, the mood in the Stribling camp was often playful. Every night as they gathered around the training table for dinner, someone could be counted on to tell their current favorite joke.

"Please pass the Schmeling salts," one of the diners would say, and everyone would break up as if hearing the gag for the first time.

W.L. was as irrepressible as ever and rarely missed a chance to pull a prank. He loved giving people the hot foot—slipping a wooden match between the sole and shoe of a distracted man and lighting it.

Several times he would sneak into one of the writer's cabins after midnight when they were asleep. He would creep across the floor and tickle the nose of the sleeping reporter with a feather, stifling his laughter as the man first rubbed his nose with a finger and then, as the irritant continued, came upright slapping at his face.

In the third week of June, Russell believed W.L. had reached the peak of his conditioning and convinced Pa to cut back on his training schedule. Pa then decided it was time his son stopped other activities as well, such as giving diving demonstrations in the lake and making newsreels with the photographers.

W.L. was restricted to roadwork, swimming, and skipping rope. As the days passed, he grew bored and edgy.

30

On June 27 both camps announced their fighters were ready. The swarming sportswriters watched the last sparring matches and made their own judgments. The consensus was that Schmeling was ready, but Stribling might have been a bit too finely trained.

Schmeling took it easy for the rest of the week and planned to finish up the time at his camp by hosting a soccer match between two local German American teams. Stribling relaxed in a different way.

On Tuesday afternoon, he slipped away from camp. Disregarding warnings from Pa and the Garden promoters, he borrowed a plane and flew across the border into Pennsylvania.

Schmeling was in the middle of a light workout when the drone of an engine was heard above the camp. Everyone on the ground looked up and saw an airplane performing a series of swoops and loops above their heads. Then, as the plane made a slow, low pass over the ring, the motor was shut off.

In the sudden quiet there came a voice, "Yoo-hoo! Maxie! Whatcha doin'?"

W.L. then restarted the plane, climbed into the sky, and disappeared.

But even with the diversion of flight, W.L. remained restless and a bit nervous. To add to the stress, he knew that many of his friends bet on his matches, and this one would be no different. Sometimes they would wager everything they had, so sure were they that he would win. The knowledge was an extra burden on the young fighter.

Clara returned to Ohio that week, and on Thursday the Schmeling and Stribling parties moved into Cleveland hotels. W.L. kept a low profile the day before the fight, avoiding reporters and resting in his room.

When the fighters had their official weigh-ins on Friday night, Schmeling tipped the scales at 192. But Stribling registered only 177½ pounds, ten pounds below his usual fighting weight.

The size of the crowd at the outdoor Cleveland Stadium wasn't as large as the promoters had hoped, and the weather may have been to blame. The humidity was stifling, and at fight time the temperature was in the high 80s.

After the preliminary bouts, the two stars of the evening were introduced. Stribling and Schmeling shook hands as the crowd gave them an ovation. Then they slipped off their robes and prepared for battle.

Stribling began cool and cautious, scoring points and looking confident. But Schmeling matched him punch for punch. Through the first four rounds W.L. appeared to be leading, but in the fifth his stamina began slipping away.

By the seventh the tide had turned, and W.L. was forced into a defensive posture. Schmeling staggered him with blow after blow. The southerner rallied a bit in the eighth and ninth rounds, but the fight from then on was all Schmeling's.

When the last round began, Schmeling seemed to be the sure winner, but W.L.'s supporters hoped he would at least salvage his pride by lasting until the final bell.

But it wasn't to be. Schmeling rushed Stribling into the ropes, battering him unmercifully. Stribling went down, and the referee reached nine in the count before W.L. managed to get to his feet again and stagger a few steps forward.

The German fighter moved in on him again, and some people in the crowd shouted, "Stop it! Stop it!" That's exactly what referee George Blake did. With only fourteen seconds remaining in the match, he declared Schmeling the winner by a technical knockout.

As soon as the referee dropped his arm, Schmeling crossed to where W.L. had slumped to the mat. He picked him up, carried him to his corner, and gently set him on the stool.

After a minute or two, Stribling got to his feet and went over to shake Schmeling's hand. The champion was surrounded by reporters and photographers, but he shouldered through all of them to accept W.L.'s congratulations.

Then, unsteady and bloody, W.L. was helped to his dressing room by his father. Clara and Ma followed close behind. It was a sad, quiet procession. As reporters crowded around him minutes later, asking questions, W.L. through nearly shuttered eyes and bloodied and puffed lips, offered no alibis. He had tried to finish Schmeling in the first few rounds, he said, but hadn't counted on the other man's incredible stamina.

"He fought a fair fight, a clean fight," he told them.

The atmosphere was markedly different in Schmeling's dressing room. The champion was jubilant, but he also praised the man he had just beaten.

"He's a trickish fighter and a good fighter and hard to beat."

Only minutes after the decision had been announced, Macon's mayor Glen Toole sent Stribling a telegram: "You're great. We're still proud of you."

Attendance at the fight was only 30,930, smaller than the promoters had anticipated. And that, of course, reduced the expected gate. When the money was counted and the expenses and taxes were paid, the Garden showed a slight loss. Schmeling's share was just over $100,000 while Stribling received about $33,000, half of what he and Pa had expected.

Even though W.L. had suffered his first and only knockout loss, few southern reporters weren't yet counting Stribling out. In fact, they contended that he just might be a better fighter now that the fear of being knocked out was behind him. But most sportswriters, particularly those with national readership, declared that he was through. They didn't belittle him—he had been courageous to stand up to the punishment Schmeling had delivered—but he had lost his big chance. Now, they said, it was time for him to retire.

But W.L. didn't see it that way. Back home, he addressed the subject with *Telegraph* sports editor Jimmy Jones. "I haven't the slightest idea of quitting and I'm awaiting developments while here at home. The first thing I'm going to do is get a good rest and then I'll be ready to talk about fighting anybody."

He had no harsh words for anyone, especially his opponent. "Max is a great boy. Once I fell through the ropes, and he stepped back until I could get back out again. I tried to return his sportsmanship later when I had him turned around with his back partially to me and I let him get straight. Yes, I'm glad it was a clean fight and the best man won. Max was the better man that night."

He also complimented his attendants. "I don't believe any fighter ever had any cooler men in his corner than I did that night in Pa, Bob Smith, and Nate Lewis. They never got excited, and their coolness helped me to get through the hard rounds. Nothing could excite Pa. He let me fight my fight."

He finally praised referee George Blake. "He's one of the squarest officials I ever fought under. I could have lasted the remaining 14 seconds and I'm sorry he stopped the fight, but I appreciate Blake's position. He didn't know whether I could last or not, and he didn't want to take chances on having me seriously hurt."

W.L.'s family and friends rallied around him as if he were recovering from a near-fatal illness, and that outpouring of love and concern helped him heal quickly. His friends were anxious to reassure him that they still believed in him.

Battling Mims, Stribling's chief sparring partner at Lake Geauga, wrote a letter to the editor of the *Telegraph* predicting that W.L. would be the champion in 1932 or early 1933. And a banquet in Stribling's honor was held in the Gold Room of the Hotel Dempsey. His family was there along with more than 200 friends and associates.

When it was time for W.L. to address the gathering, he was sincere in his thanks. "This is the most wonderful welcome that I ever received in my life." Then the man who had nearly set records for the brevity of his speeches addressed them for almost ten minutes. He was alternately serious and comic.

"They say I lost the fight and apparently I did," he joked at one point. "Anyway, I'm going over to the Grand and see if the fight pictures can tell me what happened."

Pa had already started work on his son's next comeback, spending time in Atlanta, Miami, and New York. But W.L. was busy with other things. On July 20 he reported to Atlanta's Candler Field for his annual Reserve training and was assigned to the operations staff as an instructor for new cadets.

His presence attracted several dozen young fans from the area who hung around the airfield every day waiting for a glimpse of their boxing hero. But they got much more than glimpses. W.L. liked children and spending time with them.

When he worked around the field they trailed after him like a pack of puppies, and when he was gone on a flight they watched every plane that landed. They would rush over once it had stopped. If a pilot other than Stribling got out they simply turned away to wait some more.

On July 27 W.L. flew with several other young officers from Atlanta to Dayton, Ohio. Once there he received permission, left the group, and made his way by train to Wichita. There he retrieved his own airplane, which had been undergoing repairs in the factory, and flew it back to Atlanta.

With his training over for the year W.L. returned home and spent time doing the things he enjoyed. He loved long rides in the country on his motorcycle, but hated leaving Clara alone. His solution was to buy her a small bike of her own. Then the two of them could ride together. He also fashioned a little box that fit on the back of his machine so that they could take along picnic lunches.

In mid-August he and Clara left the children with his parents and took a flying vacation cross-country to California. It was wonderful having some time alone and was an exciting trip. In Hollywood they took tours of the movie studios and spent time with the many celebrities who were anxious to meet them.

There was great interest in Stribling, and at one point a group of producers approached him about appearing on the screen himself. A number of sports figures—including Johnny Weissmuller, Bill Tilden, and Babe Ruth—had done so, and they saw no reason that the handsome, personable Stribling couldn't do the same.

But W.L. wasn't interested. He had no desire to appear in movies and told them so. No amount of persuasion could change his mind. So they tried another approach. They would purchase the rights to his life story and have an actor play him on screen. This time it was Clara who put an end to the idea.

"No one could be as wonderful as Strib," she told them. "It would be mockery to let anyone try to impersonate him."

So W.L.'s shot at movie stardom passed him by, and on Wednesday, August 26, the couple left Los Angeles for the flight home.

It was important that they be in Ochlocknee in plenty of time for Herbert's marriage to Edith Nolan the following Sunday. Edith had been Pa's secretary for a year, and she and Herbert had grown close during the time they had spent at Lake Geauga.

They arrived in South Georgia in plenty of time for the ceremony, which the Reverend J. Gorsham Garrison of the Ochlocknee Baptist Church performed in his study. Afterward Herbert handed the minister an envelope containing a sum of money and a curious note:

> To Mr. Garrison. You will find $4.00 in here for the license, and $10.00 for you. I know you give one tenth of all your earnings to the church so am putting $1.00 to cover the $10.00 I am giving you for marrying us, and I find when I put $1.00 in I have to put a dime in to be ten-percent on the dollar, and also placing one penny to cover up the dime so as to be sure you will get the $10.00.
>
> You have made me a good teacher, a good lodge brother, a good preacher and on top of all this what I get more pleasure in saying than all the rest of the other combined you have always been a good sport.
> Edith & Herbert

On Monday, W.L. and Clara left Georgia again, this time flying to Cleveland for the National Air Races. Herbert and Edith traveled with them, making the journey part of their honeymoon.

The Air Races included cross-country flying, landing contests, and glider demonstrations, but the most popular events were those where the pilots raced their crafts around a series of pylons on a closed twenty-five-mile course. W.L. competed that year. He averaged 144 miles an hour and won second place in the sportsman race.

Reporters still followed him around, and every one of them asked about his future. W.L. was intentionally vague.

"I'm going to play around for a while. I haven't made any definite plans for the future."

And play he did. On a warm Friday night in September W.L. and Clara, along with other members of the Macon Motorcycle Club, were invited to a watermelon cutting in nearby Jones County. W.L. and his wife arrived early because he had certain arrangements to make.

Unbeknownst to Clara, W.L. had a quiet word with the host before the other club members arrived. When the guests began to show up, the host regretfully told them he hadn't been able to get any watermelons.

"But you can go down that road just a little ways and pick up a few out of that field," he said. "They'll probably never know they're gone."

The group thought this sounded like a wonderful idea. The prospect of engaging in a little petty theft that wouldn't hurt anyone and for which they wouldn't get in trouble seemed like a lark. Off they roared on their bikes to the neighbor's field where they began piling up melons.

"Be still—every one of you!" came a shout from the bushes.

Then two shots rang out overhead and full-scale panic ensued. The cyclists fell all over themselves getting out of there. One ran into a fence and another laid his bike down on the dusty road. Clara jumped in front of W.L., pushed him to the ground, and laid on top of him to protect him.

But the only danger facing W.L. was that he was laughing so hard he could hardly breathe. When they had all made their way back to their friend's place, W.L. confessed he had set up the whole thing with the neighbor. They had been victims of another Stribling practical joke.

Fall was approaching, and W.L. didn't have a single match scheduled for the rest of the year. He had never had so much free time, and he was growing restless. That's when he and three friends—Harry Burch, Lewis Brewer, and Frank B. Simpson—came up with an idea. They would make a cross-country air trip, visiting as many states as they could. Their route was tentative, at best, but with one definite stipulation. They wouldn't fly over any large bodies of water.

"I'm going to fly over land," W.L. declared. "I can't find Candler Field after leaving Macon, and I certainly am not going out over a big pond of water and try to find Paris or Tokyo."

Clara stayed home with the children and would have preferred to keep her husband nearby as well.

"But you know he's the original gypsy," she told friends. And, as usual, she wanted W.L. to do anything he chose.

The four began their trip on September 24. When they returned over two weeks later, they had visited eighteen cities, including a stop in St. Louis to see the sixth game of the '31 World Series.

While his son had been crisscrossing the nation, Pa was working hard. W.L. had barely time to greet his family before he learned that Pa had arranged a fight for him a week later in Wichita. So Stribling returned to the Midwest and fought Salvatore Ruggeriello on October 19, knocking him out in the second round.

Two notable but very different Americans were in the news that month. eighty-four-year-old inventor Thomas Edison died at his home in Orange, New Jersey. A week later Al Capone was sentenced to eleven years in prison for income tax evasion. The powerful man who had tried to purchase W.L. Stribling's contract was now a federal prisoner.

31

October was a difficult month for Pa Stribling. While in New Orleans for a Battling Bozo fight, his car was struck by a streetcar. No one was seriously injured, but the car was wrecked.

Only a few weeks later, he filed suit in Bibb County Superior Court to try and recover a $3,000 check that he had left with the Merchants and Mechanics Bank in Macon. Pa was a stockholder in the corporation and had also been named to the board of directors, but none of that helped when the bank failed in August after its president embezzled $91,000.

Whether or not Pa had simply left the check with the bank for safekeeping, as he said, or had actually deposited it didn't matter to the state banking department. He was listed as a general depositor right along with the hundreds of other people who lost their money.

In November W.L. knocked out two more fighters in Missouri and Oklahoma and won a third match in a decision over Pietro Corri in Birmingham. But his run of bad luck wasn't over yet. His left hand, the cause of so many problems in the past, was injured once again in the Corri fight. Because of that, a match with leading heavyweight contender Ernie Schaaf had to be cancelled.

At least W.L. could still fly. When Wiley Post, pilot to Will Rogers, and George Shealy made a stop in Macon on December 12, W.L. met them at Miller Field and flew with them to Atlanta where Post had a radio interview scheduled. But it was a short trip. He was back home the next day in time to act as an official timekeeper for the Motorcycle Club's hill climbs at the Indian Mounds in East Macon.

And when the navy airship U.S.S. *Akron*, the largest dirigible in the world, flew over Macon the morning of December 16, W.L. joined the thousands of people who poured out of homes and businesses to get a glimpse of the enormous craft. With a crew of 53, it was big enough to carry five airplanes and could travel 10,000 miles without refueling. The roar of its eight motors could be heard all over town, and it flew low enough that its flag, fluttering in the wind, was clearly visible.

Pa was not in town when the dirigible made its appearance. He was busy that December in Florida, where he had landed the job of director of activities at Miami's Biscayne Arena. He was also in charge of promoting the winter fights at Madison Square Garden's open arena there.

In fact he was so involved in Miami that he was not able to accompany his new light heavyweight fighter Clyde Chastain to Chicago for a match on Wednesday, December 30. He asked his son to take his place, and W.L. immediately agreed—he liked anything that gave him a reason to fly.

W.L. invited *Telegraph* columnist Ed Ray to go with him, and the two met at Miller Field before dawn on Tuesday morning. Together they pushed Stribling's airplane out of the hangar, but before they could take off, an airport official brought W.L. the weather forecast for his planned route—zero visibility from Chattanooga to Evansville, Indiana.

They waited a little, hoping the news would improve, but after another check there was no change in the forecast. W.L. didn't want to risk flying.

"We don't live but once," he told Ray, "and I'm not ready to die now."

His next option was train travel. They knew the *Dixie Flyer* would be leaving Macon on its northbound route at 7:50 that morning.

"We might make it," W.L. said as the two sped off toward downtown in his car.

But they were ten minutes late to Terminal Station, and the train was already gone. Standing beside the track, they considered their options. There would be another train that day, but it didn't leave until afternoon and wouldn't arrive in Chicago until late the next day. W.L. was afraid that would be cutting it too close.

He hurried to find the station master. "Where does the *Flyer* stop next?"

"There's only one scheduled stop between here and Atlanta," the station master told him. "That's Griffin. But if you drove fast to Forsyth, you could have the stationmaster stop the train and get on there."

W.L. didn't know any other way to drive but fast. He opened up the car on Forsyth Road and was making pretty good time until a police officer pulled him over.

Of course nearly everyone in Middle Georgia knew W.L., and he was at his most charming as he explained his predicament. The officer, now feeling as if Stribling were one of his buddies, let them go.

Just outside of Forsyth, they spotted the train up ahead through the trees to their right. W.L. caught up and passed it, but when they got into town, they couldn't find the station. Once more the *Flyer* passed them by and once more they were back in the car, speeding northward.

W.L. found a rutted dirt road that ran beside the railroad tracks and floored the accelerator. With dust flying behind them and Ray desperately hanging on, fearful of being bounced out of the car, they overtook the train one more time.

They made it to Barnesville in time to persuade the station master to flag down the *Flyer* so that W.L. could board it. He was finally on his way to Chicago and Ray drove the car back to Macon—at a greatly reduced rate of speed.

Herbert Stribling rejoined his father's stable of boxers in 1931, and the following January 7 he fought Pat Flaherty in Savannah. W.L., who was now taking on more and more managerial responsibility from Pa, was in Herbert's corner that night as the match ended in a draw.

The same week the National Boxing Association released its annual ratings of fighters, and W.L. was listed in fifth place, behind Schmeling, Sharkey, Mickey Walker, and Ernie Schaaf. A match with Schaaf now looked probable for February. If he won, W.L. could once again start fighting his way back to the top.

In the meantime W.L. refereed some matches for Pa in Florida and, on January 20, appeared in an exhibition match with Babe Hunt. A few days later, he and Hunt met again—this time on the jai alai court. Neither man was in danger of giving up boxing for jai alai, but W.L. did win by a score of 10-8 and had added yet another sport to his repertoire.

On January 30 arrangements for the fight with Ernie Schaaf were finalized. The two would meet in Chicago on February 26.

W.L.'s mother-in-law Clara (Mrs. W.O.) Kinney was preparing for a fight of her own. Having been elected to the city council in 1927 she was serving her third term. But she was ready for something more. When U.S. Representative Samuel Rutherford died on February 4 a special election was called for March 2 to fill his unexpired term. She declared herself a candidate for the office.

W.L. was pleased to do some campaigning around Macon for her and spoke at several political rallies, but the time soon came for him to head to Chicago for the Schaaf fight. If the headlines on the sports pages were to be believed, W.L. would be defending his right to remain in the ranks of recognized heavyweight contenders.

The fight with Ernie Schaaf took place at Chicago Stadium as planned on February 26. But that was the only thing that went like the Striblings expected. Schaaf overwhelmed W.L. from the start.

Although Stribling stayed in the ring for the full ten rounds and even managed a few spirited attacks of his own, he was badly beaten. By the time the unanimous decision was announced and Schaaf's hand was raised in victory, both of W.L.'s eyes were nearly swollen shut, blood ran freely from several gashes on his face, and he was nearly limp with exhaustion.

It was a resounding defeat. Pa insisted his son hadn't been hurt much, but even he had to admit W.L.'s appearance after the fight was gruesome.

"He certainly looked bad, didn't he?"

Pa wouldn't discuss W.L.'s possible retirement from the ring, but sportswriters were nearly unanimous in labeling him finished. Even Ed Ray, columnist for W.L.'s hometown *Telegraph*, declared that Stribling would never be champion.

W.L. understood he had been beaten, but he didn't understand why he had not been feeling like himself, even before coming to Chicago. The day after the fight, he went to a doctor for a complete physical.

Later he told friends that the doctor found he was lacking "a certain element in his blood to a large degree," an element which affected his strength and endurance. While it was never defined more clearly than that, the symptoms could easily have been anemia. Whatever the ailment, he assured his Macon pals that treatment was under way and he felt stronger already.

Two days after the Schaaf fight, the Striblings were back in Macon. After another day campaigning for Mrs. Kinney, W.L. went on to Miami where Clara and the children were waiting. But he left his airplane behind in Macon for use by the Kinney campaign.

The biggest news in Middle Georgia that week was that the navy was building another huge dirigible—this one to be named the USS *Macon*, in honor of the city. The mayor and other dignitaries were already making plans for travel to Akron when the $5,000,000 ship was christened later in the year.

But on March 1 all headlines about airships, politics, or anything else were wiped off front pages across the nation to make room for the news that Charles Lindbergh's 20-month-old son had been kidnapped. A ransom was paid, but the child was not returned. Two months later the little boy's body was found not far from the Lindberghs' New Jersey home. But it would be several years before an arrest was made in the case.

W.L.'s help wasn't enough to win Mrs. Kinney's election to Congress. She made a respectable showing, coming in third in a field of five candidates, but when the votes were counted, Carlton Mobley was the new congressman.

That spring W.L. divided his time between Macon and Miami, resting and building up his strength. In spite of his loss to Schaaf, fight offers kept coming in. Jeff Dickson wanted him to face Primo Carnera in London in May, and he was offered a bout with Tommy Loughran in April, but Pa wasn't ready to commit his son to anything just yet.

W.L. was growing weary of hearing about his own retirement. "Just because I lost a couple of fights some want me to quit," he told reporters in Atlanta in late March. "Well, I think when a man goes into the ring 330-odd times and loses only 18 bouts, including probably a bad decision or two, it's not necessary that he give up the game. I'm not walking around on my heels yet. Before I get into that punch-dizzy predicament, I'll retire. Don't worry about that."

His math was a bit off—he had only fought 270 matches at the time and lost just 9—but his point was well taken. No one else in the country had entered the ring as many times as Stribling had.

In late April, Pa received an offer that was too attractive to turn down. He was contacted by Australian fight promoter Hugh McIntosh who offered W.L. three matches in that country at very profitable terms.

"I believe the trip to Australia will do W.L. lots of good," he said. "We would be there five months or more, and he could get back into real condition."

They made plans to sail from Los Angeles in early June, and it wasn't such a bad time to leave the country. Riots continued across the nation. When 3,000 men staged a hunger walk in Dearborn, Michigan, the event erupted into chaos and several marchers were killed. In New York, Governor Franklin Roosevelt announced a plan to assist the unemployed by moving them to farms.

But even in the face of such problems life went on. Couples married and children were born. Students still filled schools, and Hollywood continued to divert the population with movies like *Tarzan, the Ape Man* and *The Big Broadcast of 1932*.

Pa wanted W.L. to be in tiptop shape before his Australian tour and accomplished that in the way he always had—by scheduling a series of fights for him.

In May W.L. fought four times—in Tennessee, Toronto, North Carolina, and Alabama—and won four times. He seemed as healthy and fit as ever.

Father and son, accompanied by Clyde Chastain, sailed from Los Angeles on June 4. They docked in Sydney two weeks later, and W.L. immediately began training.

They were out of the country when, on June 21, Jack Sharkey defeated Max Schmeling in Long Island. It was a controversial decision with one newspaper declaring "The best man lost," but Sharkey was the new heavyweight champion of the world.

The news reached them, even in Australia, but they didn't dwell on it. W.L. had his own matches to worry about. His first fight in Australia was against Ambrose Palmer, the dominion's champion and a

214

formidable opponent. It was quite a battle, but W.L. finally won with a technical knockout in the tenth round.

With W.L.'s next fight still weeks away, the Striblings had some time on their hands. The three men might have passed the time seeing the sights, but when W.L. and Pa were offered a nice sum to perform in vaudeville, they jumped at the chance.

They put together an act combining jokes, banter, shadow boxing, and rope skipping and had a hit on their hands after the first performance. It was like old times for the Striblings. Their only regret was that they had just a week to spend on stage before it was back to training.

W.L. quickly became a favorite with Australian fans. People were impressed with his good manners and pleasant demeanor, and women were thrilled by his movie-star good looks.

On July 15 he fought Frankie Wine in Sydney and won a fifteen-round decision. Observers noticed that he rarely used his left hand in the fight, fueling speculation that the recurring problems with that hand were not yet resolved. But when he was asked about it, W.L. said he had only hurt his thumb and expected a full recovery.

By the end of July, Ma, Clara, and the children were on their way to Australia. They traveled across country to Los Angeles where the Olympics were under way and sailed from there on July 30.

It was an exciting trip for Clara. Although she had been to Europe, the Pacific was new territory for her. Along the way the ship stopped in Hawaii, Tahiti, and Fiji before landing in Sydney on August 19.

W.L. was so anxious to see his family that he couldn't stand waiting on the dock. He got the captain of a tugboat to take him out into the harbor as the ship came into sight.

The family soon spotted him and waved happily from the deck. That's when W.L. opened his arms wide.

"Jump to me, Tee!" he shouted. "Jump to me!"

His five-year-old son, accustomed to being tossed around by his father and grandfather, started to climb up on the railing, ready to leap, but the tug captain quickly put a stop to such a stunt. W.L. had to wait until the ship docked to embrace his son.

32

Australia warmly welcomed the Striblings. It seemed that everyone they met wanted to be sure they saw the best of that country. They were invited to dances and dinners and were entertained in clubs and private homes. W.L. and Pa played countless rounds of golf. They traveled to Brisbane and Melbourne and even took the train across the continent to Perth.

While the family had a glorious time, W.L.'s boxing experience there was not without problems. Although he won six of the seven matches he fought, his performances were inconsistent. He managed four knockouts, but had to go a full fifteen rounds in two others before winning by decision.

When he met Johnny Freeman for the second time in Sydney on October 29, the bout was a disappointment to all concerned. After a slow eight, clinch-filled rounds, the crowd had been reduced to booing, and the referee stopped the match and declared it a "no contest."

By the middle of November the Striblings were ready to leave Australia, but the news from home didn't make them want to hurry back to the States. Although Franklin Roosevelt had been elected president on November 8 the country's future was still uncertain.

So the Striblings boarded a ship in Perth and set out across the Indian Ocean for the 5,000-mile voyage to South Africa. The ship provided onboard childcare and entertainment for the little ones. The children had a wonderful time while their parents were free to relax during the days and dance the nights away.

The Striblings stayed in South Africa for six weeks. W.L. had only one match during that time, so they were free to see the sights and experience the exotic country. One of the highlights of their trip was a visit to the Johannesburg Zoo where they rode elephants. Jostling along on the backs of the huge beasts, laughing and a little fearful at the same time, was an experience none of them would ever forget.

When W.L. did enter the ring in South Africa 15,000 people were on hand. Under the stars, Stribling defeated Dan McCorkindale. It was a good fight, and Willie later reported they had made $32,000.

The Striblings might have been half a world away, but distance couldn't protect them from the trouble at home. While they were still in South Africa, they received word that Clara's father had lost his business and learned that their own holdings were experiencing serious reverses as well. A chain of filling stations in which they had invested had gone bankrupt, and W.L. and Willie, along with the other stockholders, were being sued by the company's creditors.

They considered canceling the rest of the trip, but going home wouldn't help anything and Willie had already scheduled matches for W.L. in Paris and London. So their travels continued.

After Christmas in Johannesburg they boarded the German liner *Uaambara*—a smaller ship than they were used to that carried both passengers and cargo—and set off up the eastern coast of Africa, making numerous stops along the way.

In Mozambique they were driven through the streets in bicycle-powered rickshaws. They heard fantastic stories about the Pasha who kept a harem there when they visited Zanzibar. They marveled at the fragrant, white-blossomed frangipani bushes that scented the air in Dar Es Salaam and bought oranges at ports on the Gulf of Aden.

In Cairo they stayed for several days in Shepheards Hotel, the elegant social center of town for visiting Europeans. A side trip took them to Giza where they rode camels to see the pyramids by moonlight. But their visit to Egypt was short, and several days later their party passed through the Suez Canal into the Mediterranean.

As February came to an end, they finally docked in Southampton, England. They were all thrilled to check into a London hotel that afternoon and sleep that night in a bed that didn't roll with the ocean waves.

Early the next morning W.L. and Willie met with Jeff Dickson and learned he had already arranged for W.L. to fight Pierre Charles in Paris five days later. It wasn't especially good news for Stribling. He had been living aboard a ship for most of the past two months and wasn't in the best condition. Although he knew he didn't really have time to get into shape, he never hesitated. He would go on with the match as he always did and try to make a good showing.

The family left immediately for Paris and settled into an apartment. The city was just as beautiful as it had been the last time they visited, but the weather was now cold and damp and the children came down with what appeared to be colds the first day they were there.

W.L. began working out hard at a nearby gym, but was soon feeling ill himself. In two days the entire family was sick, and the diagnosis was influenza. But the Striblings came from a vaudeville background and believed that the show really did have to go on.

So on the night of March 6 W.L. climbed into the ring in Paris, willing to fight although he was in no condition to do so. The action was about what would be expected given his illness. After the first few rounds, his energy began to flag. A better fighter than Charles would have been able to take advantage of W.L.'s lessened abilities and finish him off, but the Frenchman couldn't do it. So the fight dragged on.

W.L. rallied a few times but wasn't able to put Charles away, and in the eighth round, the referee stepped in. He disqualified W.L. for holding and declared Charles the winner.

Losing the fight was bad enough, but the next day the French Boxing Federation suspended Stribling for three months. And the International Boxing Union, of which the French organization was a member, announced it would honor the suspension as well. The only bright spot in all this was the fact that the suspension wouldn't affect any fights that had already been scheduled.

Willie was angry and told the Associated Press reporter, "My son was ill with influenza and got out of bed to fight so as not to disappoint the public. I don't believe the Federation knew my boy was ill."

Sportswriters who covered the match believed that Stribling was treated unfairly. Sparrow Robertson wrote in the Paris edition of the *New York Tribune*: "Stribling met with disqualification in his match with Charles for what was called a foul, which he did not commit."

Still unhappy about the situation, the Striblings returned to London where W.L. was scheduled to fight Don McCorkindale on April 6. By then he had recovered from his illness and started training for the bout as soon as they were settled. But during a sparring match on April 4, W.L. twisted his leg, slipping a cartilage in his right knee.

It wasn't a new injury. He had done the same thing several times in the past, but had always been able to shift it back into place by performing a snap-kick or two. This time, however, nothing he did could fix it. The doctors they consulted in London advised that surgery would be necessary to correct the problem.

The McCorkindale match was canceled, and the Striblings took the first ship home they could get. It was a rough crossing, and everyone felt a bit queasy, with Clara becoming quite seasick. She was so ill, in fact, that she went to the ship's doctor for relief, but the pills he gave her did little good. She was relieved when they docked in New York on April 18.

W.L.'s progress down the gangplank that morning was uncharacteristically slow. Reporters noticed he was wearing a slipper on his right foot and using a cane for support. They rushed to get the story from the fighter himself, and the next day papers across the country carried an account of his injury.

Pa and Ma stayed in New York for several days, but W.L. and his family were in the big city only for the time it took to make their way from the docks to the train station where they boarded the *Crescent Limited* for Atlanta.

Nearly 100 friends and relatives met them at Terminal Station the next night. Clara's parents were there, as were Foy and Merle Boone, and Roy Barrow.

Mary Virginia laughed with delight when she saw Barrow. She threw herself at him, locking her little arms around his neck. "So this is America!" she exclaimed. "I wouldn't have thought it."

His friends were naturally concerned about W.L.'s knee, but he assured them it wasn't overly serious.

"Those crazy English doctors were too anxious to use the knife," he said. "When they told me that an operation would be necessary for it to be healed and that I'd have to walk on crutches for several months afterwards I decided then and there that home was where I belonged."

He announced he would soon be going to Miami to see Dr. Cecil Ferguson to learn what should be done. "If I have to go under a knife, I'd rather do it at home."

When the tired family arrived at their Nottingham Drive home that night, they were greeted with vases full of blossoms in every room. The whole house was filled with their fragrance. It was a welcome-home gift from Clara Kinney.

W.L. traveled to Miami the next week where Dr. Ferguson operated on his knee. After a short time in therapy, his knee significantly improved. When he returned home on April 30, he was still walking with a cane, but was confident of a full recovery. He didn't, however, plan to do anything strenuous for at least six weeks.

W.L. wasn't the only Stribling who visited a doctor that April. Clara's physician confirmed what she had already suspected. There was a reason the pills she was given on the ship didn't help her nausea. She wasn't seasick, she was pregnant!

The Striblings were thrilled at the news. They celebrated that summer by planning for their third child and spending as much time together as possible in Macon and at the farm.

They played miniature golf, and W.L. spent many afternoons with his children in nearby Baconsfield Park. He was a great favorite with the neighborhood children, not because he was a famous boxer, but because he was always willing to play games with them just like another kid.

And as he recovered, he also played a lot of golf. He particularly wanted to excel in golf, just as he had in other sports. So determined was he to do so that the year before he had gone to George Norrie, golf professional at Idle Hour Country Club, for instruction. He had started out scoring around 100 on 18 holes, but within a month he had dropped into the high 80s. Now he regularly averaged 80 and he confided to Norrie that, after boxing, he hoped to become a professional golfer. Norrie had watched the determination with which Stribling had tackled the game and had no doubt he could do it.

But his relaxing summer came to an end in late July. W.L. and his father decided it was time to try out his knee. While rope skipping and sparring gave them some idea of how his knee was recovering, the way it held up in a real match was what would determine Stribling's future in the ring.

Willie scheduled a fight for him in West Virginia on August 2. No opponent was named at first and it really didn't matter whom he faced. The test wasn't whether he could defeat another man, it was whether his injured knee could ever perform again.

Sportswriters called the coming match in West Virginia a warm-up fight or the first step on W.L.'s comeback trail. The opponent was finally named. He would be facing George Neron in Beckley, West Virginia. The two men weren't strangers. They had fought the year before when Stribling had defeated him in Australia.

W.L. didn't expect any real trouble from Neron, but his knee was another matter.

"It hasn't bothered me at all for several weeks now," he said the night before he and Pa left Macon, "but I'm not sure yet how it's going to stand up."

His knee, encased in a stiff brace, held up just fine. In his first fight on U.S. soil in over a year, W.L. took a 10-round decision and returned home feeling more optimistic about his future than he had in months.

Pa was so pleased that he immediately started looking around for more matches and arranged for W.L. to fight Benny Odell in Rome, Georgia. Odell wasn't a pushover by any means. A veteran of over 100 fights, he held the New York state heavyweight title.

W.L. buckled down to real training, and when he entered the ring in Rome on August 29, spectators could easily have believed they were watching the old W.L. Even with the brace that now covered his right knee, he danced around the ring, moving in and out on Odell and hitting him at will. The New Yorker was punched down to the canvas five times before he finally took the full count in the second round.

Stribling seemed to be well on the way to another comeback. It was a long way to a title match, but Pa believed that his son could get there. He had done it before.

W.L. had hardly arrived home before Pa announced his next fight. And this was an important one. He had signed W.L. to fight Maxie Rosenbloom, the world's light heavyweight champion, in Houston, Texas, on September 22.

W.L. was pleased to be matched against such a strong opponent, but he had another concern at the time. The baby was due the end of September, and he wanted to be with Clara for the birth. However, she assured him she would be fine whether he was there or not.

"Do what you need to do," she told him. "Don't worry about me."

So a week before the fight Pa and W.L. drove to Houston, and as is so often the way in such things, the baby arrived soon after they left Macon. On Wednesday, September 20, Clara gave birth to their second son. As they had already decided, the boy was named Guerry Boone, honoring both Clara's beloved grandfather and W.L.'s closest friend.

While he wanted nothing more than to be at home with his wife and new son, W.L. knew he couldn't leave Houston. The fight was only two days away, and traveling to Macon and back would be exhausting. He had to stay as fit as possible for the match. So he tried to be content with long-distance calls to his wife, knowing he would see her and the new baby soon enough.

Twelve thousand people saw the Stribling–Rosenbloom match in Sam Houston Hall on September 22. It wasn't a title match, being scheduled for only ten rounds, but it was still an important fight for Stribling. He started strong and never wavered. His performance was decisive enough to win the decision over Rosenbloom.

33

Pa's reaction to the win over Rosenbloom was to turn his sites on New York. He believed it was time for another shot at Madison Square Garden. But W.L. was interested in only one thing—getting home. He drove all the next day and half the night to arrive in Macon early Sunday morning.

A few hours later he showed up at Macon Hospital with flowers and presents. Then he crawled up onto the bed with his wife and held her close. The moment he set eyes on the new baby, he fell in love with him, just as he had with the two older children.

W.L. was so excited about the new baby and being back home with his family that he couldn't seem to decide where to spend his time. He whizzed between home and the hospital on his motorcycle, playing with Tee and Virginia, then rushing downtown for a few happy hours with Clara and the baby.

The local press was clamoring for a picture of Guerry Boone, calling the Stribling house several times a day with the request. On Friday, September 29, W.L. finally relented.

A reporter and a photographer joined the family at Macon Hospital. The nurses had waived their rules and allowed Tee and Virginia into the room. They played quietly on the floor beside their mother's chair while their father paced. When the baby was brought in, the nurse handed him to W.L., and moments later he was photographed holding Guerry Boone and gazing down at him with absolute adoration.

The photo of them appeared in the paper's Sunday morning edition, but it was doubtful W.L. even saw it. It was a perfect day for golf, and he had time for a round before visiting hours at the hospital.

In Middle Georgia the first day of October didn't mean autumn. The days were still hot, but there was a taste of the cool, dry weather to come in the morning air. The summer haze had cleared, leaving behind brilliant blue skies. W.L. climbed on his motorcycle and rode to Idle Hour Country Club where he met several friends and played 18 holes of golf, finishing just before noon.

His partners invited him to join them for lunch, but he declined. He was going to see Clara and the baby at the hospital and wanted to pick up some flowers on the way.

But he did take a minute to buy and drink a Coke at Tyson's Grocery across the street from Idle Hour. A few blocks away he stopped again when he saw Roland Scott and Jack Kinney hitchhiking. He pulled over and talked with the two teenagers a few minutes, then flagged down a car for them. Then he was back on his motorcycle and on his way.

Traffic was moderately heavy with cars full of homeward-bound churchgoers. W.L. was driving slowly, about 35 miles an hour, just relaxing and enjoying the beautiful day. As he headed south on Forsyth Road, his good friend Roy Barrow was driving the opposite direction with his fiancée Frances Jones.

"There's Strib!" she said when she spotted the motorcycle coming toward them. She leaned forward to wave to him at the same moment Barrow noticed a car up ahead waiting to turn left. He slowed and put his arm out the window, hand down, signaling a stop.

In the car behind him R. V. Johnson chose that moment to pass. He swung around Barrow's car directly into Stribling's path.

Neither had time to avoid the collision. Johnson's bumper slammed into Stribling, crushing his left side and throwing him into the air. The bike went one way and W.L. went another. He landed on the roadside, his head only a few feet from the pavement.

"My Lord!" Barrow shouted. "Strib's hit!"

He slammed on his brakes and stopped the car in the middle of the road, then flung open his door and ran back to where W.L. lay. Frances was right behind him. They were confronted by an unbelievably gruesome sight. W.L. was severely injured. He was bleeding from numerous cuts and scrapes, but the worst was his left leg. His foot had been nearly severed from his leg and was attached by only a strip of skin.

The sound of the crash brought people out of the Buck Ice and Coal Company, just south of the accident site, and cars were stopping up and down the street. People ran to the scene, forming an awkward circle around the injured man. Some gasped in horror; others started talking among themselves.

Frances Jones was a nurse, and it was she who took control of the situation. "Phone for an ambulance!" she shouted. "And everybody calm down. You can't help him by talking."

Barrow dropped to his knees beside his friend and took his head in his lap, gently wiping the blood and dirt from his face.

W.L. looked up at him. "If I had wished for anybody to be here now, Wheel," he said, using his nickname for Barrow, "I wouldn't have wished for anybody better than you."

Jones was quickly assessing his injuries. Blood poured from his leg, and she removed her cape and wrapped it around the stump as a makeshift tourniquet. It slowed the flood a bit, but not nearly enough.

"Can anyone get me a real tourniquet?"

J. P. Williams, a Buck employee, hurried off to retrieve one from the company's first aid box.

W.L. took a deep, shaky breath. "Wheel, am I going to die?"

"Of course not," Barrow told him with more confidence than he felt. "You've got too much nerve to die. Besides you've too much to live for."

His friend gave a weak smile. "Yes, I've got the sweetest wife and the sweetest kids in the world." His mouth was bleeding, and he ran his tongue around inside it. "My bridge got knocked out. Can somebody find it?"

They assured him they would as Williams returned with the tourniquet. He and a couple of others helped Jones get it into place and tighten it to the point that the bleeding stopped.

After several minutes in which the ambulance still had not arrived, Barrow couldn't bear to wait any longer. He flagged down a milk delivery truck, then he and several other men carefully lifted Stribling into the truck.

"Don't forget my foot," W.L. told them. "And Wheel, if I die on the way in, tell my folks that I died fighting to live."

His injuries were horribly painful. His fists were clenched so tightly that the muscles in his arms were taut and pronounced, but W.L. never cried out. Instead he tried to keep things light.

After struggling to get a look at his left leg and the barely attached foot, he told Barrow, "Well, kid, I guess this means no more roadwork."

They reached Stanislaus Circle at the same time as the approaching ambulance. One of the men got out and waved it down, and W.L. was quickly transferred to the faster vehicle. Barrow climbed in after him.

"And to think I was just riding along casually," W.L. managed to say a moment later. "Any other time, I would have been going at a breakneck speed and nothing would have happened."

News of the accident spread quickly. Within minutes someone called WMAZ radio and word of Stribling's accident was announced as a bulletin. Foy Boone had heard it and was already walking into the emergency room when the ambulance arrived at Macon Hospital.

As they wheeled him past on a stretcher, Boone could see that his friend's injuries were serious. Stribling understood that as well.

He spoke calmly to the doctors who rushed to attend him. "The first thing I want you to do when you take me to the operating room is to examine my pelvis. It's in bad shape."

They rushed W.L. away, and Boone staggered out of the emergency room, shocked at what he had seen. He was so overcome with grief and fear that he collapsed on the sidewalk outside.

Up on the third floor of the same hospital Clara was feeding her new baby. W.L. was a bit late, but not so much that she worried about him. However, when Dr. A. P. Kemp came in the room, his face grim, she knew something was wrong. As gently as possible, he told her that W.L. had been in an accident.

"I want to see him!"

"Not now. He's in surgery. But you can see him as soon as he's out of recovery."

Clara's parents had already heard the news and rushed to the hospital where they joined her for a long, frightening day of waiting. Roy Barrow, Foy and Merle Boone, Mary Jim Oliver, and other friends kept a vigil there as well.

All day long Macon Hospital was flooded with telephone calls from people wanting to know Stribling's condition. Scores of people walked in off the street, many offering to donate blood if it was needed.

Surgeon A. R. Rozar, assisted by Dr. Kemp, performed the surgery on W.L. They amputated his left foot and stitched his torn upper lip. As he had feared, W.L.'s pelvis was severely fractured, but he wasn't stable enough at that time to survive the extensive surgery such an injury required. Instead the doctors took X-rays to determine the scope of the damage and called in Dr. O. H. Weaver as a consultant about future surgery.

While W.L. was being rushed into the operating room, R. V. Johnson was still at the accident scene talking to the police. His wife and seven-year-old son stood nearby, both in tears. While the crowd had diminished somewhat, a lot of people continued to mill around.

"We were on our way to Newnan," Johnson told the officer in a breathless voice, "to visit relatives. We approached a group of cars. . . near the Buck Ice and Coal Company." He gestured toward the business with his head. "I braked my car because the driver of the car right in front was holding his hand out—I thought he meant to stop."

Johnson, a twenty-eight-year-old bond salesman for the Franklin Loan Bank, was still visibly upset. He was breathing hard, and his hands were shaking.

"How fast were you going?"

"About 15 or 20 miles an hour, that's all. I was driving as close to the right side of the pavement as I could—I always do. Looking around the other car, the road seemed clear. Stribling must have been near the center of the road ... because it seemed clear. So I turned to the left to pass the car in front.

"I saw Stribling first about ten yards away. . . .Everything happened so quick. . . . I hardly know what happened. The front bumper seemed to hit him."

W.L.'s motorcycle still lay twisted and broken on the side of the road. From time to time a passerby would stop and strip off a piece or two as a souvenir.

J. P. Williams watched this activity for a while and finally decided he had to do something. He retrieved the motorcycle and half-wheeled and half-dragged it into the Buck Ice and Coal building for safekeeping.

Later that day, Sheriff J. R. Hicks announced that his investigation indicated that the accident was unavoidable. No charges would be filed against Johnson. "It was simply one of those things that will happen. Nobody can be blamed."

Stribling's friends were outraged, but the decision had been made.

It was six in the afternoon before W.L. regained consciousness, and he immediately asked about his wife.

"She's fine. She wants to see you," the nurse told him.

"Well, I surely do want to see her."

They rolled Clara into the room in a wheelchair. She had already been told his foot had been amputated, but she wasn't prepared to see her strong, young husband lying there, pale, hurt, and barely conscious. She took his hand and told him she was there.

His eyes fluttered open. "Hello, baby."

She tried to assure him that he was going to recover, but his major concern was that she and his parents might scold him for taking chances as they had in the past. "I'm sorry, honey. I was careful. It wasn't my fault."

"I know," she said. "It's all right."

He gave her a smile, but still wanted to explain what happened. "I was on my way to the hospital, on the right side. All of a sudden a car loomed up. I cut as far to the right as possible, but it happened. The car hit me."

The nurses interrupted then, saying her husband needed rest. They promised she could see him again later that night.

Devastated and feeling helpless, Clara returned to her room where her parents waited to try and comfort her. W.L. was put into a room on the floor below Clara's, and at nine that night she was allowed another short visit with him.

Afterward she spoke with his doctors. He was in very serious condition, they told her, but had a good chance of recovering. They released the same statement to the press an hour later.

The rest of the Stribling family was out of town that day. Friends frantically tried to contact them and first reached Herbert in Greensboro, North Carolina, where he was arranging a boxing match. He got to Macon as quickly as he could and entered his brother's hospital room just after 8:00 that night. Herbert must have looked horrified when he first saw W.L. After a few minutes his older brother tried to reassure him.

"It's all right, kid," he said. "Come back in the morning."

Herbert's wife Edith had been visiting family in Kentucky. She joined him at the hospital about midnight. And Monroe Braswell and Cuy Harrell arrived soon after that from South Georgia.

But no one had been able to get in touch with Pa and Ma. All their family knew was that they were driving home from Texas. Late Sunday night they were on an unpaved stretch of road between Birmingham and Atlanta. The radio was on, but the bouncing and rattling of the car made it hard to hear. They did, however, recognize one phrase when they heard it: "W. L. (Young) Stribling, the heavyweight fighter of Macon, Georgia." They couldn't make out anything else, but knew something must have happened.

The next town they came to was the small community of Heflin, where Pa found a phone and soon learned the devastating news. Shaken, he climbed back into the car and headed for Macon. When they finally arrived at the hospital about 2:30 a.m., they went straight to W.L.'s room.

He lay in the bed, pale and so weak that talking was a huge effort for him. His parents tried to assure him he would be fine, but they couldn't convince themselves of that. Ma was barely able to stand when she came out into the hallway a few minutes later. "My boy doesn't have a chance," she said, tears streaming down her face.

All day Monday, telephone and telegraph offices were overwhelmed with requests for updates and calls and wires of support and sympathy. The vigil at Macon Hospital went on.

For a while W.L. appeared to rally, but as morning became afternoon his temperature began to rise. Doctors administered morphine to help him sleep, but he seemed to struggle against its effects, as if staying awake was the best way he could fight his injuries. His doctors repeatedly told him that sleep would help him gain strength, but even when he tried he was not able to drift off.

Clara's parents stayed with her, trying to keep her spirits up. Because she was recuperating herself, her doctor permitted her only two short visits with W.L. during the day.

She was sitting by his bed, holding his hand that afternoon when he told her, "This is really stormy weather, honey."

W.L.'s parents rarely left his bedside. Although Pa managed a quick nap in the early morning hours, Ma neither slept nor ate. And neither stopped encouraging their boy.

"Listen, son," Pa said at one point, "we're in the tenth round now, and we've got to fight. I'm your manager, and you've got to do what I say. And I say 'Fight!'"

W.L. smiled up at him and nodded.

But when Pa left the room, his confident smile disappeared. Friends asked what they could do, but he just shook his head.

"What we need is someone to perform a miracle," he told them. "It will take that."

That afternoon, W.L. began asking if he was going to die.

"Ma, how am I getting along?"

She hesitated, then said, "Well, son, you're a good patient. You're doing everything the doctors tell you."

"But how do they say I'm getting on?"

"Fair," she finally said.

"Well, come here and kiss me then."

She leaned over the bed and kissed him, then went outside the room, face white, tears brimming.

Late Monday afternoon, the doctors admitted to the family that W.L.'s condition was worsening. His temperature was 104°, and his pulse rate had jumped to 150.

Dr. Kemp went into his room during this period, and W.L. asked him a direct question.

"Doc, am I going to die?"

"Of course not," Kemp reassured him. "We're not going to let this thing lick us."

"Oh, I'm not afraid," W.L. said, "I just want to know what's going to happen and whether or not I'm going to die. I'm leaving it up to you."

Just before 7:00 that evening, the three doctors met to consider the situation. Stribling was suffering from shock. His foot had been amputated, but they still hadn't been able to treat the compound fracture of his left hip. Even more disturbing was the extreme rigidity of his stomach that indicated internal bleeding. The situation was grim. None of them expected their patient to recover.

Late in the afternoon Dr. Kemp had told Clara he didn't want her to visit W.L. again that evening. He thought another trip to her husband's bedside would be too stressful for her. She agreed, but made him promise to send for her if his condition worsened.

When a nurse came to her room at midnight to wheel her down to W.L.'s room, she knew hope was just about gone.

Pa, Ma, and Herbert were already at his bedside. The nurse positioned her chair close to the bed, and Clara took her husband's hand in both of hers. W.L. looked up and gave her one last smile.

"Hello, baby," he said, then slipped into unconsciousness.

Clara's parents, her brother Fred, and Edith Stribling were brought into the room then, and the sad little group stayed there the rest of the night. There was almost no talking. Each person thought his own thoughts and prayed his own prayers.

As the sky outside the window lightened with dawn, W. L. Stribling took his last breath and was gone.

After a moment, Clara's mother pushed her wheelchair out of the room. Pale and shocked, Clara tried to smile at the friends who had gathered in the hallway, but could not. They crowded around her, taking her hands and telling how sorry they were, but the words were just meaningless babble.

Herbert and Edith left as well, but Pa and Ma stayed in the room. They needed just a few more minutes with their son, the golden boy they had loved so dearly.

34

It was hard for people in Macon to comprehend that W. L. Stribling had died. They had followed his fortunes, his ups and downs, for years. They had been with him through his triumphs, and when he had been down, they had stood by him as he gathered his considerable strength to start over. It was difficult to grasp the fact that this time there would be no comeback.

Telegrams poured in from all over the world. Max Baer and Johnny Weissmuller sent condolences from California. Edward Foster, president of the National Boxing Association, and Dr. C. B. Ferguson from Miami sent telegrams of sympathy.

Jack Dempsey wrote, "Accept my heartfelt sympathy in your hours of sorrow." And Max Schmeling cabled from Germany, "I am heartbroken. All my sympathy is with you."

Senators, congressmen, and governors joined actors, prizefighters, and thousands of everyday people in expressing condolences to the family while sportswriters all over the country devoted columns to Stribling's life and death.

Before daylight Wednesday morning, people began lining up on the steps of Macon's Municipal Auditorium, waiting for the doors to open. W. L. Stribling's body lay in state all day. Members of the National Guard stood at each end of the bier, honoring one of their own. And in that large arena where he had fought and played so many times, thousands of people filed past his open casket.

The doors were closed only once that day—when the family came. Clara, brought in from Macon Hospital, joined her two oldest children and W.L.'s parents and brother. She spent several minutes talking quietly with Tee and Virginia, then walked to the casket and stood looking down at the husband she had adored. The whole family was in tears when they left the building.

Then the doors reopened, and the crowd resumed its slow progress past the casket. It was a silent procession and one filled with great respect and sorrow. When the doors were closed again at 6:00 p.m., 15,000 people had taken the solemn walk to say good-bye to the city's friend and most famous athlete.

All city playgrounds were closed from 4:00 to 5:00 Thursday afternoon to honor the man who had been such a glowing example of sportsmanship and athletic excellence. At the same hour a public funeral was held for W. L. Stribling in the auditorium. It was the largest ever seen in Macon. Thousands of people filled the arena, and thousands more stood solemnly on the terraces surrounding the building.

Macon was not just saying good-bye to a famous citizen, they were bidding farewell to one of their own. W.L. was a friend and neighbor. He was a golden boy who had grown up in their midst to become a fine man they counted among their friends and acquaintances. He had not been a remote celebrity. He was someone to whom, when they saw him on the street they could call out, "Hello, Strib!" and often as not he would respond, using their names.

The capacity crowd in the auditorium stood as the family entered the building and were taken to the section cordoned off for them. Clara and Ma were pale, but dry-eyed, keeping themselves in tight control, but Herbert couldn't hold back his tears. Tee and Virginia sat still, silently watching their mother and grandparents with large, frightened eyes. The Kinneys, relatives from South Georgia, and several close friends completed the family group.

It was a simple service, marked by old familiar hymns, and Dr. James E. Sammons presented the eulogy. Dr. William Mackay offered a prayer, but had to pause at one point as the drone of several airplanes filled the air, announcing that W.L.'s flying companions had come by to pay their respects.

When the ceremony ended, the attendants began slowly moving the casket up the center aisle. As it passed Pa and Ma, they both broke into sobs, and Ma reached forward with both arms to embrace the casket.

The funeral cortege comprised a hearse and five automobiles that slowly wound through the crowded downtown streets. Other vehicles pulled over to let it pass, and hundreds of people lined the sidewalks, watching in silent respect.

W.L. was laid to rest on the highest point in Riverside Cemetery, overlooking the Ocmulgee River. Hundreds of people left their cars along Riverside Drive and climbed the rocky paths in the hundred-year-old cemetery, but police officers kept them from coming too close to the family.

The area around the gravesite was covered with wreaths and floral arrangements, so many that they had to be piled on top of each other. The Macon Drum and Bugle Corps arrived to the beat of muffled drums, and the Floyd Rifles Company lined up some distance away. After the pallbearers had placed the casket over the grave, Dr. Sammons spoke briefly and Dr. Mackay gave one more prayer.

At a command from Captain D. C. Harris the seven riflemen each fired three times, the staccato salute startlingly loud in the quiet of the hilltop. Then a bugler played "Taps," and each slow note was softly echoed by a second bugler standing out of sight down by the river. Finally three airplanes appeared in the brilliant blue sky. Twice they swooped down over the group standing by the grave, then they wheeled across the sky and flew out of sight.

As the roar of the engines faded, Captain Harris turned to the huge crowd that had gathered on the hillside and asked that they now leave so that the family could be alone. While some did go, more people kept coming.

A few ventured close enough to the gravesite to try and take a flower for a souvenir. Police and National Guardsmen rushed forward to stop them, but the family intervened and told them to let the flowers go.

So the beautiful floral tributes were given to the crowd to be torn apart as mementos of the occasion. Later that evening souvenir seekers even combed the hillside to find the ejected shells from the rifle salute.

Clara and her children returned to the waiting cars, but Pa and Ma remained at the grave, still standing there as the sun receded and finally dipped below the western horizon.

When W.L. fought his last match in Houston, he would been attended by Dr. Milton L. Brenner. Worried that a cut he had sustained over his eye in training would reopen during the fight, W.L. had asked Brenner to be at ringside that night.

Sure enough, a blow from Rosenbloom started the cut bleeding again in the second round. As soon as the bell rang, Brenner hurried to W.L.'s corner and closed the wound so efficiently that it gave Stribling no trouble through the rest of the fight.

After winning the match, W.L. had been surrounded by fans. Several of them clamored for the gloves he had worn, but he just shook his head. When they were cut off his hands, he presented them to the doctor.

"These gloves go to Doc Brenner and no one else," W.L. said with a smile.

The day after the funeral, Brenner sent the gloves to Macon. He believed that his widow and children should have the last gloves Young Stribling ever wore.

A few weeks later, a smooth granite stone was erected at the Stribling gravesite. Clara had requested that a Robert Browning quote be engraved on it:

"Earth changes, but thy soul and God stand sure."

35

R. V. Johnson was exonerated of any responsibility for W. L. Stribling's death by a coroner's jury, but he had been deeply shaken by the accident. The hostility he and his family felt from the community was disturbing. Neither he nor his wife ventured out in public unless it was absolutely necessary.

He was reluctant to get behind the wheel of any car again, but there were occasions when it was necessary. On the morning of October 11, less than two weeks after the Stribling accident, Johnson was driving down one of the many alleys that crisscrossed the blocks in downtown Macon. At the intersection of two of these alleys, he struck a car driven by Collier Sargent, slightly injuring Sargent's passenger.

Johnson was charged with responsibility for the accident, but rather than pay his ticket, two weeks later he went to trial in Recorder's Court. The decision to do so was probably more the result of wanting to have his say about the Stribling accident than to avoid paying a fine for failing to yield the right of way.

When he took the stand in his defense, he declared he had been so traumatized by the accident in which W. L. Stribling was killed that he hated to drive an automobile at all. In fact, he said, he had now decided never to drive again.

As for the current charges, he swore he had been traveling at a very low speed down the alley and that the accident had been unavoidable because the wall of a building blocked the Sargent car from his view until the moment it entered the alley. But after all the testimony had been heard, Judge Felton Hatcher found Johnson guilty and fined him $25.75.

W. L. Stribling's death was like most terrible events. Those involved were shocked and grieved, but then life intruded and they had to find a way to move on. Clara Stribling started slowly putting her life back together with the help of her family and friends. She concentrated all her attention on the children. She knew it was now up to her alone to provide them with a stable, happy life.

Her family and friends were at her side, ready to help, as was a young Episcopalian minister named Randolph Claiborne. He was always there to listen to her fears and doubts and did not condemn her for the anger she felt at the awful turn her life had taken. In the years after her husband's death, Claiborne would become one of her most steadfast friends.

Herbert Stribling was reexamining his path in life. Three months after his brother's death, he fought his last professional match, defeating Wildcat Monte in Miami. The fight had been scheduled for months and Herbert kept his commitment. But after that he was through.

Although he refereed matches from time to time, he never boxed professionally again. Quitting just two months before his 28th birthday, he finished his boxing career with a record of which he could be proud. He had fought in 89 matches, winning 57 and losing 14, with 18 draws.

The elder Striblings carried on, pouring their energies into their various businesses. They spent most of the year after W.L.'s death in Ochlocknee, but traveled frequently to Miami and Atlanta.

W.L.'s hometown did not forget him. On February 9, only four months after his death, the Stribling Memorial Foundation was formed. The two main sponsors were the Junior Chamber of Commerce and the Macon YMCA, but nearly every civic club in the city was involved. Their goal was to raise money to erect a life-sized memorial to the late fighter that would stand in front of the YMCA and to create a Stribling Room inside the building in which photos and memorabilia of his career would be displayed.

Their first fund-raising effort was an all-star boxing benefit on March 5. They sent invitations to the prominent fighters of the day, and the first man to accept was Primo Carnera, who had recently won the world heavyweight champion title.

When reporters asked Carnera why he was so quick to accept an invitation to travel to Georgia, he said, "Primo no forget his friends." He had always maintained that his two fights with Stribling were what first brought him international attention.

Maxie Rosenbloom, the light heavyweight champ and W.L.'s last opponent, also agreed to come. Previous commitments prevented Max Baer and Jack Dempsey from appearing at the benefit, but Johnny Risko sent word he would be there. Advance sales were good, and NBC radio planned to broadcast the program.

Carnera arrived the day of the benefit. The huge man attracted attention everywhere he went, but he managed to slip away that afternoon to visit W.L.'s grave. He laid a large wreath there, adorned with a banner that read: "In memory of my dearest friend—Primo Carnera."

Nearly 4,000 people jammed the auditorium for the boxing benefit that night. There was a brief memorial service, then the action began. Carnera was the first man into the ring.

The champion displayed his prowess in four exhibition rounds with a variety of sparring partners. He was followed by Maxie Rosenbloom and Johnny Risko, who squared off in an exhibition bout.

The benefit was a success, but the Foundation soon learned that commissioning a statue such as they wanted was not a cheap proposition. At the request of the Foundation, local sculptor Marshall Daugherty had fashioned a four-foot model of Stribling in clay. It was a beautiful piece, reminiscent of statues of the Greek and Roman gods, and photographs of it were printed in the local papers.

The Foundation met with Daugherty soon afterward. But when they heard his plans for the monument and what it would cost, they realized that the project would have to be put on hold until more money was raised. But as the years passed, they were never able to have the statue completed.

The sculptor kept the model in his Mercer University office for years. Then Macon businessman Bill McCowen approached him with an offer. He purchased the head and had it bronzed, and the resulting bust of W. L. Stribling was given a place of honor in his home. The body of the model was eventually discarded.

But the Foundation did go ahead with part of their project. By April 6, 1934, work had begun transforming a space at the YMCA into the

Stribling Room. The family donated numerous photos and mementoes to the project, and several sporting goods manufacturers donated equipment. When the room was dedicated in early September it functioned as both a memorial to Stribling and an auxiliary gymnasium.

Gradually the accolades stopped, and the public's attention was caught by other people and other things. In the boxing world more distractions came and went. Carnera lost to Max Baer. Baer, in turn, surrendered the title to Jimmy Braddock. And on the horizon was Joe Louis.

Pa and Ma invested in the lumber business in South Carolina. Herbert went to work for them, and the three lived there for a while, but in 1936 they moved to Hattiesburg, Mississippi.

The house on Nottingham Drive that Clara and W.L. had so lovingly renovated, that was the heart of their young family, was now more a repository for memories of another happier time than a home. Clara's parents and grandmother had moved from Cherokee Avenue to 600 Napier Avenue, and it came as no surprise to anyone when Clara and the children moved in with them.

But W.L.'s memory was still occasionally honored in Macon. In June 1935 the new Stribling Bridge over the Ocmulgee River was dedicated to him. A bronze plaque on the end pillar of the bridge read: "In Memory of W.L. 'Young' Stribling, Jr." Along with his birth and death dates was the inscription: "To live in the hearts of men is not to die in vain."

And in January 1938 the final matches of the Middle Georgia Golden Gloves Tournament were dedicated to Stribling. Pa, Ma and Herbert all came back to Macon for the event and one newspaper referred to their meeting with Clara and the children as a happy family reunion.

Unfortunately that description was inaccurate. Relations had been strained between Clara and her in-laws for some time. W.L. had always told her not to worry, that his parents would take care of her if anything happened to him, but she no longer believed that.

W.L.'s will had left his entire estate to Clara and the children, but many of his interests had been in his father's name and still were. Clara had never been given the details of her husband's partnership with Pa.

She knew that real estate had been purchased and sold and investments made, but she had no knowledge of the details. She had repeatedly asked for an accounting of the assets Pa had acquired with W.L., but so far had not received it. Now she found herself with three children to raise, struggling to make ends meet.

Ma and Pa attended the boxing matches on January 25 with eleven-year-old Tee. Herbert was there, serving as referee for one of the matches, but Clara and the two younger children were absent.

She told reporters she was staying home that night because Guerry Boone was ill, but none of the children were sick. Clara simply did not want to be anywhere near her former in-laws. That morning her attorney had filed an action in Bibb County Superior Court, and just before the elder Striblings were introduced from the ring, they were served with copies of that lawsuit.

In her petition to the court, Clara alleged that her husband had "earned several hundred thousand dollars" and that a portion of the money had been invested for him by his father in some form of partnership. Her father-in-law, she stated, had never accounted for the money in spite of her many requests. After the suit was filed, the judge issued a temporary order restraining Pa and Ma from disposing of any of the real estate, bills, or accounts pending an accounting.

The elder Striblings were furious, but they masked their anger until they were out of Macon that night. Once home in Mississippi, Pa issued a statement about the lawsuit. He had, he said, given Clara a very detailed accounting the previous year. He was sorry that family differences were being aired in public, but vowed that he and Ma would fully cooperate with the court.

Legal proceedings in 1938 didn't move any more quickly than their present-day counterparts do. It wasn't until August 7, 1941, that the two factions of the Stribling family finally reached a settlement and Judge Malcolm Jones issued a final decree in the case, laying out the specific division of the disputed property.

Clara was awarded the house and two vacant lots on Nottingham Drive; 148 acres of farmland, half interest in a 103-acre farm, and a two-and-a-half-acre lot in Ochlocknee; two lots in Miami; a lot on Sea Island; and seven shares of stock in the Bank of Ochlocknee.

Pa received the house in Miami; 980 acres of Thomas County farmland; 25 shares of stock in the Bank of Ochlocknee; and a $500 bond in the Beneficial Loan Society.

It is doubtful that either side was completely satisfied with the outcome, but at least the dispute was finally over.

36

W.L. Stribling's fame might have faded, but he was not forgotten. In 1965 he was inducted into the Georgia Sports Hall of Fame. A year later he received the same recognition from the International Boxing Hall of Fame in New York. And 1969 brought the publication of *King of the Canebrakes,* a Stribling biography written by former *Telegraph* sports editor Jimmy Jones.

Pa and Ma Stribling eventually settled in Miami where they reconnected with old friends and continued to manage their various real estate interests. Pa retired from business after having a stroke in 1945, but he was not idle. He and Ma were very involved with the First Christian Church in Miami and devoted much of their time to the ministries there.

On Valentine's Day of 1954 the two celebrated their 50th wedding anniversary by renewing their vows. Unlike their first wedding, this one was planned and took place before a crowd of nearly 400 friends and family members. Ma wore an elegant periwinkle blue lace dress, and Pa slipped a second wedding band—this one made of platinum—onto her finger.

The following year, Pa suffered a heart attack on October 13. He died two days later with his beloved wife by his side. He was 70 years old. After funeral services in the First Christian Church, he was buried in Miami.

But years later, Ma decided that their family should remain together forever. She had Pa's body moved to Riverside Cemetery in Macon, where he was reinterred beside W.L. And when she passed away a year later on May 3, 1959, she, too, was buried in the Stribling plot in Macon.

Herbert Stribling kept his resolve not to fight again, but he engaged in several other exciting careers during his lifetime. For a while he taught flying in Wichita, Kansas, and then served with the air force in World

War II, retiring with the rank of colonel. He even returned to the stage for a while as a magician and nightclub entertainer. But he always ended up back with his parents, working in their various businesses.

His first marriage to Edith Nolan ended in divorce. Some time after his parents' deaths, he married Alma Critchlaw and lived with her and her two sons, Robert and Gary, in Miami until his own death at the age of 59 on January 3, 1967. He was laid to rest with the rest of the family in Riverside Cemetery.

Clara and the children were frequent visitors to St. Simons Island in the years after W.L.'s death. It was a familiar place that held happy memories for them. By the time Guerry was ready to start school, the family was living there full-time. Clara involved herself in the community, but she also kept in touch with many old friends from Macon, including Randolph Claiborne. In later years he became a frequent visitor to the St. Simons house.

Her children were grown and living their own lives in 1955 when Clara decided she was ready to do the same. Randolph Claiborne proposed and she accepted. He had just been appointed bishop of the Atlanta Diocese when they married.

They honeymooned in New York and were welcomed back to Atlanta with a reception at St. Phillip's Cathedral. The couple settled into the large manse in Ansley Park, and another chapter in Clara's life began. For many years she was happy as the bishop's wife, immersed in the myriad details and duties that were involved.

Randolph's health began to fail in the early '70s, and in 1975 he retired. He and Clara moved to Dunwoody, Georgia, where they purchased a house overlooking a lake on Waterton Court. They traveled when they could, tended the garden together, saw family frequently and kept in touch with their old parishioners. It was the retirement they always hoped to have.

Twelve years later Claiborne passed away, and Clara was a widow for a second time. She left the house in Dunwoody and moved into an apartment at Canterbury Court, a nonprofit, high-rise senior living facility in the heart of the Buckhead district of Atlanta. She passed away in 1996 after suffering a series of strokes.

W.L. and Clara's children inherited many of their parents' character-istics. Each was successful, determined, athletically inclined, and focused on family.

Tee joined the navy right after his 17th birthday in 1944. After he was discharged, he attended the University of Georgia and graduated from Georgia State. He and his wife, Anne Willingham Stribling, had a daughter and three sons. For many years Tee worked for the Georgia Marble Company and, after that concern merged with them, the Jim Walter Corporation in Tampa. He died on October 8, 1977, at the age of 50.

Virginia attended the University of Georgia, where she was a member of the water ballet swim team. A gifted athlete and avid sports fan, she played championship-level tennis and golf. She was married to David Blackshear for 54 years. Together they had a daughter and a son. Virginia died at 76 on February 15, 2005.

Guerry, the youngest of the Stribling children, was a Georgia Tech graduate. He was a successful real estate developer and built neighborhoods and resorts in the United States and the Caribbean. Like his father, he loved flying. He also played polo and golf. He and his wife Sandra Thompson Stribling had two sons and two daughters. He was 75 years old when he passed away on May 8, 2009.

W. L. "Young" Stribling was called by some "the greatest champion that never was." Exactly why the championship eluded him isn't clear. Perhaps, as Jack Dempsey and Jim Corbett both said, he lacked the killer instinct, preferring to score points rather than inflict pain. Or maybe it was just bad luck.

But looking back, the title he *never* held is unimportant. W. L. Stribling's legacy can be seen in his children, grandchildren, and great-grandchildren, and in the memories of those who knew and loved him. He might never have achieved the lasting fame that belonged to some others, particularly those who wore the championship belts, but it was never about fame and recognition for W.L. The important things for him were sportsmanship, honor, and doing his best. He never did less.

W. L. "Young" Stribling
Boxing Record

287 Fights - 224 Wins - 12 Losses - 14 Draws - 36 No-decisions - 2 No Contests – 125 Knockouts.

1921

Date	Opponent	Location	Result
Jan 17	Kid Domb	Atlanta	W
Feb 9	Kid Nappie	Atlanta	W
Feb 15	Tim O'Dowd	Atlanta	W - KO
Feb 18	Kid Sullivan	Atlanta	W - KO
Mar 23	Benny Harvey	Milledgeville	W
Mar 30	Dick Leonard	Savannah	L
Apr 5	Battling Mishound	Atlanta	W
May 5	Lou Gomez	Macon	W - KO
May 26	Dick Leonard	Macon	W
Jun 7	Dick Leonard	Atlanta	W
Jun 13	Duette Allred	Birmingham	W - KO
Jun 23	Jim Waites	Macon	W - KO
Jul 4	Kid Bartlett	Macon	W - KO
Jul 12	Kid Cy Young	Atlanta	W - KO
Aug 4	Kid Peck	Macon	W
Aug 15	Freddie Boorde	Atlanta	W
Sep 5	Fearless Ferns	Macon	D
Sep 29	Red Keenan	Columbus, GA	W - KO
Oct 10	Rabbit Palmer	Macon	W
Oct 25	Joe Matranga	Atlanta	W
Nov 9	Freddie Boorde	Macon	D
Nov 29	Dick Leonard	Savannah	W
Dec 5	Fearless Ferns	Atlanta	W
Dec 19	Freddie Boorde	Macon	W

Dec 26	Battling Budd	Atlanta	D

1922

Jan 16	Jack Bradley	Columbia, SC	W - KO
Jan 23	Freddie Boorde	Birmingham	D
Feb 2	Battling Budd	Macon	W
Feb 13	Sailor Blanque	Birmingham	W
Mar 7	Larry Avera	Atlanta	D
Mar 13	Battling Kelly	Birmingham	W
Mar 23	Spike Maloney	Macon	W - KO
Mar 28	Battling Budd	Atlanta	L
Apr 6	Terry Nelson	Albany, GA	W
Apr 21	Battling Kelly	Nashville	W
Apr 25	Larry Avera	Atlanta	D
May 3	Battling Budd	Macon	D
May 19	Battling Budd	Albany, GA	D
May 24	Joe Marks	Macon	W
Jun 2	Larry Avera	Americus, GA	W
Jun 6	Johnny Flynn	Chattanooga	W
Jun 12	Battling Budd	Charlotte	ND
Jul 4	Jake Abel	Macon	W
Jul 27	Frankie Lewis	Macon	W - KO
Aug 4	Jimmy Conway	Savannah	W
Aug 9	Kid Suby	Columbus, GA	W
Aug 17	Bill Kennedy	Bainbridge, GA	W - KO
Sep 4	Red Herring	Macon	D
Sep 14	Eddie Hanlon	Americus, GA	W - KO
Sep 29	Red Johnston	Thomasville, GA	W - KO
Oct 4	Red Herring	Macon	W
Oct 14	Young Wallace	Havana	W - KO
Oct 20	Tiger Toro	Johnson City, TN	W
Nov 9	Jack Denham	Macon	W
Nov 18	Tony Marullo	Havana	W
Dec 1	Bill McGowan	Quitman, GA	W
Dec 7	Jimmy King	Macon	W
Dec 26	Frankie Lewis	Johnson City, TN	W
Dec 29	Jack Denham	Birmingham	W - KO

1923

Jan 1	Jack Middleton	Macon	W - KO
Jan 18	George Shade	Macon	W
Jan 26	Tony Marullo	New Orleans	W - KO
Jan 30	Harry Krohn	Atlanta	W
Feb 7	George Kuhn	Macon	W
Feb 27	Bill McGowan	Rome, GA	W
Mar 1	Johnny Klesch	Macon	W
Mar 9	Jackie Clark	Atlanta	D
Mar 20	Leo Leonard	Savannah	W
Mar 26	Kid Suby	Augusta, GA	W
Mar 29	George Kuhn	Columbus, GA	W - KO
Apr 19	Happy Howard	Macon	W
Apr 23	Red McLachlin	Miami	ND
May 4	Frank Carbone	Atlanta	L
May 17	Al Nelson	Atlanta	W - KO
Jun 4	Jimmy Darcy	Columbus, GA	W
Jun 14	Jack McCarron	Macon	W
Jun 18	Vic McLaughlin	Savannah	D
Jun 25	Happy Howard	Shreveport, LA	W
Sep 10	Sailor Martin	Miami	ND
Sep 19	Jimmy Conway	Rome, GA	W - KO
Oct 4	Mike McTigue	Columbus, GA	D
Oct 15	Tommy Burns	Detroit	ND
Oct 18	Steve Choynski	Macon	W - KO
Nov 26	Joe Eagan	Boston	W
Dec 15	Eddie McDonald	Johnson City, TN	W - KO
Dec 18	Bill McGowan	Knoxville, TN	ND
Dec 21	Harry Krohn	Miami	ND

1924

Jan 1	Dave Rosenberg	Newark, NJ	ND
Jan 3	Kid Numbers	Fayetteville, NC	W - KO
Jan 9	Mike Nester	Miami	W - KO
Jan 14	Norman Genet	West Palm Beach	W
Jan 21	Harry Fox	Indianapolis	ND
Jan 29	Billy Shade	Atlanta	W

Feb 4	Vic McLaughlin	Columbus, GA	W
Feb 11	Jack Schoendorf	Cincinnati	ND
Feb 15	Roughhouse Ross	Savannah	W - KO
Feb 25	Jimmy Slattery	Buffalo	L
Feb 28	Jack Perry	Raleigh, NC	W - KO
Mar 31	Mike McTigue	Newark	ND
Apr 11	Joe Quinn	Appleton, WI	W - KO
Apr 14	Tex McEwen	Philadelphia	W - KO
Apr 25	Walter Rollo	Norfolk, VA	W - KO
May 2	Tommy Burns	Toronto	W
May 9	Bill Conley	Youngstown, OH	ND
May 20	Dan O'Dowd	Atlanta	W
May 28	Ray Neuman	New Haven, CT	W
Jun 26	Tommy Loughran	New York	W
Aug 12	Leo Leonard	Charleston, SC	W - KO
Aug 18	Jack Stone	Johnson City, TN	W - KO
Aug 27	Paul Berlenbach	New York	D
Sep 1	Bob Fitzsimmons	Macon	W
Sep 5	Bill Clemens	Knoxville, TN	ND
Sep 9	Glen Clickner	Columbus, OH	W - KO
Sep 13	Mike Nestor	Portland, ME	W - KO
Sep 16	Tommy Robson	Boston	W
Sep 24	Ad Stone	Newark	ND
Sep 27	Vic McLaughlin	Raleigh, NC	ND
Sep 29	Jimmy Cox	Memphis, TN	ND
Nov 11	Fay Kaiser	Greenville, NC	W - KO
Nov 27	Harry Fay	Atlanta	W
Dec 12	Joe Lohman	Grand Rapids, MI	ND
Dec 15	Johnny Klesch	Dayton, OH	ND
1925			
Jan 12	Hugh Walker	Miami	ND
Jan 14	Mike Wallace	St. Petersburg, FL	ND
Jan 21	Jimmy Delaney	Grand Rapids, MI	ND
Feb 2	Joe Burke	Columbus, GA	W - KO
Feb 20	Ted Jamieson	Savannah	W - KO
Feb 27	Jimmy Delaney	Milwaukee	ND

Mar 3	Dan Dowd	Kalamazoo, MI	ND
Mar 9	Harry Fay	Pittsburgh	W
Mar 28	Tommy Loughran	San Francisco	W
Apr 7	Hugh Walker	Augusta, GA	W
May 7	Quintin Romero	Boston	W - KO
May 19	Hugh Walker	Kansas City	ND
May 25	Chief Metaquah	Hutchinson, KS	ND
Jun 5	Buck Brady	Greensboro, NC	W - KO
Jun 8	Bearcat Clemons	Baltimore	W - KO
Jun 15	George Cook	Boston	W
Jun 29	Bud Gorman	Detroit	ND
Jul 2	Johnny Risko	Chicago	ND
Jul 9	Billy Freas	Grand Rapids, MI	W - KO
Jul 17	Jack Matlock	Wichita, KS	W - KO
Jul 28	Harry Perkins	Colorado Springs, CO	W
Aug 4	Johnny Lee	Salt Lake City	W - KO
Aug 18	Jimmy Delaney	Los Angeles	W
Aug 22	Jack Lynch	Phoenix	W - KO
Aug 25	Red Fitzsimmons	El Paso, TX	W - KO
Aug 27	Jack League	San Antonio, TX	W - KO
Aug 31	Peck Warren	Dallas	W - KO
Oct 10	Sailor Huffman	Los Angeles	W
Oct 22	Tom McKiernan	Columbus, GA	W - KO
Nov 2	Soldier Buck	Memphis	W - KO
Nov 27	Billy Britton	New Orleans	W - KO
Dec 4	Tony Burns	Grand Rapids, MI	ND
1926			
Mar 25	Jimmy Slattery	New York	W
Apr 12	Chuck Burns	Wichita, KS	ND
Apr 13	Tommy Marvin	Oklahoma City	W - KO
Apr 26	Billy Britton	Topeka, KS	W - KO
Apr 30	Joe Lohman	Kansas City	W
May 14	Johnny Risko	New York	W
May 24	Ray Neuman	Atlanta	W
Jun 10	Paul Berlenbach	New York	L
Sep 17	Buck Ashton	Tampa	W - KO

Sep 21	Chuck Burns	Atlanta	W
Sep 29	Frankie Busch	Memphis	W - KO
Oct 15	Lou Rollinger	Waterloo, IA	W - KO
Oct 18	Soldier Buck	Louisville, KY	W - KO
Nov 11	Battling Levinsky	Des Moines, IA	ND
Nov 18	Ed Smith	Miami	W
Nov 26	Big Boy Peterson	Tampa	W - KO
Dec 20	Joe Lohman	Macon	W - KO

1927

Feb 7	Eddie Huffman	New York	W
Mar 3	Leo Gates	Atlanta	W - KO
Mar 10	Eddie Civel	Macon	W - KO
Mar 17	Maxie Rosenbloom	Boston	W
Mar 23	Art Weigand	Buffalo	W - KO
Apr 4	Red Fitzsimmons	Canton, OH	W - KO
Apr 6	Jack Melrose	Memphis	W - KO
Apr 18	Benny Ross	Buffalo	W
May 3	Tommy Loughran	Brooklyn	L
May 13	Jimmy Byrne	Louisville, Ky	ND
May 19	Tiny Herman	Columbus, GA	W
Jul 4	Chuck Wiggins	Macon	W
Jul 21	Otto von Porat	Minneapolis	ND
Aug 12	Chuck Wiggins	Indianapolis	D
Aug 29	Ed Smith	Tulsa, OK	W - KO
Sep 6	Leo Diebel	Omaha, NE	NC
Oct 28	Mike Arnold	Wichita, KS	W - KO
Nov 4	Angus Snyder	Spokane, WA	W
Nov 10	Harry Dillon	Portland, OR	W
Nov 21	Andy Palmer	Valdosta, GA	W - KO
Dec 9	Lou Scozza	Buffalo	W
Dec 15	Tom Kirby	Wilkes-Barre, PA	W

1928

Jan 9	Chuck Wiggins	Wichita, KS	W
Jan 23	Martin Burke	Miami	W - KO
Jan 29	Chuck Burns	Tulsa, OK	W
Feb 6	Marine Toliver	Birmingham	W - KO

Feb 13	Sailor Maxted	Jacksonville	W - KO
Feb 23	Joe Clancy	Montgomery, AL	W - KO
Feb 27	Al Friedman	Miami	W - KO
Mar 6	Chuck Wiggins	Cleveland	W
Mar 11	George Avera	Dothan, AL	W - KO
Mar 16	Pat Joyce	Augusta, GA	W - KO
Mar 30	Earl Blue	Tampa	W - KO
Apr 3	Jack Blackstock	Sarasota, FL	W - KO
Apr 11	George Gemas	Goldsboro, NC	W - KO
Apr 15	Jack Herman	Jacksonville	W - KO
Apr 23	Joe White	Chattanooga	W - KO
Apr 30	Rough Rowsey	Miami	W - KO
May 8	Andres Canstano	West Palm Beach	W - KO
May 10	Pete Angeles	Orlando	W - KO
May 18	Marcello Gubinelli	Tampa	W - KO
May 22	Charles Rammell	Pensacola	W - KO
May 25	Tommy Stone	Albany, GA	W - KO
May 30	Johnny Urban	Chattanooga	W - KO
Jun 5	Ted Cook	Meridian, MS	W - KO
Jun 8	Harry Fay	Jacksonville	W - KO
Jun 12	Joe Packo	Montgomery, AL	W - KO
Jul 2	Wild Bill Rowe	Daytona	W - KO
Jul 4	Buckeye Harris	Macon	W - KO
Jul 20	Tom Kirby	Chicago	W
Jul 24	Bill Jordan	Highpoint, NC	W - KO
Aug 6	Jack Ryan	Wilmington, NC	W - KO
Aug 13	Martin Burke	Mobile, AL	W - KO
Sep 6	Johnny Squires	New York	W - KO
Sep 20	Frankie Wine	Grand Rapids, MI	W
Oct 30	Sid Terris	Atlanta	W - KO
Nov 30	Ray Neuman	Charlotte, NC	W - KO
Dec 18	Billy Feas	St. Louis	W - KO
Dec 20	Pancho Castano	Macon	W - KO
Dec 21	Marshal Blackstone	Augusta, GA	W - KO

1929

Jan 1	Jack League	Kansas City	W - KO
Jan 9	Tommy Stone	Durham, NC	W - KO
Jan 18	Art Malay	Norfolk, VA	W - KO
Jan 21	Sully Montgomery	Memphis	W - KO
Jan 25	Ralph Smith	New Orleans	W - KO
Feb 27	Jack Sharkey	Miami	L
Jun 17	Babe Hunt	Wichita, KS	ND
Jun 23	Jack Lee	Flint, MI	W - KO
Jul 4	Tony Fuentes	Birmingham	W - KO
Jul 11	Jack DeMave	Knoxville, TN	W
Jul 18	George Cook	Kansas City	ND
Jul 28	Frankie Wine	Nashville	W
Jul 29	Babe Hunt	Tulsa	L
Aug 12	Harry Fay	Little Rock	W - KO
Aug 19	Joe Sekyra	Kansas City	ND
Aug 29	Joe Packo	Evansville, IN	W
Sep 2	George Cook	Macon	W - KO
Sep 24	Johnny Gibson	Cairo, GA	W - KO
Nov 6	Maurice Griselle	Paris	W
Nov 18	Primo Carnera	London	L
Dec 7	Primo Carnera	Paris	W

1930

Jan 22	Jack DeMave	Atlanta	W - KO
Feb 17	Joe Packo	New Orleans	W - KO
Feb 21	Pietro Corri	Tampa	W
May 8	Hans Schoenrath	London	W - KO
Jun 5	Frankie Wine	Birmingham	W
Jun 20	Otto von Porat	Chicago	W - KO
Jul 28	Phil Scott	London	W - KO
Oct 31	Meyer Christner	Boston	W - KO
Nov 11	Arthur DeKuh	Atlanta	W
Nov 19	Whitey Gorasline	Grand Rapids, MI	W - KO
Dec 12	Tuffy Griffiths	Chicago	W

1931

Mar 29	Champ Clark	Matamoros, Mexico	Exh
Jul 3	Max Schmeling	Cleveland	L
Oct 19	Salvatore Ruggeriello	Wichita, KS	W - KO
Nov 3	Fred Fitzsimmons	Springfield, MO	W - KO
Nov 11	Pat Fay	Muskogee, OK	W - KO
Nov 23	Pietro Corri	Birmingham, AL	ND

1932

Feb 26	Ernie Schaaf	Chicago	L
May 10	George Neron	Johnson City, TN	W
May 16	Joe Doktor	Toronto	W
May 23	Sid Terris	Winston-Salem, NC	W - KO
May 30	Johnny Freeman	Huntsville, AL	ND
Jul 4	Ambrose Palmer	Sydney	W - KO
Jul 15	Frankie Wine	Sydney	W
Aug 10	Jack Renault	Brisbane	W - KO
Sep 24	Johnny Freeman	Melbourne	W
Oct 29	Johnny Freeman	Sydney	NC
Nov 5	Tony Gora	Adelaide, Australia	W - KO
Nov 7	George Thompson	Perth, Australia	W - KO
Dec 17	Don McCorkindale	Johannesburg	W

1933

Mar 6	Pierre Charles	Paris	L
Aug 2	George Neron	Beckley, WV	W
Aug 29	Benny Odell	Rome, GA	W - KO
Sep 22	Maxie Rosenbloom	Houston	W

Sources

Associated Press

Atlanta Constitution

Atlanta Journal

Jack Banks - interview by James C. Bryant

James Barfield - interview by James C. Bryant

www.boxingscene.com

Virginia Cason - interview by Beatrice Griffin

Annie Laura Dixon Chastain - interview by Beatrice Griffin

Cleveland Plain Dealer

Frances Croft - interview by Beatrice Griffin

From Boxer to Bishop - A Biography of Clara Kinney Stribling Claiborne

Elizabeth Blackshear Flinn, copyright 1991 by Elizabeth Blackshear Flinn

Claude Green - interview by James C. Bryant

Cuy Harrell Jr. - interview by James C. Bryant

Mary Harris - interview by James C. Bryant

History of Macon, Georgia, Ida Young, Julius Gholson, Clara Nell Hargrove - Press Lyon, Marshall and Brooks, 1950

www.hoopedia.nba.com

Kansas City Star

King of the Canebrakes, Jimmy Johnson, Southern Press, Inc., 1969

Macon Telegraph

J. B. Maddox - interview by James C. Bryant

Miriam Garrison Minter - interview by James C. Bryant

Morning News - Florence, South Carolina

New York Journal American

New York Sun and Globe

New York Tribune

Ochlocknee: Land of Crooked Water, Georgia Beatrice Griffin, Ed.D, privately printed by Ochlocknee Community Civic Club, Inc., 1982

Philadelphia Bulletin

Will Rogers, The McNaught Syndicate

Savannah Morning News

Pauline Braswell Singletary - interview by James C. Bryant

Pauline Smith - interview by James C. Bryant

Sports Illustrated

Guerry Boone Stribling - interview by James C. Bryant

Tampa Tribune-Times

The Georgian

The Ring Magazine

Index

Paul Walsh